THE IMPERIOUS ECONOMY

DAVID P. CALLEO

THE
IMPERIOUS
ECONOMY

HARVARD UNIVERSITY PRESS
CAMBRIDGE, MASSACHUSETTS, AND LONDON, ENGLAND 1982

For AHB

Anche una gioia per me, Signora. . .

Second printing, 1982

The lines from *The Rake's Progress*, libretto by
W. H. Auden and Chester Kallman,
music by Igor Stravinsky, are reprinted by permission
of Boosey & Hawkes, Inc., copyright 1949, 1950,
1951, copyright renewed 1976, 1979.

Library of Congress Cataloging in Publication Data

Calleo, David P., 1934–
The imperious economy.

Bibliography: p.
Includes index.
1. United States — Economic policy — 1961–
2. United States — Economic conditions — 1961–1971.
3. United States — Economic conditions — 1971–
I. Title.
HC106.6.C275   338.973   81-20066
ISBN 0–674–44522–8   AACR2

Contents

S ECURE from need, the cause of crime,
The world shall for the second time
Be similar to heaven.
F OR, so it please, there's no fantastic lie
You cannot make men swallow if you try.

W. H. Auden and Chester Kallman,
The Rake's Progress

Introduction

The Pax Americana and Its Future

THE FIRST three or four decades after World War II have often been called the *Pax Americana*. From our present perspective, the label seems not inappropriate. In these postwar years, American power, imagination, and energy have induced the greater part of the world into a pattern of American design. That design is the American version of the Western liberal dream—a closely-knit world system of vigorously prosperous democracies, enjoying security from military aggression, permitting the free movement of goods, money, and enterprise among themselves, and promoting the rapid development and integration of those nations whom liberal progress has left behind. Manifold blemishes notwithstanding, the postwar system has been a more than tolerable approximation of that liberal ideal.

What place will this *Pax Americana* occupy in the history of the century? Will it prove, as hoped, the founding of a durable new world order, or will it seem merely a passing episode of American supremacy?

By the 1980s, the prevailing mood is less inclined to self-congratulation over the system's past accomplishments than to serious doubts about its future. From today's perspective, the 1960s and the 1970s reveal not so much unfolding strength as accumulating debility. Instead of evolving solutions, there seem worsening contradictions. Not only is the *Pax Americana* seen to be faltering, but pluralist democracy, the domestic political and economic formula upon which the *Pax Americana* is based, is said to be facing a crisis of "governability." Above all, the United States itself seems more troubled and uncertain over its own domestic political economy than at any time since the Great Depression of the 1930s.

The mood, to be sure, is more troubled than despairing. All systems have their tensions and contradictions. The economic and political problems within the postwar order have proved manageable, if not solvable. Despite numerous shocks, prosperity has continued. With all their difficulties, the sixties and seventies also display an unprecedented growth and progress in the world economy, as well as in the United States itself. Capitalist countries have enjoyed extraordinary prosperity, spread through an increasingly open and interdependent world framework. World trade has never been more free, and capital and enterprise have flowed across national borders with an ease impressive by any historical standard. Development has brought notable success to many countries as economic ties with the Third World have gradually evolved toward forms more suitable to national independence.

All this being said, the mood of the eighties is not optimistic. Disruption and uncertainty have been growing rather than diminishing. The deterioration appears to have deep-seated causes, which even the greatest tactical skill will find increasingly difficult to contain.

The tensions undermining the postwar system may be described in several ways. In one common view, the problems are laid to some absolute decline in American power, imagination, and will. To be more realistic, they should be ascribed to the relative rise of other powers. The postwar system, initially organized and dominated by the United States, has been evolving into a more plural structure in which other powers grow more active and powerful. In itself, such an evolution should not be surprising. The extraordinary conditions of the postwar period, with Europe, Japan, and the Soviet Union in ruins, could hardly have been expected to persist. American policy itself generously promoted the recovery of Europe and Japan, as well as the development of the old and new states of the Third World. Recovery and development were bound to lead to a world with American power less overwhelming and American leadership no longer unquestioned, even among close allies and dependencies. And if the Soviet Union, America's great geopolitical rival beyond the pale of the *Pax Americana*, has also been growing relatively stronger, that, too, should be no cause for surprise. For the United States, despite the billions spent on arms, has never sought to destroy its rival, but has rather tried to contain and accommodate it. Such a policy was bound to mean, in the end, a weightier international role for the Soviets, as well as a world environment conducive to greater independence among the middle powers. In short, the slow transition from American hegemony to a more plural world is not, in itself, a defeat for American policy. On the contrary, it is precisely the outcome that might have been expected to follow from the policy itself.

Historically, the test for American statesmanship should therefore be not how long it manages to cling to a deteriorating and overextended hegemony, but how well those liberal domestic and international arrangements it has fostered can adapt themselves to the stresses of the more plural order. In other words, the real test of American statesmanship is whether the postwar world system can survive the relative decline of American power. As American supremacy diminishes, will the system remain liberal and integrated, or will it fragment into hostile blocs?

Most examinations of this question focus on the difficulties other countries have remaining within a liberal system without American power and generosity to keep them there. The economic experience of the sixties and seventies, however, suggests a different threat. For in large part it has been the United States itself, with its diminishing relative economic, political, and military superiority, that has had the greatest trouble fitting within the mutual constraints of an integrated world system. Increasingly, America's domestic aspirations have been in tension with its responsibilities to a liberal international order. To be sure, the responsibilities themselves have been unusually heavy. Throughout the 1960s and 1970s, the United States, as the principal architect and manager of the *Pax Americana*, had not only a heavy stake in the existing international order but also a disproportionate part of the burden of maintaining it. This disproportionate burden made American policy increasingly unstable. For despite its historic role in forming the system, the United States was also, in many respects, less sensitive and vulnerable to international disturbances than other industrial countries within the postwar order. Moreover, with a vast and varied territory, a relatively autarchic and advanced economy, and a racially diverse society, the United States had rather special domestic problems and ambitions. Throughout the sixties and seventies, America's special domestic claims and exceptional foreign responsibilities proved increasingly difficult to reconcile. Most other advanced democracies also had increasing difficulty in participating in an interdependent world system while managing their economies in response to domestic needs and pressures. But the American situation was unique, not only from the country's unusual problems and responsibilities, but also from its special privileges. Among these privileges was the capacity to set aside certain international rules inconvenient to itself. This capacity for self-exemption proved not only a danger for the system as a whole, but also a mixed blessing for the domestic problems of the United States.

This book analyzes American economic and foreign policy through the five administrations of the sixties and seventies. These administrations form a certain pattern. Two administrations, those of John Kennedy and Richard Nixon, were periods of great creativity. Both set the broad lines of policy that dominated the rest of their decades. The Johnson, Ford, and Carter Administrations, by contrast, inherited their policies and managed, well or ill, the possibilities and problems inherent within them.

The differences between policies in the two formative administrations reveal how much the world was changing. Kennedy opened the 1960s with what seemed the maturity and flowering of America's postwar leadership. He saw himself as the heir to Franklin Roosevelt's domestic and world designs. A bold domestic program for growth was to transform American society, while vigorous international leadership was to complete the *Pax Americana*. To Kennedy, those national and international goals seemed not only compatible, but complementary. America's leadership in the world was to be based upon the strength and exemplary achievements of its political system at home. And the domestic system was seen to depend upon an orderly and congenial world environment, sustained by American power and leadership.

Kennedy, of course, hardly invented these views. His postwar predecessors in the Presidency had all served the same broad ideals, with notable success. Not only was the *Pax Americana* well established by 1961, but the domestic economy was prosperous and stable. Nevertheless, Kennedy felt America was losing its vision and fervor. Its energy would run out long before the new world and domestic order could be completed. He summoned his countrymen to a new burst of idealism and vigor to fulfill the Roosevelt heritage. Growth would be speeded at home; American leadership reasserted abroad.

By contrast with Kennedy, fate cast Nixon in an unrewarding role. Instead of Eisenhower's fat legacy in 1961, he inherited Johnson's bankruptcy in 1969. Johnson left Nixon not only a lost war, but a deteriorating trade balance, a collapsing currency, and domestic stagflation. Nixon's first two and a half years in office witnessed, in effect, the last act of the Kennedy-Johnson economic policy. The dollar's debacle and the end of fixed exchange rates in August 1971 formed the final scene. Nixon's way out of the crisis, his "New Economic Policy," set the lines for American policy in the seventies. By 1979, the Nixon policies began to appear as bankrupt as the Kennedy policies they had replaced. As the 1980s opened, the country was once more in search of a viable strategy.

Looking at government policy over five administrations helps reveal a number of themes which, if not invisible in a shorter perspective, are more sharply apparent in the longer stretch. Most obvious is the close connection between domestic and foreign economic policy. In retrospect, a good part of American foreign economic policy seems the attempt to make an international system out of the consequences of the economic policies pursued at home.

The longer perspective also makes the cyclical nature of economic patterns stand out more clearly. Contemporary economic managers and analysts often talked as if they were eliminating traditional business cycles. Observed in retrospect, however, government policy did not so much eliminate cycles as acquiesce in inflation.

The misperceptions of much contemporary economic analysis

throughout the two decades provide a third rather depressing theme. Economic punditry was always being surprised by "exogenous" variables. That so many determining forces should have been thought accidental reflected the too narrow compass of the analysts as much as the unpredictable nature of human affairs. Cycles went on as they always had, a revelation only to those without historical memory. As usual, power, with its own shifting balance, pervaded and shaped national as well as world economies. Power could be ignored in economic analysis only at the risk of unanticipated shocks. In short, as the two decades illustrate all too well, economic analysis lacking a sense of history or politics must expect many surprises.

To a considerable extent, the limitations of analysis in this period became the shortcomings of policy. American policy grew increasingly ahistorical, fragmented, and hectic. By the end of the seventies, this loss of direction, combined with nostalgia for outworn hegemonic formulas, pointed toward increasing conflict between American policy and the realities of a more plural world. If not checked, such a trend meant a time of great trouble in the world and perhaps a deep historic tragedy. For the eighties, some restoration of distance and gravity to analysis seems essential if America is to rise to its historic responsibilities to the world system it has created. Under such circumstances, a critical look at the evolution of American policy over twenty years and its consequences seems a useful task. A clearer notion of where we have been may suggest a clearer idea of where we should be going.

ONE

THE KENNEDY DILEMMA
1963-1971

1

Kennedy's
Grand Design

I F THE WORLD were only a theater, the Kennedy Administration
would have to be counted a great success. Aside from Roosevelt
himself, no President in this century so stirred the imaginations
and moral energies of his countrymen. Among other things, Kennedy embodied the advent of a new generation to power. But while
his Administration had a wonderful capacity for projecting youthful vigor, its ideas, in retrospect, do not seem very fresh. After the
New Deal, pressing for growth through Keynesian demand management was hardly a novelty in domestic economic policy. And
after Truman and Eisenhower, American "leadership" in the postwar world system had become routine. Even accommodation to
the Soviets, if not as yet christened "detente," was already under-
way by the later fifties.

Such ideas, though not new in 1960, nevertheless seemed in need
of youthful renewal. In a certain sense, Eisenhower, with his concern with inflation and excessive federal power, had been the real in-
novator in American policy. His fears of inflation had helped
dampen the domestic boom of the Korean War into a mild recession. And perhaps, because of his fear of power, he had deliberately
sought to take the enthusiasm out of foreign policy. In these respects, Eisenhower now seems ahead of his time.[1] Kennedy's policies, by contrast, seem the militant return of conventional wisdom.

Kennedy and his followers, to be sure, saw things differently. To them, Eisenhower's caution in pursuing traditional goals was not the self-restraint of maturity, but the indolent complacency of middle age. At home, Eisenhower's stress on inflation seemed selfishly indifferent to the poor and disadvantaged. Abroad, his diffidence seemed fatuously lethargic before nuclear dangers, Soviet ambitions, and explosive expectations in the Third World.

Kennedy's Administration brought traditional American policy not only a renewed ardor and urgency, but also a taste for coherent and articulate philosophizing, a public art that had fallen into a particularly low state during the Eisenhower period. Kennedy's government was partial to "grand designs" that tied traditional and diverse policies into coherent rhetorical packages. Although the Administration was as prone to unexpected crises and adventitious solutions as any other, its economic and political initiatives were consciously linked to a broad general strategy for domestic and foreign policy. The essential elements of the strategy were traditional: expansive growth and social improvement at home, world integration and American leadership abroad. But the rhetoric was fresh, and the goals were pursued with unusual ingenuity and dedication.

Thus traditional New Deal policies for domestic growth became the "New Frontier" and the "New Economics." Together, they evolved into an unusually active form of Keynesian demand management. Policies to regain the initiative abroad began with a new cycle of Cold War fears and crises leading to a major American rearmament, soon supplemented by an equally vigorous pursuit of detente. New approaches to the Russians were matched by renewed attempts at consolidation in the West. A series of ambitious military and economic initiatives sought to promote the familiar goal of closer integration within the Atlantic Alliance. Not all Europeans were pleased. Europeans like Charles de Gaulle hoped detente might lead to a mutation in the postwar order, a mutual withdrawal of the superpowers from their blocs. But detente, as Kennedy saw it, meant that each superpower would respect the integrity of the other's system. Detente was not to mean the end of the postwar blocs, but their consolidation.

At the same time as Kennedy's policy sought to reinforce the Atlantic political-economic core, it was reaching out to reanimate

American leadership in the Third World. A sophisticated theory of "development" superseded the rather simple-minded and unappealing military emphasis of the Dulles era. According to the fashionable doctrine of the sixties, after a certain stage, development could become self-sustaining and favorable to democracy. Communism was a childhood disease, to be held off by force, if necessary, until development had proceeded to "take off."[2] Liberal faith in progress thus combined with Hobbesian faith in power. Hence, two characteristic innovations of the Kennedy Administration: the Peace Corps and the Green Berets.

For the rest of the decade, American policy moved forward on these broad Kennedy themes—growth, social improvement, rearmament, detente, Atlantic integration, and Third World development. The idealism early in the decade and the actual situation at the end make a painful contrast. But the links are all too clear, no less in the economic policies that led to inflation than in the broader military policies that led to war. The economic policies cannot in fact be understood apart from the Administration's broader political and military goals.

In economic policy, three Kennedy initiatives proved crucial for later developments at home and abroad: the domestic growth policies, the Kennedy Round of tariff cutting; and the "ad-hoc" response to the international monetary problem. Each had its own special character. In the end, all were in tension with each other.

Growth the Panacea

To Kennedy's Administration, growth seemed the first and best answer to the country's problems. Growth would provide the sharply increased federal revenue needed for foreign ambitions and domestic reforms. Growth would reverse the worrisome trends showing European economies gaining on the American. Growth was even supposed to help the dollar. For domestic growth, it was agreed, meant increased investment and productivity at home, less American investment and more American trade abroad.[3]

Kennedy was fortunate to inherit an economy ripe for expansion. Eisenhower had taken office in the throes of the boom set off by the Korean War. Understandably, his policies had been sensitive to the dangers of inflation. But after several years of Eisenhower's fiscal stinginess, inflationary fires appeared to have burned out. A mild recession in 1960 had pushed unemployment to 6.9%, and the public dissatisfaction with the sluggish economy had helped elect Kennedy.[4]

During its first two years, Kennedy's Administration used relatively traditional policies combining welfare transfers, public projects and financing, investment tax credits, and more generous depreciation allowances.[5] But signs of expansion, particularly business investment, were too slow for the Administration's high expectations. By 1962, Administration economists feared the economy might slip back into recession. Kennedy's economic advisers, most notably Walter Heller, had already set to work persuading the President to adopt bolder countercyclical policies, in particular a tax cut. Still deficient in Keynesian economics, the President nearly foiled his advisers' plans by considering a tax increase instead. Kennedy was disturbed because federal expenditures in 1961 had outstripped receipts by $3.4 billion, thanks, it seemed, to the increased defense spending in reaction to the Berlin crisis of that year. His advisers gave the President a crash course in Keynesian demand management and thereby rescued the country from a balanced budget.[6]

A major tax cut began to be discussed in mid-1962. That deficits were legitimate and beneficial in the midst of a recession was, of course, part of official postwar orthodoxy. But 1962 was not a recession year. Indeed, real GNP was to rise a healthy 5.8%. A tax cut was nevertheless needed, according to the Administration's reasoning, because a considerable gap existed between actual output and potential output at "full employment." By this formula, fiscal deficits were called for not only when the economy was actually in recession, but whenever its performance dipped below its optimal state.

To legitimize such a formula required a major educational campaign, not only in Congress but in business circles generally. The Administration set about to popularize the concept of a "full-employment budget." This notion, in effect, combined hypothetical revenues with actual expenditures. Tax revenues were estimated as if the economy had already expanded enough to achieve full employment. These imaginary revenues were then compared with actual expenditures. In a period of recession, like the early sixties, such a computation yielded a hypothetical surplus. In other words, at the existing level of spending, the federal budget would have been in surplus if only the economy had been running at full employment. From this hypothetical calculation, with its phantom surplus, Kennedy's advisers argued a portentous conclusion: it was the phantom surplus that was blocking expansion to full employment.[7] Their reasoning was complex.

In a downturn, as the government's traditional deficit spending took effect and the economy moved back toward full employment, overall income in the private sector would naturally begin to rise. As private incomes rose, so would government revenues. With progressive income tax rates, government income would tend to rise faster than private income. Under these circumstances, insofar as the government's spending remained the same or declined, the government's revenues would accumulate and thereby reduce or even eliminate the government's deficit. The phantom surplus would become more and more actual. And whereas the original deficit would act to stimulate the economy, the government's growing unspent revenue would begin to deaden it. Once recovery reached a certain stage, the "fiscal drag" of increasing government revenue could be expected to hold back further progress. Ironically, the very growth of government revenues that would stall recovery would prevent a balanced budget. For without recovery, a balanced budget could not be achieved. Too much government revenue, too soon in the cycle, would actually reduce the government's revenue in the long run.

The "New Economics" was ready with the solution. The budget should anticipate its phantom surplus. The revenues that stimulation would bring to the government should be spent before they arrived. Expenditures should be raised or taxes cut in advance. Applying these calculations in Kennedy's actual situation yielded a clear prescription. By January 1963, full employment calculations showed a $9 billion budget surplus and a shortfall between actual and potential production of $30 to $40 billion, along with an actual unemployment rate of 5.6%.[8] To revive the economy and balance the budget, Kennedy formally proposed a tax cut to offset the fiscal drag.

These advanced notions proved difficult to get through Congress, perhaps because real GNP growth rates turned out to be relatively high after 1961:[9]

    1961 + 2.6
    1962 + 5.8
    1963 + 4.0
    1964 + 5.3
    1965 + 6.0

In any event, Congress finally passed a tax cut in 1964, as a sort of memorial to the murdered President. The passage marked a major shift in American fiscal management. Henceforth, fiscal deficits became the rule in good times or bad. Between fiscal 1965 and fiscal 1980, the American federal budget was out of deficit in only one year.[10]

Although Kennedy's belated education in economics brought him to full employment budgets, both he and his tutors were not unmindful of the dangers of inflation. But their policies suggested that they saw inflation as the consequence more of monopolistic structures than of expansionist government policies. Thus, wage and price guidelines were their preferred remedies and indeed formed an integral part of the Administration's expansionist package. The President, moreover, stood willing to defend the guidelines, as his celebrated confrontation with the steel industry in April 1962 made clear. Prices, in fact, did not rise ahead of productivity throughout the Administration's lifetime, and wages exceeded it by only a small margin.[11] But in the long run, controls were unlikely to be able to hold back inflation in the era of the perpetually expansive government policies demanded by the full-employment budget. Kennedy's early instincts, in economics at least, were perhaps superior to his belated education.

The Trade Expansion Act

While the Administration's domestic economic policy grew increasingly interventionist, its foreign economic policy remained resolutely committed to Cordell Hull's venerable dream of a worldwide free market. Thus, the sophisticated neo-Keynesianism of the full-employment budget contrasted starkly with the Administration's major foreign economic initiative, the militantly orthodox Trade Expansion Act of 1962.[12] This international side of the Administration's program was, again, hardly a radical departure. Free trade and monetary convertibility were major elements in Kennedy's liberal internationalist heritage and consistent principles of the postwar *Pax Americana*. The new Trade Expansion Act gave the President broad new authority to negotiate mutual trade concessions with the European Economic Community and Japan. Thus fortified, the Administration launched an ambitious campaign of trade liberalization, the "Kennedy Round." Trade liberalization moreover, seemed a natural part of the Administration's policy to renew American world leadership and tighten the Atlantic Alliance. In particular, the sixties seemed a crucial moment to fix the emerging European Economic Community in a liberal, "outward-looking" mold, an Atlanticist orientation compatible with a close political and military relationship with the United States. Thus, pushing the British into the Common Market became a major Administration foreign policy initiative, along with the Kennedy Round itself.[13]

At the same time that it was pressing forward with trade liberalization, the Administration was apparently determined to defend the liberal system of fixed exchange rates outlined in 1944 at Bretton Woods. These monetary arrangements, suspended throughout the period of European reconstruction, had in fact only just come into operation with the general return to currency convertibility in 1958.

Tension Between Domestic and Foreign Policies

While these liberal trade and monetary policies fitted well with traditional American internationalist interests, political as well as economic, the Administration's international liberalism and domestic Keynesianism coexisted uneasily at best. "Fine-tuning" a budget to perpetual full employment was to become increasingly incompatible with sustaining a more open world economy. The practical difficulties were complicated by a certain philosophical astigmatism. Anyone familiar with Keynes ought to have remembered the difficulties of reconciling his rediscovered "neomercantilism" with his inherited liberalism. Indeed, the same broad tension between domestic intervention and internationalist free trade had characterized Roosevelt's New Deal.[14] But neither the Kennedy Administration nor its successors seem to have been prepared intellectually for this tension. If the Kennedy Administration's rhetoric is to be believed, free trade and a favorable balance of payments were simply assumed to be complementary with stimulated domestic growth.[15] Lower tariffs, for example, were expected to make it more advantageous to export from home rather than manufacture abroad. American corporations would thus invest more in their home production. More domestic investment would mean not only more growth but higher competitiveness and, hence, an even more favorable trade balance. More favorable trade and less foreign investment would also strengthen the balance of payments.

As a practical matter, these suppositions, though eminently conventional, were highly conjectural. Nothing guaranteed that the Kennedy Round, for instance, would improve the US trade balance. Immediate gains for industrial trade were doubtful, since American tariffs were often higher than European. Presumably, the Administration was counting on gains in agriculture, where the United States had an unquestioned comparative advantage as well as a chronic and politically troublesome problem of overproduction.[16] Ending restrictions on American food exports to Europe would resolve a serious American domestic problem, powerfully bolster the dollar, and firmly link the interests of American agriculture to the *Pax Americana*. But even if such expectations were economically plausible, they were politically naive. American plans for a common trans-Atlantic market in agriculture were, as it happened, in direct contradiction to Europe's aspirations for a continental economy of its own, in particular to France's national interest in that economy.

Predictably, Kennedy Round negotiations dragged on interminably, and the agreement finally reached in 1967 continued to restrict American access to Europe's agricultural market. Meanwhile, a by then inflated US economy had grown even more vulnerable to foreign competition in industrial goods. In short, whatever the theoretical long-range benefit, trade liberalization was not a panacea for America's economic problems. Quite the opposite. Nor was it an easy way to reaffirm America's political leadership and the Alliance's solidarity. On the contrary, the Kennedy Round revealed an unexpected depth of trans-Atlantic economic tension, as well as fundamental contradictions in American domestic and foreign goals.[17]

The Weak Dollar

Contradictions between the Administration's domestic Keynesianism and international liberalism emerged most clearly in its foreign monetary policy. Its international policy on money was as orthodox as its policy on trade. But while the new Administration was aggressive in pressing free trade, circumstances made it defensive about monetary convertibility. As Eisenhower had discovered, no sooner had the open monetary system actually come into being in 1958 than the United States found itself unable to live within the rules it had pressed upon others.

The postwar international monetary system had been structured in the Bretton Woods negotiations of 1944. The Americans had insisted not only upon an integrated liberal system, with fixed rates and free convertibility of currencies, but also upon systemic sanctions weighted against countries running balance-of-payments deficits. Keynes, representing the British and trying to provide enough leeway for countercyclical full-employment policies, had pleaded in vain for more generous credits to debtors and automatic sanctions against surplus countries.[18]

The arrangements decided at Bretton Woods proved highly premature in any event. After the terrible destruction and dislocation of the war, European powers could not sustain the exchange rates of their currencies against the dollar without tight exchange controls. Britain, under intense American pressure, tried to restore the pound's convertibility in 1946. Within a few weeks, sales of pounds for dollars were so heavy that Britain ran through most of its reserves of foreign exchange, including a large loan from the

United States. Thereafter Britain, like all the other European states, maintained exchange controls.[19] Europeans developed a "payments union" that permitted a relatively free exchange of goods and money among themselves, but strictly limited purchases and investments in dollars.[20] Meanwhile, throughout the fifties, the United States began running large annual balance-of-payments deficits to finance the Marshall Plan, NATO's rearmament, and development for the Third World, along with the growing overseas investments of US corporations. Tight exchange controls continued until 1958 when, Europe having recovered, the liberal convertibility envisioned at Bretton Woods finally came into effect. By this time, America's overseas liquid debts already exceeded its monetary reserves.

Contrary to earlier expectations, the pattern of American balance-of-payments deficits established in the period of currency controls continued after restrictions had been lifted. Not only did the United States run deficits from the start of the Eisenhower Administration, but after 1958 the deficit immediately grew worse. In 1959 the United States actually ran a payments deficit not only on capital flows and government spending but on the entire current account. Under such circumstances, currency traders began to wonder how long the United States could sustain the dollar's convertibility at the official price. Signs of serious trouble first became apparent in the fall of 1960, with a major speculative run in the London Gold Market.[21]

The gold market had a special significance in the Bretton Woods system. Bidding up the price of gold was, in effect, bidding down the value of the dollar. For the dollar was both the system's *numeraire* and its principal reserve currency. Being *numeraire* meant that all other currencies were valued in terms of dollars, while the dollar was valued in terms of gold. Being a reserve currency meant that other countries could hold dollars in their monetary reserves as a substitute for gold itself. There were advantages in holding dollars rather than gold. Gold reserves, for example, earned no income, whereas dollar reserves were generally held in the form of interest-bearing US government securities. Gold was nevertheless supposed to be available from the Federal Reserve when a foreign central bank wished to exchange its dollars.

This convertibility of dollars into gold, at $35 per ounce, was the system's theoretical anchor, justifying other countries' holding dollars as reserves in place of gold. Technically, the whole arrangement was called the "gold exchange standard." The pound was also a reserve currency, and the British, too, were supposed to have either dollars or gold available to meet all claims.[22]

While only foreign central banks were able to get gold for dollars from the US Federal Reserve, private holders were supposed to be able to buy gold at the official price in the open market. Bidding up the dollar price of gold on the private market was thus a speculation against the dollar itself. Traders were betting against the ability of the United States to provide enough gold to sustain the official price. The London Gold Market remained dangerously unsettled until 1961, when the United States succeeded in negotiating a multilateral arrangement, the London Gold Pool, to supply enough gold to keep the open market price steady at the official rate.[23] The gold market nevertheless remained a point where a weak dollar was particularly vulnerable.

Why was the dollar weak? For a start, there was the continuing American balance-of-payments deficit. Each year saw fresh deficits, and as the fifties wore on into the sixties, the net outflows showed no signs of diminishing. A significant part of America's dollar outflow ended up in private hands rather than in foreign central banks. This phenomenon reflected, in turn, the growing size of private transactions in what might be called the cosmopolitan economy of transnational firms and investors. Ths nonnational economy operated chiefly on a credit base of expatriate dollars that had initially flowed out of the American national economy and hence had been registered as a negative flow in the American balance of payments. The correlative of these deficits was the larger and larger dollar accumulations of foreigners or nonresidents, including multinational corporations. A good part of these cosmopolitan dollars were reserves and working balances, held in liquid, short-term forms of investment. Such funds were necessarily volatile, with their managers naturally searching both for safety and for higher interest rates.

Even by Kennedy's time, the movement of these short-term funds had become more significant for the American balance of payments in any given year than either the trade balance or long-term capital movements. And as the size of these nonresident liquid holdings kept growing in relation to US monetary reserves, they became an increasing danger for convertibility.[24] A loss of confidence or a sudden change in relative interest rates could, and did, result in the large-scale selling of dollars. Though the American government tended to view the movement of short-term capital as irrational speculation, it represented, in effect, the appearance of an international capital market in dollars, a development of great significance not only for the world but also for the American domestic economy.

"Ad-hocery"

From the start, the Kennedy Administration was concerned about the country's continuing balance-of-payments deficit and was particularly sobered by the gold run of 1960. If nothing else, Britain's growing troubles with the pound suggested the political liabilities of a weak reserve currency. But the Administration was puzzled about how to react.[25] In the long run, plans for domestic economic rejuventation and trade liberalization were supposed to resolve the dollar problem. A stronger domestic economy, it was thought, would mean a stronger dollar. Meanwhile, the Administration counted on its banking experts to figure out how to defend the dollar against speculative runs without in any way deflecting foreign or domestic policy from its real concerns. The result was the temporizing policy known as ad-hocery, a series of expedients designed to bolster the dollar during what was imagined to be only a temporary period of weakness. Credit lines were arranged against sudden waves of speculation. In keeping with good internationalist principles, the credits were multilateral, like the gold pool or the "swap" lines among the major central banks. To reassure foreigners about convertibility, official US obligations began to be denominated not in dollars but in foreign currencies.

In addition to arranging advance credits, the Administration also sought to limit or mitigate forms of outflow. An item-by-item breakdown of America's foreign accounts suggested a connection between the dollar's weakness and America's heavy overseas responsibilities. Except for 1959, US current account was always in surplus. But five large negative items regularly threw the overall basic balance into deficit: overseas military expenditures, foreign aid, direct capital investments abroad by American corporations, short-term capital flows, and tourist expenditures. Except for the short-term capital flows and perhaps the tourists, the rest seemed costs of the *Pax Americana*. They represented official military or economic subventions or private capital investments to shape a new world economy.

Controlling this "imperial" deficit seemed to depend on special measures to reduce the outflows. Kennedy's ardor for world leadership precluded any serious reduction in military and aid commitments. On the contrary, the American role in European defense increased greatly. And the Alliance for Progress, the Peace Corps, the emphasis on counterinsurgency tactics, and the Vietnam commitment all testified to a heightened concern with the Third World. Attempts to counter the government's "imperial" outflows were thus limited to various measures to mitigate their negative effects rather than to curtail the activities themselves. Among these mitigating measures were bilateral arrangements for early debt repayments to the United States, offset payments for US troops stationed abroad, and aid programs tied to purchases in the United States.[26]

Nonpolitical outflows were less sacrosanct to the Administration but not much easier to reduce. Capital outflows were the major problem. Kennedy's plans for domestic growth and worries about domestic productivity made him unenthusiastic about the heavy long-term foreign investments of American corporations, even though he was familiar with the usual arguments about the ultimate benefits for the balance of payments. But aside from general inducements to domestic investment or attempts to change tax laws that favored foreign over domestic earnings, the Administration avoided direct curbs.[27] Controls did grow increasingly direct under Johnson, however, until Nixon reversed the whole trend as part of his revolution of 1971.

Resisting Monetary Integration

The issue of limiting long-term corporate investment abroad was only one aspect of the problem created by international monetary integration. In a liberal international monetary system, capital markets can be expected to grow more and more integrated. Where money flows freely, monetary conditions in one market can be expected to resemble those in others. Without controls, for example, interest rates in an offshore dollar capital market and interest rates in the domestic dollar capital market may be expected to converge.

Until Nixon's time, however, official US policy essentially sought to insulate the domestic from the world capital market. In particular, the United States sought to protect its market for long-term investment capital from the effects of the higher interest rates that prevailed overseas. "Operation Twist," one of the resulting policies, was designed to push US short-term interest rates toward world levels, while simultaneously keeping US long-term interest rates down. Thus, it was hoped, high interest rates for short-term capital would keep dollars from flowing outward while low interest rates for domestic long-term capital would encourage domestic investment for industry and housing.[28] The Interest Equalization Tax, recommended in 1963, tried to close the US long-term capital market to foreign borrowers by imposing a special tax on foreign issues sold in the United States.[29] These measures had indifferent success and unintended consequences.[30]

An Interest Equalization Tax inside the United States could not, for example, keep a world dollar market from developing in London, nor its rates from affecting those in New York. This "Eurodollar Market" became, in effect, a huge "offshore" extension of the American capital market, nourished by and inciting further US payments deficits.[31] The whole effort to insulate the domestic economy from that market was, in fact, misguided and naive. When the dollar continued as a reserve currency in a world of free convertibility, a world market in dollars was bound to develop. Domestic economic management would eventually have to conform to the realities of that world market. In a liberal international system, dollar rates in New York could not be kept insulated from dollar rates in London.

The Dollar Strategy in Retrospect

The Kennedy Administration's balance-of-payments strategy was not even a cosmetic success during its own lifetime. Heavy dollar outflows continued, Operation Twist and other policies not-withstanding. As the dollar's temporary defenses grew more in-genious, the pressures built inexorably toward its later crises and ultimate fall. The fall, to be sure, was to take over ten years. But until Nixon's revolution in August 1971, the basic balance-of-payments policies laid down in the Kennedy Administration were un-changed. As with domestic economic and trade policy, Kennedy's broad strategies continued to govern his successors.

In retrospect, the fatal weaknesses in the Kennedy dollar strategy seem obvious. The elaborate ad-hoc defenses, however necessary, did not constitute, in themselves, a serious policy. The payments problem was to prove not adventitious and temporary, but deep-seated and persistent. From the start, American re-sponses were inherently contradictory. Trying to reduce overseas capital flows, for example, was incompatible with American global ambitions, public and private. American business was no more prepared to reduce its "imperial" spending overseas than the Am-erican government. And trying to insulate domestic capital mar-kets from international conditions ran counter to the whole thrust of American liberal plans for integrating the world economy. In short, the Kennedy Administration was unwilling to abandon its overseas ambitions and policies, but could not understand or face their consequences for the balance of payments, or for domestic monetary policy and financial markets. Instead of seeing capital flows as the sign of an integrating world economy, the Administra-tion regarded them as alien, speculative, often irrational, and in no sense organically related to the way the American domestic econ-omy was or ought to be managed. The Administration, of course, had good reason for its blindness, for had it accepted the full im-plications of this integration of financial markets, it would have had to abandon either the domestic Keynesian expansion that made money cheaper in America or else the international integra-tion that allowed the cheaper money to flow outward.

The Administration's problems with the balance of payments can be described in both economic and political terms. Economi-cally, American policy was caught between promoting an ambi-tious Keynesian expansion at home and a liberal market system for the world. This fundamental contradiction was to break down the Bretton Woods system and lead to floating exchange rates—not,

however, before successive administrations had tried a long cata-
logue of ineffective measures designed to square circles. In Kennedy's time, the problem had not yet grown acute. What was a failure of imagination in the Kennedy Administration became a blind
resistance to experience in its successor.

In due course, America's balance-of-payments problem began
to have serious consequences for its foreign policy. The monetary
system became an increasing bone of contention between the
United States and its European and Japanese partners. These tensions had a larger political meaning. The world's monetary system
is generally a metaphor for its political system. In this perspective,
Kennedy's problems in the international monetary system reflected, sooner than in most spheres, America's changing geopolitical position. Still immensely powerful and confident under
Kennedy, the United States was unwilling to check its expansive
ambitions either at home or abroad. But America's political system
was unwilling, or unable, to mobilize the real resources needed for
its ambitions. Meanwhile, resistance from within the reviving international state system grew increasingly effective.

It is difficult to draw any final account for an administration cut
off so tragically in its prime. As Kennedy read the history of his
time, the moment had come for a dramatic reassertion of American activism, both at home and abroad. With his articulate intelligence and wonderful élan, Kennedy stirred the moral energies of
his countrymen. His administration set the grand lines of American policy for the rest of the decade. Tragically, but perhaps inevitably, the outcome was inflation, war, and a collapse of the dollar. While Kennedy can hardly be held responsible for all
Johnson's mistakes, the dreams of Camelot are surely a large part
of the nightmare that followed. History will perhaps be kinder to
Kennedy's predecessor, for even if Eisenhower was less ardently
concerned with prosperity and social improvement at home, or
security and power abroad, he was more sensitive to the dangers of
overextension. As it happened, caution was the better guide for a
country no longer able to run the world by itself.

2

From Boom
to Stagflation

ALTHOUGH IT TOOK two years, the Kennedy Administration finally saw the start of a major American domestic boom. It was to last from 1963 to 1969, with a significant pause in 1966. In effect, the economy moved within the decade from slump to boom and back to recession. In itself, a cyclical pattern was hardly exceptional, except for politicians and journalists with short attention spans, or economists who had thought the business cycle abolished. Genuinely noteworthy and alarming, however, was the rise in the inflation rate from one recession to the next. From barely 1% per year in 1961, it rose to nearly 6% in 1970. This was a change full of unhappy consequences not only for the domestic economy but also for the dollar, the international monetary system, and the *Pax Americana* in general. This rise in the basic American inflation rate was, in all likelihood, the most important and harmful development in the world economy during the decade. How did the rise take place? The answer lay in the American economy itself.

Johnson's Boom

Until the first half of 1963, despite the government's ministrations, business investment had remained low and unemployment high compared to the better years of the fifties. When Johnson came into office in November 1963, Kennedy's growth policies seemed finally to be working, even though the "full-employment" tax cut had not yet been passed through Congress. Johnson nevertheless continued to push for the cut. By the time it was passed in February 1964, the economy had already been growing strongly for seven months.[1] Thereafter, expansion accelerated, fueled by rising business investment, increased consumer spending, and growing outlays of state and local governments. The Federal Reserve felt able to help with easy money since, with the trade balance improving and the Interest Equalization Tax expected to cut long-term capital outflows, prospects for the dollar seemed much improved.[2] Even after the tax cut, moreover, fiscal policy continued to pile on new fuel for expansion. Congress's enthusiasm for cutting taxes grew with practice. The next several months saw cuts in excise taxes, along with more liberal depreciation allowances and investment tax credits.[3] With all this accumulating encouragement, the GNP rose a startling 5.9% throughout 1965. By December 1965, unemployment had fallen to the magic 4%.

The New Economics, in fact, had overreached itself. The dollar was heading into serious trouble abroad. Inflation was in the air at home. Through 1963, when the upswing started, the consumer price index rose at an annual rate of 1.2%. Through 1964, the annual rate was 1.3%. From December 1965 to December 1966, the rate was up to 3.4%; by August 1966, to 5.4%.[4]

Spending for Vietnam seems to have had little to do with these early stages of the inflation. Defense outlays actually declined rather sharply from the end of fiscal 1964 through fiscal 1965. Rises did not begin until the latter half of 1965, and even then by a relatively modest $3.5 billion. Federal spending in general stayed fairly level from the second quarter of 1962 to the second quarter of 1965. No doubt America's growing Vietnam commitment did begin to encourage inflationary expectations. And by the latter months of fiscal 1966, as defense outlays jumped $13 billion, rising military orders unquestionably fanned the inflationary fire. Inventories rose sharply as businessmen, fearing shortages, began to build stocks of raw materials and intermediate goods for the defense industries. At the same time, Johnson's "Great Society" programs began to involve major increases in nondefense spending, increases that were to continue rising sharply over the next few years.[5]

By 1966, the logic of Keynesian "fine-tuning" clearly called for a reversal of fiscal policy. The President's Council of Economic Advisers recommended a tax increase. Johnson, however, was reluctant to press for it.[6] He feared that the congressional conservatives would instead cut expenditures for his Great Society, as he was later to fear that the congressional liberals would cut the spending for his war. Nevertheless, the rapid rise of war expenditures starting in 1966 made the need for some new mix of fiscal and monetary policy increasingly urgent.

Under the circumstances, the task fell to the Federal Reserve. The Fed raised the discount rate from 4% to 4.5% in December 1965, a move bitterly opposed by the President. By the second quarter of 1966, monetary growth had ceased altogether. The effects were noteworthy. Interest rates reached new heights. Mortgage money dried up, seriously affecting the already troubled housing and construction industries. Financial markets grew increasingly disorderly. The Fed came under growing attack in Congress. In short, the situation exhibited the usual problems of combining an expansive fiscal policy with a restraining monetary policy.[7] Distress and clamor over tight money grew until, in the last quarter of 1966, the Fed began to reverse itself. Tight money and inventory adjustment were bringing the economy to a pause.

In January 1967, Johnson finally yielded to his advisers and requested a 6% surtax on incomes. But with the pause at the end of 1966 already being called a serious recession, Congress was more hesitant than ever to raise taxes. Meanwhile the Fed, anticipating the tax increase and fearing a recession, had already shifted to a highly expansive monetary policy. In the first three quarters of 1967, the money supply (M1) grew at an 8.2% annual rate. And though there was still no tax increase, federal defense spending continued to rise rapidly, to a high of 9.5% of GNP in 1967, sustained in 1968. Meanwhile, spending on the Great Society welfare programs continued apace.[8]

Not surprisingly, in 1967 the economy recovered from its pause and resumed expansion. By the end of the year, the Fed had once again grown thoroughly alarmed over inflation. But with the British pound in full crisis, the delicate international negotiations to save it inhibited raising American interest rates sharply.[9] The boom proceeded. Since unemployment had fallen to less than 4% in 1966, labor shortages were acute. An inflationary psychology was again spreading throughout the economy. Wages were regularly rising at inflationary rates—4.9% in 1967, 6.2% in 1968, and 6.6% in 1969. The consumer price index, meanwhile, increased 2.9% in 1967, 4.2% in 1968, and 5.4% in 1969. With economic dislocations powerfully reinforced by growing political disaffection, the Kennedy system of voluntary wage-price guideposts simply collapsed.[10]

By August 1967, the Administration had again taken up its demand for an income tax surcharge, this time at 10%. Even under such obviously inflationary circumstances, the tax increase required a protracted struggle in Congress. A final compromise was not reached until June 1968. A 10% tax surcharge was paired with a $6 billion cut in budget expenditures, mostly in Great Society programs.[11] Meanwhile, in the winter of 1968, the dollar had been through its worst foreign-exchange crisis of the decade.

As fiscal policy finally tightened in 1968, monetary policy loosened. Once the tax bill was passed, the Federal Reserve, smarting from congressional criticism and concerned over the still parlous state of the housing industry, relaxed monetary policy still further. By the second half of 1968, the money supply was growing at roughly an 8.5% annual rate. Consumer spending continued apace. Personal savings fell sharply. Business investment, pushed by rising unit labor costs, spurted ahead. By late 1968, the Fed was again alarmed and began tightening credit severely. Thus 1969 was to see the highest interest rates and lowest level of bank liquidity since World War II.[12] With monetary and fiscal policy finally pulling together, the stage was set for the recession of 1969, an inglorious finale for the era of fine tuning.

The Early Nixon Administration

Nixon arrived in office prepared for stern measures to control domestic inflation and, in the process, to strengthen the dollar abroad. His method was as conventional as his goal. He continued Johnson's tax surcharge, reduced the investment tax credit, and cut federal spending. The Federal Reserve persevered with tight money. Nixon's advisers promised no novelty except consistent moderation. Policies were to be "gradual," free from the hectic, disruptive oscillations typical of Johnson's later years.[13]

Moderation, however, proved neither a popular nor an economic success. Instead, Nixon found himself in the toils of a "stagflation" pleasing to no one. Policies to stem inflation resulted in a recession, but without reducing inflation to a satisfactory level. The recession of 1970 was the first since Eisenhower's recession of 1958–59. Declining military expenditures and returning soldiers exacerbated the slump. By the end of the year unemployment reached 6%. Real GNP shrank by about $3.5 billion, and tight money led to a credit squeeze that thoroughly alarmed the overextended business community. Bankruptcies and near-bankruptcies proliferated, with the fall of the Penn Central Railroad the most spectacular of the many business failures.[14]

Despite the severe slump, inflationary expectations, once aroused, proved to have a momentum of their own. Even in the face of heavy and growing unemployment, labor unions were determined to sustain the real incomes of their members whatever the consequences to employment, as the prolonged, bitter, and ultimately successful General Motors strike of late 1970 was to indicate.[15] Professional associations and others with high economic and political leverage behaved in a similar fashion. So did many enterprises. When demand fell, manufacturers tried to sustain their incomes by cutting output and raising prices, while waiting for the government's next round of stimulation. Thus the annual inflation rate, although it did fall to a low of 3.3% for 1972, was even at that point two and a half times higher than the average rate for 1964, and more than three times higher than the previous cyclical low of 1961.[16]

Events soon demonstrated to Nixon the high political costs of his deflationary policy. With tight money and unemployment the leading issues, the 1970 Congressional and state elections resulted in serious defeats for the Republican Party. Political reverses and business clamor against tight money pressured the Administration toward reflation. Johnson's tax surcharge was first lowered and finally canceled. William McChesney Martin was succeeded at the Federal Reserve by Arthur Burns, Nixon's ally of the fifties against Eisenhower's fiscal conservatism. Thereafter, despite Burns's reassuring conservative rhetoric, the Federal Reserve proved exceptionally submissive to presidential prodding. Interest rates began falling in mid-1970; the money supply was pumped up as much as 11% throughout 1971. Recovery was nevertheless spotty and seemed too slow for the increasingly impatient Administration.[17]

Lethargic as the reflation may have seemed to Nixon and his domestic critics, it was more than enough to trigger a massive run on the dollar. Throughout the sixties, each surge in the boom provoked its own dollar crisis — in 1965, 1968, and again in 1971. The 1968 crisis barely avoided a dollar devaluation. By 1971, the prospects were even more discouraging.[18] It was clear that nothing would be able to save the dollar's parity short of a return to severe deflation. The United States had apparently caught the British disease of endemic stagflation. American domestic prosperity was no longer compatible with a stable currency. To put the matter in purely domestic terms, the American economy could not be kept anywhere near full employment without running a high and accelerating inflation rate. The domestic syndrome led to the foreign problem. High and accelerating inflation meant a weakening currency. To save the dollar's parity meant deflationary restraints that blighted prosperity, but reduced inflation only slowly and partially. Reflation, on the other hand, would soon provoke a new payments crisis.

Nixon was determined to escape from this predicament. In particular, he had no intention of returning to deflation before the 1972 presidential election. All through early 1971, the Administration was restlessly looking for some revolutionary new policy.[19] The demands of domestic prosperity and foreign economic obligation seemed in direct opposition. In particular, Nixon's political survival seemed in flat contradiction to the requirements of the Bretton Woods monetary regime. Rather than continue the recession to save the dollar, Nixon let the dollar depreciate and saved his Administration. At the same time, he smothered the domestic inflationary consequences by imposing mandatory wage and price controls. Nixon's new policy, depreciation abroad and controls at home, constituted, in effect, a classic mercantilist solution.

There was no shortage of liberal economists, however, ready to rationalize Nixon's decision, thanks to which devaluing did not have to be presented as the consequence of domestic mismanagement nor as a choice for inflation over stable prices. Instead, devaluation was defended as rectifying a long-standing structural defect in the international monetary system. This preoccupation with the structural framework of the international monetary order had persisted among American economists for several years. Though brilliant, sincere, and to a limited extent even correct, these sophisticated criticisms of the mechanics of the international system deflected attention from the real domestic choices involved in Nixon's devaluation. As the subsequent course of events made manifest, the dollar's weakness was the consequence of America's domestic inflation and not of some technical defect in international monetary arrangements. Thus the dollar was to depreciate not just once in 1971, but again and again throughout the 1970s. Under the circumstances, Nixon's devaluation brought only temporary surcease from both the dollar's weakness and the domestic economy's stagflation. For while the American economy could declare its freedom from international monetary rules, it could not so easily escape the consequences of its own internal disequilibrium. Those consequences were not long in coming. Thus 1973 saw an unprecedented inflation, and 1974 saw the worst recession since the war. The later 1970s were to see a similar but even more extreme cyclical pattern. At the end of each cycle, moreover, the underlying inflation rate would be found to have taken another major jump forward.[20]

Why Inflation?

What was the matter with the domestic economy? Why had its inflation become endemic? Why was the economy trapped in stagflation? Contemporary analysts were fertile sources of special reasons. But an inflationary pattern that recurs, each time more violently, suggests not random agglomerations of misjudgement and accident but some deep-seated condition.

Inflation has to do with money, more precisely, with the creation of superfluous money. Inflation is a disease of the monetary system, a cancer of the money supply. Excess money, at a given level of prices, means excess demand. One way or another, money and credit are being created faster than can be absorbed by the actual growth of the supply of goods and services in the real economy. Hence, in the classic formulation, "too much money chases too few goods." Prices of goods and services rise until the excess money is absorbed.

Rising prices are only one of inflation's two basic symptoms. A balance-of-payments deficit is the other. Where money is allowed to flow freely across national boundaries, the excess money of an inflating economy will flow into other open economies that are less or not at all inflationary. In effect, an afflicted economy "exports" some or all of its inflation to others. Thus, while the rate of price increases was relatively low in the United States until 1965, the perennial US balance-of-payments problem, particularly after the restoration of convertibility in 1958, suggests that the United States was already an inflationary economy, or rather an economy more inflationary than the norm for the system as a whole.

How does the economy get itself into this inflationary condition? The subject is complex, involving, in the end, the essential character not only of the economy itself but of the society, culture, and political system. Certain broad generalizations nevertheless permit a broad answer.

If inflation is a disordered growth of the money supply, who permits or induces that unwarranted expansion? In a modern economy, public authority actively tries to regulate the money supply, either through the treasury or the central bank. The efficient cause of inflation, therefore, is frequently government monetary policy itself. For one reason or another, the state wishes the money supply to increase. The government's own fiscal deficit is one common reason. Thus, a period of high government spending, like a war, is almost always a period of inflation. In themselves, of course, government deficits are not inflationary. If taxes do not cover expenditures, the government may borrow all the funds it needs from the existing pool of private savings in the domestic capital market. The borrowed funds are thereby used for government spending rather than for private purposes. When a government regularly borrows a large part of private savings, it may "crowd out" private borrowers and thus discourage private investment. Whether this is good or bad for the economy depends on whether the government uses the funds it preempts more productively than the private investors. In any event, the borrowing is not, in itself, inflationary.

Deficits tend to cause inflation, however, when the central bank regularly creates extra money to cover them. In such circumstances, government does not preempt capital from private uses. It simply creates the extra money it needs. An expansive monetary policy, in effect, prevents a confrontation in the domestic capital markets between the demands of the government and the demands of private borrowers. Inflation ostensibly accommodates both.

Quite apart from the state's natural tendency to outspend its income and print money to cover the difference, the postwar goal of full employment is, in itself, a further major incentive for expansive monetary policy. Conventional postwar countercyclical policy pursues full employment either by an expansive fiscal policy with a deficit monetized by an expansive monetary policy, or by an expansive monetary policy alone. To a very substantial degree, countercyclical policy is now automatic. Whenever unemployment is high, statutory jobless and welfare benefits balloon fiscal spending, while reduced incomes mean smaller tax revenues. Fiscal budgets thus move sharply toward deficits. In a recession, central banks find it politically difficult to restrict the money supply, particularly as an expanding money supply is expected to stimulate the demand for goods and services, and hence for employment. In principle, as the economy moves back to the prosperous half of its cycle, budget deficits should turn into compensating surpluses and monetary policy grow tighter. In practice, this judicious balance is difficult to maintain in the face of the government's growing appetites and the citizenry's rising expectations. The government, after all, is supposed to foster growth as well as full employment. Everyone, including government itself, is regularly supposed to have more. When growth seems insufficient, more stimulation seems the obvious prescription. Societies have thus a strong tendency to keep raising their expectations about full employment. After 1960, the American case illustrates these tendencies all too clearly.

US Monetary Policy

In all stages of the business cycle, American budgets were regularly in deficit. Not only was US fiscal policy regularly inflation prone, but US monetary policy was unusually acquiescent. Higher American fiscal deficits would not have been inflationary if it had not been for the accommodating attitude of the Federal Reserve. The Fed faced serious obstacles to imposing a more restrictive policy. It lacked both the institutional and the political base for a tighter monetary policy. As it was, the Fed's efforts aroused powerful opposition, not only in Congress but within the successive administrations. Both the Kennedy and Johnson Administrations were highly sensitive to the social and human costs of less than full employment. At the same time, both had ambitious foreign programs and were eager to avoid a confrontation between the government's foreign and domestic aspirations, each with its own political constituency. Both therefore had unusually high demands for economic growth. High growth meant high investment, which required, it was widely believed, cheap and abundant capital. America's economic advantage was supposed to lie in its ample capital and correspondingly lower interest rates, a comparative advantage that had to be conserved by active measures if needed. Hence, the various efforts to close the domestic capital market to foreign borrowing. Hence, too, a powerful aversion to restrictive monetary policies that raised domestic long-term interest rates.

In practice, it proved easier to create enough extra money to meet the foreign demand for dollars than to follow policies that would presumably restrict domestic investment and growth. Wage and price guidelines could, it was hoped, control inflationary consequences at home. Any inflation could, in effect, be "exported" abroad. Throughout the sixties, thanks to the dollar's interna tional status, no serious external sanctions prevented the United States from running balance-of-payments deficits. At the same time, after Kennedy's popularization of the full employment budget, no real restraint prevented the federal government's running fiscal deficits at all stages of the business cycle.

Under this combination of conditions, to which in due course a war was added, it was not surprising that the Federal Reserve could not find the will or the support to halt the progress of American inflation. Thus, by 1965 inflation was showing up in higher prices at home as well as in the traditional balance-of-payments deficit abroad. The "pause" of 1966, induced by tight money reacting to fiscal deficits, brought a foretaste of the stagflation of 1969 and 1970. The dollar crisis of 1968 provided a dress rehearsal for the dollar crisis of 1971. Quite naturally, the inflationary crises came at the high points of the economy's expansion. Thus, Johnson's problems with inflation grew increasingly unmanageable the closer the economy came to the full employment that was Kennedy's goal. The same pattern was to be repeated with Nixon, and with Carter thereafter.

Economics and Inflation

It is still commonplace to blame the rise of inflation in the sixties on various particular events, like the Vietnam War, or Johnson's failure to ask for a timely tax increase, or the Federal Reserve's ill-timed shifts of monetary policy. In a similar fashion, difficulties in the seventies were blamed on "shocks" — Connally, bad harvests, disappearing anchovies, OPEC, or Khomeini.

To be sure, the most obvious "exogenous shock" of the 1960s, the Vietnam War, clearly did accelerate the inflationary process. Vietnam expenditures, unmatched by cuts elsewhere or new taxes, and financed by monetary expansion, were a powerful additional source of stimulation. But the Vietnam stimulus merely exaggerated an already established pattern, so much as to obscure it. The full-employment policies spawned in the Kennedy era, including the celebrated tax cut of 1964, had already set the United States to building its inflationary momentum. The 4% unemploy ment goal was already realized in 1965, the year price inflation also became visible, and months before Vietnam expenditures had any effect on the economy.[21]

For politicians, adventitious explanations are more convenient than blaming anything as fundamental as defense spending for Amercia's world role or full-employment policies to ensure smooth prosperity and endless growth. Any such general explanation goes to the very heart of the political system and its goals. But after two decades of inflation, a string of particular causes seems a less and less convincing explanation for the pattern that has kept recurring.

Part of the reluctance to admit general causes springs from the need to defend the pretentions of macroeconomic management. If bad consequences can be traced to bad individual decisions, the significance of economic managing in general is not impugned. But, in fact, modern societies do not seem to lend themselves to fine-tuning by economists, either neo-Keynesian or monetarist. In the United States, the high point of enthusiasm for Keynesian fine-tuning was reached early in the Johnson Administration. The 1964 tax cut was widely heralded as the start of a new era of rational economic management. Explanations for that Administration's in-glorious economic record thereafter tend to make a great deal of Johnson's reluctance to ask for a tax increase in 1966.[22] But John-son's failure to heed his economists reveals not so much the Presi-dent's pusillanimity as his economists' naive expectations about managing fiscal policy. Politicians are seldom eager to raise taxes. In a democracy, tax increases, when they do come, are almost in-variably too slow for the countercyclical effects desired. The same point holds for the pretentions of fine-tuning through monetary policy. If monetary policy was unquestionably more responsive and flexible than fiscal policy in the sixties, it was not notably more successful. Monetary shifts were generally late, extreme, and coun-terproductive. Does this "failure" to maintain price stability merely reflect incompetence at the Federal Reserve? More plausibly, the weakness of monetary policy reveals the limitations of techno-cratic management in the face of powerful forces whose goals and strategies have grown embedded in the political system.

By the end of the 1960s, the pretentions of neo-Keynesian man-agement were already under severe attack within the economics profession itself. Full-employment policy was being declared not only inflationary, but ultimately ineffectual. The first part of the charge did not bother neo-Keynesians unduly. The notion that some sacrifice of monetary stability was needed to achieve full employment was widely accepted among Keynesian economists and economic managers in the 1960s. Economists regularly counseled governments to accept a certain degree of "trade-off"—a little more inflation for a better employment rate. This relationship between inflation and employment was supposed to be expressed in a country's "Phillips Curve." As economic policy grew increasingly activist and inflation rose everywhere, economists, including Keynesians themselves, looked more and more closely at the nature of this Philips Curve.[23] In due course, a prominent school of American economists, anti-Keynesian monetarists, came to spurn not only the Phillips Curve but the whole neo-Keynesians policy for full employment.

The Phillips Curve

The ratio between unemployment and inflation described by the Phillips Curve was normally explained by imperfections in the labor market or the economy in general. In the language of liberal economics, a "perfect" market would "clear." Wages would fall low enough so that those who wanted employment could find it. Such perfect conditions required not only downward flexibility of wage rates but the other ideal circumstances needed for a perfect market, such as full information, mobility, and education. Insofar as such ideal conditions were lacking, achieving a lower level of unemployment required a degree of government stimulation of the economy that would cause some inflation.

By the late sixties, analysts began noting how the ratio between employment and inflation seemed to be changing for the worse. The curve was "shifting to the left." In other words, more and more inflation seemed needed to achieve the same degree of employment. The shift was generally laid to demographic changes in the labor supply. The work force was rapidly growing larger, and its composition was changing. Thanks to the postwar baby boom and the social progress unleashed in the sixties, youngsters, blacks, and women were entering the official labor force in unprecedented numbers. Overall employment had been rising sharply, but not enough. With so many young and traditionally marginal new workers, and with all the structural rigidities of the labor market, maintaining earlier unemployment goals required ever more vigorous fiscal and monetary stimulus, hence increased inflation.[24]

To Keynesians, this kind of analysis suggested various remedies. Inflation, if unavoidable, might be made more tolerable by selective indexing. Full employment goals might be defined in a less ambitious fashion. And fundamental improvements could be promoted in the quality or organization of the labor force. Some of these ideas found their way into policy. At one point, the Nixon Administration tried to redefine full employment as 4½% instead of 4% unemployed. The maneuver was perhaps justified in theory, but had limited appeal to an electorate and political leadership accustomed to the rapid gains of the sixties.[25] The Administration's radical proposals for changing the welfare system, formally introduced in January 1971, were among its more imaginative efforts to get at unemployment and inflation through structural reform. A "negative income tax," it was argued, would not only improve benefits to the poor, but actually reduce the economic burden by shearing bureaucracy and eliminating disincentives to employment. Presumably, it might also have reduced political pressures for inflationary full-employment polices. In any event, the reforms got nowhere in Congress.[26]

The Friedman Critique of Full Employment

The shifting ratios in the Phillips Curve data also supported a far more radical critique of conventional Keynesian policy. American economists of the monetarist school, of whom Milton Friedman became the most celebrated, rejected the very hypothesis that had informed the Phillips Curve. They denied that more inflation could be traded for more employment. The inflation would remain, they argued, but the increased employment would soon vanish.

Every country, according to Friedman, had a "natural rate of unemployment," a level of wages and employment compatible with price stability. This natural rate depended upon the character of the labor force, market, and economy generally. It could not be altered without fundamental changes in the economy's structural character. Lowering unemployment below the natural rate by pumping up demand through Keynesian expansionary policies was, according to Friedman, a snare and a delusion.

Friedman's analysis relied on the usual monetarist model that tied economic activity to changes in the money supply. Keynesian policies to raise the economy's overall demand required additional monetary creation. This additional money would, in itself, raise demand for goods and services and thereby increase employment. As soon as the level of employment went beyond its natural rate, however, creating more money would naturally result in inflation. For a short time, however, inflation, too, would improve the rate of employment. In inflationary conditions, prices generally increased faster than wages. This was because workers suffered from "money illusion." Their perception of money's declining purchasing power during inflation lagged behind reality. Wage claims were not adjusted adequately to compensate for inflation. Thus inflation in its earlier stages lowered real wages. With lower real wages, labor grew cheaper and employment increased. But money illusion could not be sustained indefinitely. Economic actors, workers included, gradually learned to take adequate account of inflation in their demands for compensation. Real wages then began to catch up with inflated prices. Employment began to fall back to its natural level. To resist this declining employment, Keynesian policies had to keep building new money illusion on top of old. But as the public's credulity narrowed, more and more money bought less and less illusion. Hence, more and more inflation brought less and less growth. With each new injection of Keynesian stimulus, the real economy returned ever more rapidly toward its natural rate of unemployment. Inflation remained and unemployment resumed. Price stability was sacrificed for naught.[27]

In effect, Friedman denied what the Phillips Curve was meant to describe: a stable ratio between unemployment and inflation. Stability was impossible essentially because inflation had an inher ent psychological dynamism of its own. Friedman's broad point struck home with compelling force. Certainly the experience of most countries in the sixties and seventies has given it powerful support. Inflation has proved to be progressive, its dynamism evidently springing from its psychological effects on people's behavior in the marketplace. In effect, "inflationary expectations," once implanted in the economic culture, liberate inflation's progress even from actual monetary policy. Inflationary expectations and behavior persist, even after the initial monetary stimulus is withdrawn. In modern economies, unions, professional associations, business firms, and governments themselves can generally resist short-term market conditions. Occasional periods of restrictive policy, like the pause of 1966 or the Johnson-Nixon squeeze of 1968–1970, are thus never long or severe enough to eliminate inflationary expectations. In due course, politics forces a return to expansion. Under such circumstances, inflationary expectations are entirely rational for the individual actor, and not easily quelled. Hence, inflation rises higher and higher, faster and faster. Policies to control it, even temporarily, must grow more severe and frequent. Stagflation becomes the common state of the economy. Countries caught in such a political-economic syndrome grow increasingly "unmanageable."[28]

The Friedman critique of full employment policy provides an obvious explanation for American inflation in the sixties. Though Friedman's own sympathies linked him to the Right, his critique of Keynesian demand management was, in theory, politically neutral. Though excessive stimulation could be laid to an excessive concern for the poor or the unemployed, it could as easily be traced to rising military expenditures as to welfare expenditures, or to tax cuts for the rich as to relief to the poor. All that is needed for inflation is, first of all, a government whose commitments, whatever they are, regularly outrun its resources and, second, an accommodating monetary policy to cover the deficit. All that can be said in the American case is that the government's commitment to a 4% unemployment rate, in view of its other commitments and the economy's structure, guaranteed an accelerating inflation. Conceivably, some different mix of commitments might have avoided inflation while still keeping unemployment down to 4%. With less rearmament, for example, more productive investments might have lowered the natural rate of unemployment and Kennedy's employment goals might not have been inflationary. On these questions, Friedman's critique has nothing to say. Friedman's own prescriptions were, in fact, a good deal less useful than his critique. To stop inflation, he would simply have frozen monetary creation at a level just sufficient to accommodate real growth. With no more excess money, he reasoned, there could have been no more inflation. However, the Federal Reserve was printing excess money not because it was indifferent to inflation but because the political system demanded a certain mix of policies and compelled the central bank to finance them. Ending inflation would mean ending the substantive policies that caused it. When Nixon tried to cut back, he saw his political support evaporate. In effect, the country's political will demanded inflation.

In Defense of Inflation

The country was not necessarily wrong. To present inflation as the consequence of cherished general policies is not to condemn the policies. It is only to assess these policies at their true economic cost. Inflation may be reckoned a cost like any other. Under certain circumstances, it may be worth paying in order to achieve goals or to avoid worse evils. By any standard, the accomplishments of American society in the sixties, as in the postwar decades generally, are impressive. American power, whatever its abuses, has given much of the world a rare interlude of secure prosperity. America's GNP has remained the world's highest, and among the highest per capita. Inevitably, other advanced industrial countries have been catching up from the war, but the American growth rate remains competitive.[29] The United States, moreover, has made substantial progress toward resolving its most fundamental social and economic weakness, the racial division that is the inherited curse of American history. Progress has depended upon bringing America's blacks into the mainstream of the work force. This pressure for social improvement and integration, along with the baby boom and the great increase in women seeking work, has required a gigantic creation of new jobs. Inevitably, these changes in the size and composition of the work force have meant significant deterioration in the Phillips Curve. Thus, throughout the sixties and seventies, productivity rose substantially less than in most other industrial countries.[30] Though official documents seldom speak of it, common sense, not to mention general experience with "affirmative action," suggest a negative tradeoff, in the short run at least, between economic efficiency and social progress.

The American Phillips Curve was deteriorating not only absolutely at home but also relatively abroad. Other major industrial countries did experience some of the same general shifts in the work force. All Western countries felt the effects of the baby boom and, to a lesser degree, a rise in the number of female workers. Most also had a major shift out of agricultural labor. But few, if any, had a shift as massive or as challenging to full employment as America's migration of blacks to the cities.[31] In short, changes in the United States were more extreme and came earlier.

In such a situation, reckoning the costs and benefits of American inflation is obviously a complex and elusive calculation. Inflation, in effect, financed foreign security and domestic changes that may easily be presented as long-term investments in the stability, happiness, and productivity of American society. Certainly, a full-employment policy that overcomes barriers to economic participation can be counted a prudent investment in the society's human capital.

However worthy the goal, the calculation has a dark side as well. Good goals may go sour, particularly when not disciplined by a true reckoning of their cost. World leadership may, for example, become world exploitation. Or investment in human capital may degenerate into chronic subsidies for unproductive employment and enterprise. An extended welfare system can become a drag on future economic growth and a positive disincentive to employment. What may start out as a form of borrowing for long-term objectives can degenerate into a chronic inability to live within the collective means. If inflation sometimes takes money away from unproductive investment and directs it to new enterprise, it also can permit economies to put off painful but necessary adjustments. In short, inflation ultimately imposes real costs to be set against the most worthy goals. In due course, these costs begin to defeat the goals themselves. Inflation can make currencies unstable and thereby threaten international trade. Unless allowed to run away completely, prolonged inflation tends to mean stagflation. Stop-go policies become more erratic and extreme, and government intervention in general becomes more frequent and unpredictable. Under these circumstances, business tends to become defensive and capital to grow frightened of any long-term investments. Falling productive investment means declining growth and productivity.[32] Technological investment begins to languish. As inflation accelerated in the United States, for example, the real growth of research and development expenditures declined remarkably — from 12% per annum in the years 1953–1964, to 3% in 1964–1971, to 0% in 1971–1975.[33]

Finally, inflation disrupts growth by threatening social cooperation. Inflation inevitably takes money away from some people and distributes it to others, in a fashion that seems unfair. With incomes having to be renegotiated constantly to avoid loss, long-standing arrangements are continually called in question. Since many things in society are more easily defended by custom than logic, particularly the relative earnings of diverse occupations, an air of general contentiousness begins to pervade labor and social relations generally.[34] In summary, inflation is not a harmless placebo to divert a straitened society from its real troubles. Inflation can incite the social conflict that full employment is meant to assuage. Worst of all, inflation becomes a major obstacle to the growth it anticipates. In the end, as the 1970s would make clear, inflation undermines not only national prosperity but national power as well.

By the late sixties the more thoughtful economists in all schools were well aware of the bankruptcy of fashionable ideas and fearful of the political storms in the offing. In marked contrast to the mood of a few years earlier, doubts were widespread about the future of the American economy. The return of anxiety to economic analysis helped put postwar prosperity in a broader perspective and helped as well to give a broad explanation for worsening inflation. The 1950s and especially the 1960s saw a rate of growth surpassing even the most hectic earlier phases of Western industrial development. By the late sixties, that growth had begun to be seen less the consequence of brilliant governmental management inspired by the new economics and more the consequence of catching up from depression and war. Economists began to doubt that such rates of growth could be sustained indefinitely. Doubts were strengthened by neo-Malthusian fears of excessive population, exhaustion of raw materials, or pollution of the environment—considerations that pointed to a less abundant world. Thoughtful men began to fear the social and political consequences of an end to rapid growth.[35]

In this Malthusian perspective, the causes of inflation are all too easily understood. Prolonged growth engenders social and economic expectations which develop a momentum of their own. When these expectations confront a slowing of real growth, social and political unrest is the result. For all governments, but plural democracies especially, inflation is a natural expedient. Rising money incomes preserve the semblance of continuing growth. Money illusion becomes a sort of narcotic refuge from a too difficult world. Painful adjustments may be masked in a general confusion of unstable prices and incomes. However temporary the solution, or harmful its effects upon growth itself, politicians can always hope the latest inflated boom will last until the next election. That was Nixon's choice in 1971, when the accelerating progress of America's domestic inflation finally led to a painful choice between domestic prosperity and international obligation. The tension that had been growing between domestic and foreign goals forms the other half of the story of American policy in the sixties.

3

Decline and Fall
of the Dollar

Though the domestic economy's stagflation put Nixon in serious political trouble, it was the breakdown of foreign economic policy that actually triggered his revolutionary changes of August 1971. The prelude to the "New Economic Policy" was a massive run on the dollar, precipitated in part by a declining trade balance. These external developments were closely related to the domestic evolution. Throughout the sixties, America's external economic problems developed in tandem with its domestic economic disturbances, in particular, with its rising inflation. The basic foreign economic policies, like the domestic, were essentially set in the Kennedy era. Kennedy was worried about the dollar's weakness but lacked an adequate notion of how to deal with it. It would be resolved, he hoped, through his general policies for growth and productivity. Johnson's Administration carried Kennedy's temporizing policies forward and, under mounting pressure, grew more imaginative. Nevertheless, the policies remained unsuccessful. Nixon played out Johnson's hand until August 1971. Thereafter, he started a new game, with rules of his own choosing.

Johnson and the Balance of Payments

The Johnson Administration's first full year, 1964, revealed how intractable the balance-of-payments problem had become.

Despite a $2.4 billion improvement in the current-account balance, rising outflows of long- and short-term capital, two-thirds of it to Europe, left the overall balance still deeper in deficit.[1] These swelling capital outflows caused the Administration increasing consternation. The Council of Economic Advisers' Report of 1965 complained of the propensity of foreigners to borrow in "our highly efficient, relatively low-cost and readily accessible long-term borrowing facilities."[2] The Council was particularly disturbed by this borrowing's natural consequence: the gradual rise of America's traditionally low long-term interest rates. The growing internationalization of American capital markets had been pushing short-term American interest rates upward since the early sixties. Operation Twist was supposed to let short-term rates rise in response to world conditions while keeping long-term rates well below foreign levels. Nevertheless, long-term as well as short-term rates had risen sharply in 1964, eased somewhat, and resumed rising in July 1965. Despite the rise, monetary conditions remained easier in the United States than abroad, and American domestic rates, long or short, still remained well below European levels.[3] Hence the outflows of capital. The Administration then tried voluntary guidelines to curb US corporate investments overseas. Capital outflow was considerably reduced in 1965, at which point, however, the trade balance was deteriorating, thereby adding a new strain to the overall balance of payments.[4]

America's continuing payments deficits began to be reflected in world currency markets. The domestic boom year of 1965 saw the first serious attack on the dollar since the gold crisis of 1960–1961. Like the early signs of domestic price inflation, the run took place before any significant increase in defense expenditures for Vietnam.[5]

The Balance of Payments as "High Politics"

The 1965 crisis indicated not only the growing technical weakness of the dollar but an increasing politicization of the international monetary issue. The Western alliance was in the midst of a major quarrel between the French and the Americans which covered the whole range of foreign policy. De Gaulle seemed determined to frustrate the grand designs of the Kennedy Administration.[6] He continually attacked American detente policy as a new "Yalta" and sought to promote his rival version of a Europe from the Atlantic to the Urals. By 1965 de Gaulle was growing openly critical of American involvement in the Vietnam War. In 1966, France withdrew formally from the integrated commands of NATO.

Economic issues took a prominent place in the quarrel. By 1963, de Gaulle's veto of Britain's application to the European Economic Community had already blighted the Administration's hopes for trade liberalization. By 1965, he had forced the EEC to adopt the Common Agricultural Policy and had dashed hopes for a Europe wide open to American farm products.

In 1965, de Gaulle also attacked US monetary policy. The American deficits, he charged, were exporting inflation to Europe. In his celebrated press conference that dealt with the monetary question, held on February 4, de Gaulle attacked the whole reserve-currency system.[7] By permitting endless American deficits, he argued, the system was unsound as well as unfair. The exported dollars were pumping the world full of inflation and, as American debts began to exceed American reserves, building financial instability that threatened "world-wide upset." Stability, according to de Gaulle, could be restored only by returning to the gold standard, a system without special privileges. Everyone would then be required to settle external imbalances promptly in a neutral medium, not in a fiat currency that one government could issue at will.

De Gaulle also touched on the political aspects of the question. Under the gold-exchange standard, American deficits that other countries were expected to hold made those countries, in effect, America's unwilling creditors. This involuntary extension of credit coincided with heavy American direct investment abroad. Certain countries were thus experiencing "a sort of expropriation of some of their business firms," takeovers that they were themselves financing by holding the surplus dollars. In broad terms, America's monetary hegemony reflected a political relationship between Europe and America that was growing increasingly inappropriate.

Without being unfriendly to America, European states, in the nature of things, wished "to act independently in every field of international affairs." Arrangements natural in the period following Europe's postwar debilitation appeared "inadequate, even abusive and dangerous," as the European states recovered "their substance." Changes should be made before the monetary and political problems grew unmanageable.

French Critique of the Gold-Exchange Standard

De Gaulle's notion of "exported inflation" reflected a critique of the reserve-currency system put forward by the Bank of France in the 1920s and revived after World War II. The economist most closely connected with this critique was Jacques Rueff, prominent both in the prewar theories and in their postwar revival.[8] After de Gaulle's return to power in 1958, Rueff became his close economic adviser. Rueff had long ago concluded that monetary stability was incompatible with the use of reserve currencies. The gold-exchange standard had amply demonstrated its failings in the 1920s, Rueff argued. It had nevertheless been reborn in the Anglo-American arrangements of Bretton Woods.

The rebirth was not a coincidence. The reason for the use of the dollar as a reserve currency after 1945 was the same as for its use after World War I. After each war, the world's economies, save for the United States, lacked sufficient monetary reserves to restore normal international business. To do so required large credits in dollars, the only currency with sufficient gold backing to be acceptable for international transactions. After World War I, the United States obliged with huge public and private loans. The British managed to restore the credibility of sterling and, by the mid 1920s, were themselves pumping "liquidity" into the international economy. Under the circumstances, it was not surprising that countries kept dollars and pounds as monetary reserves. The system broke down when the British could no longer sustain the pound's convertibility in 1931. The system's ruin was sealed by Roosevelt's defection from the gold standard in 1933. The situation of the international economy was even more desparate after World War II. American loans again came to the rescue. Hence, the return of the gold-exchange standard, with dollars the principal reserve currency.

As Rueff saw it, such an international system would inevitably break down once again. Any gold-exchange standard was doomed to fail, Rueff believed, because permitting the use of a national currency as a reserve in place of gold precluded those corrective adjustments that, under the classical gold standard, had worked automatically to restore equilibrium. Without these automatic tendencies toward adjustment, the international monetary mechanism led ineluctably to inflation and collapse.

Rueff's analysis based itself upon a classic monetarist model. Under the gold standard, Rueff noted, a United States running an external deficit would automatically have had to cover that deficit with gold. The gold transfer, while lowering the money supply and hence aggregate demand in the United States, would have raised the money supply and aggregate demand in the countries receiving it. With demand thus lowered in the United States and raised abroad, Americans would have been induced to export, and their imports would have fallen. Trade would have made the necessary adjustment to equilibrium.

Under the reserve-currency system, by contrast, dollars flowing abroad increased demand outside the United States, but without reducing it inside. When the United States was in deficit, foreign central banks, instead of receiving American gold, held dollars in the form of US Treasury instruments. This influx of dollars resulted in a corresponding increase in the national money supply on the European side, as the European central bank issued its own currency in return for the dollars brought to it. On the American side, however, no corresponding reduction in the money supply occurred. The Treasury instruments given to the foreign central banks were simply added to the American national debt, with no loss required for the US monetary base. Consequently, no reduction followed in America's national money supply. The outflow of dollars produced no corresponding reduction in domestic American demand and hence no corresponding impulse to export in compensation. In short, under the gold-exchange standard, whatever the United States acquired abroad did not have to be extracted from domestic US resources.

Considerations of equity aside, the system was relentlessly inflationary. Surplus dollars flowing into Europe caused European money supplies to grow too rapidly and made inflation inevitable. American debts would pile up higher and higher, Rueff reasoned, until the system would become so unmanageable that countries would have to abandon fixed parities and protect themselves by capital and trade controls. The international economy would disintegrate and the 1930s return.

Rueff was convinced that only the gold standard could restore stability, and he outlined a series of practical steps leading to its return. De Gaulle's own defense of gold, while no doubt perfectly genuine, could also be taken as symbolic.[9] In practice, as long as national reserve currencies were eliminated, any objective standard not subject to extensive manipulation or wild fluctuation would do. Nothing in de Gaulle's pronouncements, for example, ruled out using some multilaterally determined unit as the international standard of value and reserve in place of gold. Revaluing gold by multilateral agreement, Rueff's blueprint for returning to the gold standard, was not, after all, so different from creating "Special Drawing Rights" (SDRs) by agreement in the International Monetary Fund (IMF). It was essential, however, that creation of new international money not be inflationary, and therefore not be controlled by the United States in particular or by debtor countries in general. In the end, it was difficult for the French to imagine any arrangement as satisfactory as gold. As a commodity, it had a real value of its own, determined by the cost of increasing its supply. It also had many sources, and its price was therefore not easy to manipulate over a long period of time. Furthermore, after a lifetime as odd man out in various clubs dominated by the Anglo-American special relationship, de Gaulle was disillusioned with the possibilities of multilateral management.

Rueff's views were widely misunderstood at the time, even among the monetary experts. In fashionable opinion, defending gold represented atavistic nationalism and antediluvian economics. Keynes's strictures about the foolishness of digging gold out of the ground and then putting it back into vaults could always be used to give a sophisticated gloss to arguments that, in effect, evaded the essential issue.[10] That real issue was whether the United States was serious about ending its balance-of-payments deficit and whether it could expect to do so without a much stricter international discipline over its domestic and foreign policies. Even if conventional American official thinking in the mid-sixties still imagined a return to equilibrium, an international order that would seriously constrain the United States to do so was instinctively rejected. American rhetoric may not yet have adopted the frankly hegemonic arguments popular among the British, to the effect that the world system requires a leading country whose special responsibilities give it special rules. But American thinking was drifting in that direction.[11]

American Concern over Liquidity

Ironically, instead of taking on the real issues raised in the gold question, contemporary American academic discussion preoccupied itself with resolving the problem of "world liquidity," a difficulty that was expected once the American deficit was stopped. In the late fifties, a Belgian economics professor at Yale, Robert Triffin, had formulated the liquidity problem into what became known as the "Triffin Paradox."[12] Triffin took it for granted that a weakening dollar would sooner or later force the United States to end its balance-of-payments deficits. What would happen, Triffin asked, when US deficits finally did stop? The dollar had become the principal reserve currency as well as the principal medium of payment for international transactions. With the volume of these transactions growing by leaps and bounds, swings in national balances of payments were growing larger and larger. If US deficits ended, the supply of internationally usable funds would no longer be regularly augmented. In particular, the increased volume of transactions meant that countries would no longer accumulate adequate reserves to finance temporary imbalances. Lack of liquidity would force governments to restrict trade and capital flows or follow wasteful stop-go policies.

Triffin agreed with Rueff that no national currency could provide a viable substitute for gold. It was in the nature of national reserve currencies to grow weak and to collapse. But something would have to replace those dollar deficits that had provided the

world with the money it needed. In other words, the regular aug-
mentation of liquidity that Rueff believed to be inflationary, Triffin
believed to be essential. Triffin recommended turning the money-
creating function over to the multilateral mechanism already in
place, the IMF, which by agreement among its members could
regularly issue and distribute new reserve units.

Had the United States ended its deficits as Triffin assumed, his
liquidity problem would doubtless have become real enough. In
this respect, Triffin's analysis was more realistic than Rueff's. Returning to Rueff's gold standard would have required a whole
series of other domestic and foreign changes, requiring a more
rigid self-discipline from modern nation-states than was probable,
at least without the intervention of some universally traumatic experience with inflation. But as events actually transpired, Triffin's
concern was misplaced. Since the United States was never to end
its payments deficit, the problem of liquidity was its actual excess
rather than its putative deficiency. Under these circumstances, creation of new liquidity by the IMF had a practical appeal to American policy for quite opposite reasons from what Triffin had intended. Since the United States dominated the IMF, had by far the
largest IMF quota, and would presumably also be the major recipient of the new reserve units, the Triffin scheme seemed an ideal
way to finance dollar deficits in the future. In effect, Triffin's concern for a hypothetical liquidity shortage, after the dollar deficit
was ended, provided the rationale for a new multilateral way to
finance a continuation of that deficit. The aims of US policy were
eminently simple. The United States looked to the IMF as a way of
legitimizing America's unquenchable deficit and providing credit
to sustain the dollar. In due course, both ends were served by
politicizing the simmering academic debate over liquidity.

The new American initiative developed over several years. As
early as 1963, Douglas Dillon and Robert Roosa, then the Treasury's Secretary and Under-Secretary for Monetary Affairs, realized that the payments deficit would prove difficult to cure and that
the world's tolerance for ad-hoc improvisations would grow
shorter. Managing the dollar's difficulties, they concluded, required some structural reform of the international monetary
system itself, a reform that would in turn require multilateral polit-

ical support.[13] In 1965, a new team at the Treasury, Joseph Fowler and Frederick Deming, made the creation of a new international liquidity mechanism a major American campaign. According to the proposal that evolved, the IMF was to issue regular credits, or Special Drawing Rights, to its members. In effect, creating the SDR mechanism became the Johnson Administration's major long-range strategy for resolving the balance-of-payments problem.

This major American monetary initiative, like the Kennedy Round, ran into great opposition from the French, augmented by considerable, if varying, support from the other EEC countries, Germany in particular. Both France and Germany shared a growing concern about the "abuses" of the reserve currency arrangements. Both realized, however, that the United States could not end its deficits abruptly without great disruption. Neither wanted to bring down the entire postwar liberal system. Quite the contrary. Both were handicapped by seldom being able to agree on a policy for reform. The Germans wanted to use Europe's growing financial power to curb US "extravagance" abroad, but without producing a major confrontation and without ending the reserve-currency system. The French were convinced that the system's abuses could be ended only by eliminating reserve currencies altogether. With Europe divided, the United States finally had its way. The SDR scheme was accepted in 1968 and went into effect in 1970.[14] But European hesitations greatly limited its scope. Ironically, in view of Triffin's concerns, SDR creation began just as the world was witnessing an unparalleled explosion of international liquidity.[15]

Though creating SDRs was not to prove very significant in itself, the whole initiative and debate marked a notable step toward bolder conceptions in American strategy. As the American government began to face up to the intractability of the payments deficit, it started to rethink its commitment to fixed exchange rates, the very foundation of the Bretton Woods system. The drift of American thinking was reflected in the semiofficial "benign neglect" arguments that began to be found among academic experts in the late sixties.[16] Countries unwilling to absorb more dollars, the experts argued, ought to be willing to revalue their own currencies upward. Psychologically and technically, the occasional revaluation of one or two allied currencies would be far less disruptive than some across-the-board dollar devaluation. This line of thinking gradually gained ascendancy inside the beleagured Treasury and prefigured Nixon's revolution in 1971. It had the advantage of shifting the onus for action away from the United States to the surplus countries, who could thus be isolated and singled out for particular pressure.

Power and Persusasion

The SDR campaign indicated not only more radical American views on monetary questions but also a growing willingness to use power to make these views prevail. As America's economic strength diminished, its political power came into more obvious use. US international monetary policy became more frankly hegemonic. Defense of the dollar in the late sixties came to depend primarily upon direct political pressure applied on America's major creditors.

Canada, Germany, and Japan were the special objects of American solicitude. Canada was wooed with a special status that made it, in many respects, a favored part of the US national economy. Thanks to the automobile agreement of January 1965, Canadian industrial goods were given privileged access to the American market, a powerful encouragement to multinational investment. Canada was, moreover, exempted from the Interest Equalization Tax and from later US restrictions on the outflow of capital. In return, Canadians were expected to see to it that the dollars they accumulated did not return as claims on US monetary reserves.[17]

Germany was a more powerful country, traditionally resistant to inflation and highly dependent upon world trade. For the Germans, absorbing a large regular dollar inflow into the domestic money supply prompted domestic expansion and risked inflation. Inflation would, in turn, injure exports by raising costs. The openness of the German economy, however, made it difficult to sterilize the dollar inflow. Revaluing the German mark was the most obvious alternative but ran counter to the interests of the export industries, which remained the backbone of the German economy.

The Germans' dilemma made them increasingly resentful of American economic policy. They also resented American insistence on "offset" payments for troops in Germany, a payment with overtones of occupation and tribute. But the Germans had few options. The Kiesinger "Great Coalition" of 1966 was less complacently pro-American than the Erhard regime that preceded it. But the new government was a diverse coalition, and the Social Democratic partners were preoccupied with pressing their *Ostpolitik*, impossible without American forbearance. In any event, the realities of the German military situation had not changed. For all its economic power, the Federal Republic was still an American military protectorate with Russian troops poised across its border. Berlin was a raw nerve exposed to pressure at any time. The Czech invasion of 1968 reminded the Germans of how precarious their own situation might easily become. It also, incidentally, estranged them from the French, who found the Great Coalition's *Ostpolitik* clumsy and provocative. In short, the Germans were in no position to sustain a determined opposition to US policy. Instead, they complained, dragged their feet on offsets, and protected themselves from dollar inflows as best they could. When the pressure grew too intense, as in 1969, they revalued the mark. Whatever the long-range costs to their industrial development, their trade was expanding and their domestic prosperity was at record levels.[18]

Of the three countries receiving special American attention, Japan drove the best bargain. Like the Germans, the Japanese had done very well since losing World War II. The *Pax Americana* had given them secure access to the world's raw materials and to the American domestic market. At the same time, they had successfully exempted themselves at home from most of the liberal rules that supposedly governed the rest of the system. Japan's import restrictions were notoriously impenetrable, its export subsidies flagrant, and foreign investments resolutely excluded. Despite complaints from time to time about the more outrageous aspects of Japanese policy, the American government had a strong interest in preserving the status quo. For while Japan ran a large surplus with the United States, the accumulated dollars were sterilized and safely locked up in Japanese reserves. Since the Japanese tended neither to buy nor invest abroad, Japan was a sort of "black hole" into which surplus dollars disappeared forever. The supposed defects of the mercantilist Japanese, their invincible trade and exchange controls, were precisely what permitted them to carry out such a policy with success.[19] In summary, in the face of America's mounting domestic inflation, the dollar was increasingly sustained by America's power and in particular by the manipulated cooperation of its three economic "allies."

The Crisis of 1968

In early 1968, the Johnson Administration's luck nearly ran out. The domestic economy's "pause" in 1966 had temporarily calmed the dollar's international troubles. Thereafter, the Federal Reserve, under severe congressional pressure, had relaxed its tight money policy. Domestic expansion quickened in 1967, but Britain's sterling crisis inhibited again raising US interest rates, lest the pound be weakened still further.[20] Prime Minister Harold Wilson's long struggle to sustain the pound finally collapsed in late 1967. Speculation began to turn directly against the dollar. Passage of the tax increase in early 1968 induced the Federal Reserve to relax monetary policy still more.

The Administration tried to head off the crisis. In the State of the Union Address in January 1968, Johnson finally imposed mandatory controls on direct investment abroad and again asked Congress to remove the domestic gold cover and thus make the entire gold stock available to defend the exchange rate.[21] The storm broke with the announcement of the 1967 balance-of-payments figures in February 1968. The payments deficit in 1967 had risen to $3.7 billion and was rising especially rapidly in the last quarter. Political factors were also undermining confidence in the dollar. The war in Vietnam was convulsing the United States with political dissent and economic dislocation. The war was widely believed to cause, in itself, a large outflow of dollars. No end seemed in sight. The American commander General William Westmoreland was asking for yet another "escalation." By March, an enormous rush had developed in the gold market. On March 14, the United States gave up supporting the gold pool, and Johnson asked Wilson to close London's gold market.[22] In effect, the United States defaulted on its obligations under the gold-exchange standard.

Gold, of course, had always been the weak link in Johnson's hegemonic monetary policy. Whereas the United States had an infinite supply of dollars, it had only a limited supply of gold. As long as foreign dollar holders had the right to ask for gold, the United States might at any time be faced with bankruptcy. Though central banks might be pressured, the private gold market was harder to control. An American policy moving toward open hegemony naturally drifted toward renouncing the gold commitment. In late 1966, an internal Treasury memorandum had already suggested untying the dollar from gold.[23] In 1967, the United States had extracted from the Federal Republic of Germany a pledge not to ask for payments in bullion.[24] By March 1963, when the great run developed in the private gold market, the Administration was psychologically and intellectually prepared to "demonetize" gold.

America's traditional hegemonial style, however, required that unilateral repudiation be dressed up as multilateral reform. By solemn international agreement, the empty gold pool thus became the "two-tier" gold market.[25] Under the new arrangements, the United States would maintain its hypothetical commitment to pay out gold at the official price to central banks, a pledge that American political power and economic weakness had already emptied of substance. In the private market, however, the gold price would henceforth be left to fluctuate. In other words, America's hegemony over its allies was no longer to be mocked by the private market. Gold was effectively demonetized. The world was on a de facto dollar standard.

From breaking the link to gold, however, it was only a short step to the end of fixed exchange rates altogether. Bretton Woods still committed the United States to sustaining the dollar's parity against other currencies, but with the gold tie to the private market out of the way, private holders grew less and less inclined to accept dollars for strong foreign currencies except at a discount, that is, at higher and higher interest rates. When those interest rates were no longer available, the flood of dollars into foreign central banks became unbearable. By the time of the next great run on the dollar, in 1971, the psychological barrier to breaking the dollar's parity had already given way. Europeans had lost their faith; the United States had lost its desire. Benign neglect was blossoming into a defense of floating rates.

The Johnson Administration was spared this last step by a series of domestic changes and foreign catastrophes. The Federal Reserve's abrupt switch to tight money in 1968 removed the immediate pressure after the March crisis and gave foreign dollar holders the high interests rates they demanded. Moreover, within two months of the March run in the gold market, fortune favored the dollar with a series of political and economic explosions in Europe. The May events in Paris nearly toppled the Gaullist regime, and the Russian invasion of Prague in August forcefully reminded the Europeans of their military dependence. The French franc came under strong pressure, and a great flow of European capital moved to the United States.[26] The fall of the dollar, like the fall of Vietnam, was left to Nixon.

Like the Americans, the Europeans also learned something from the monetary crises and debates of the later sixties. While European opinion outside France was still slow to evolve toward radical solutions, the monetary debates and general turmoil of the later sixties pushed European political leaders toward a more conscious awareness of their common interest in the monetary issue. While Americans contemplated floating, Europeans began thinking about a monetary union of their own.[27]

Nixon's Balance-of-Payments Crisis

Europe's misfortunes and the Federal Reserve's tight money gave the Nixon Administration respite from balance-of-payments problems through 1969. America's domestic deflationary policies, with their high interest rates, sucked short-term capital from Europe's overheated and nervous economies. Squeezed American banks borrowed heavily from their European branches. As a result, the United States itself enjoyed a massive inflow and hence, in 1969, saw its first positive balance of payments since World War II. The Fed's switch to easy money in 1970, along with Nixon's reflation, quickly reversed the flow. As cheaper domestic credit again grew abundant, American banks paid off their foreign loans. The US balance-of-payments deficit in 1970 jumped to an unprecedented $9.8 billion. As American easy money continued into 1971, the flight from the dollar accelerated.[28] With no reversal of Nixon's reflation in sight, private foreign holders began dumping their dollars. An unprecedented panic seized the foreign exchange markets. On the third of May, the Germans gave up supporting the dollar and let the mark float upward. The shift of dollars continued apace. By the third quarter of 1971, the American payments deficit stood at an astounding $11.9 billion.[29] Under the circumstances, Nixon's devaluation on August 15 was inevitable.

America's Declining Trade Balance

While the dollar was faltering in early 1971, it became known that the US trade balance, positive since the last century, was about to register a deficit. The decline in the American trade balance appears to be one of the more significant long-range developments of the Johnson period. Deterioration had gone on for some time. From 1964 to 1971, US exports of manufactures had risen 69%, while imports had jumped 144%.[30] Even earlier, the Kennedy Administration had been worried about America's trade and productivity compared with the more rapid rise of Europe and Japan. But the relative declines of the early sixties could easily be seen a natural concomitant of industrial recovery abroad. The trend was supposed to be reversed, moreover, by Kennedy's renewed American growth. As the US economy moved toward fuller capacity, productivity was supposed to improve. Greater domestic demand was expected to stimulate greater domestic investment. The outflow of investment capital abroad was to diminish, and American money was to return to rebuild American domestic industry. With a more modern plant, home products would thus be more competitive. Finally, trade liberalization would stimulate American firms to export rather than manufacture the same products abroad.

Though the notion that domestic growth would spur exports

was rather quixotic, Administration optimism seemed justified for a time by the actual performance of the trade balance as the economy initially expanded. The year 1963 saw not only the beginning of the Kennedy-Johnson boom but also a substantial jump in the surplus for merchandise trade; 1964 saw the highest trade surplus since 1947. But by 1965, as the domestic economy grew increasingly inflationary, the trade balance began to decline. Thereafter, with the usual lags, the balance followed domestic inflation. By 1966, the surplus had dropped to about half of what it had been in 1964. The pause of 1966 arrested further deterioration in 1967, but decline resumed dramatically in 1968, with the traditional surplus falling to a mere $635 million and staying at the same low level through 1969. The 1969 domestic downturn restored the trade balance somewhat in 1970. Nixon's reflation in that year pushed 1971 trade to a substantial $2.3 billion deficit.[31]

Throughout most of its life, the Johnson Administration was struggling to complete the great round of trade negotiations launched in the Kennedy era, the Kennedy Round. These negotiations had been an important part of Kennedy's grand design for domestic rejuvenation and Atlantic leadership. The Johnson Administration pursued the negotiations vigorously. Together with SDR negotiations, they were the Administration's major strategic initiative in international economic diplomacy. Progress was not rapid. Kennedy Round negotiations dragged on until 1967, with the Americans growing increasingly disenchanted that their grand design had degenerated into "a lower-key commercial operation." The final results were nevertheless impressive, at least for industrial products.[32] Indeed, liberalization was rather more sweeping than Congress proved willing to accept, as its subsequent refusal to ratify some of the key concessions of American negotiations made embarrassingly clear.[33]

The Kennedy Round's trade liberalization came at a bad time for the American economy. Thanks to the rapid progress of domestic inflation, the period 1965–1968 saw a striking deterioration in America's price stability, unit labor costs, and productivity relative to its major international competitors. By the time the tariff cuts occurred, the US domestic economy was in the midst of an inflationary boom that encouraged imports, discouraged exports, and left a highly overvalued dollar.[34] The credit squeeze and recession starting toward the end of 1968 did lead to a modest recovery of the trade balance in 1970, but they also caught many firms in a severe liquidity crisis. An overvalued dollar abroad and an acute shortage of liquidity at home did little to encourage domestic American industry to invest in aggressive export strategies. Meanwhile, foreign firms, traditionally more oriented toward international sales, were quick to position themselves in the American market. Under these circumstances, liberalization appeared to make American trade problems worse. The American deficit began to seem less a reflection of short-term conjunctural factors than a structural decline in American industrial competiveness and commercial vitality. In short, Nixon had apparently inherited from Johnson not only inflation and a feeble dollar, but also a structural trade deficit.

The Nixon Administration had these trade questions very much in mind as it faced the dollar crisis in 1971. In devaluation, Nixon began to see not only the unavoidable consequence of his domestic reflation but also the opportunity to reverse, in one dramatic shock, the steady deterioration in America's international economic standing. Instead of a defeat, devaluation began to seem a victory. Instead of being pressured to support the dollar, American allies would now be pressured to let it fall. As American power had restored the economies of Europe and Japan, so now it would restore that of the United States.

4

**Nixon's
Revolution**

THE TRENDS leading to the dollar's collapse in August 1971 were
the same as those that had steadily weakened the dollar
throughout the 1960s. Nixon's dollar crisis was, in effect, a
resumption of Johnson's. Nixon's dilemma was the same as Kennedy's: how to escape from stagnation at home without weakening
the dollar abroad. Like Kennedy, he could not find the answer.
But after ten years of deterioration, very little credit remained
available. Still another improvisation to avoid devaluation was improbable. Nixon had convinced himself, however, that both international and domestic politics ruled out any further shocks to
American prestige abroad. Just as defeat in Vietnam had to be hidden behind an elaborate series of diplomatic initiatives designed to
demonstrate America's continuing control of the world situation,
so the dollar's fall had be be masked by spectacular initiatives in
the economic sphere. The United States could not afford to seem a
"pitiful, helpless giant" who had lost control of the monetary situation. The United States could hope, moreover, that its affluent industrial allies, the Europeans and Japanese, would prove less resistant to American face-saving than the intractable Vietnamese.[1]

The New Economic Policy

By August 1971, with domestic inflation again rising and the
dollar clearly heading for a fall, Nixon was ready with his political

masterstroke, the "New Economic Policy." On August 15, with the currency markets in crisis, Nixon himself announced the new policy. The measures amounted to a sort of mercantilist revolution in domestic and foreign policy. The dollar's official convertibility into either gold or foreign currencies was suspended indefinitely, and a temporary surcharge of 10% was imposed on dutiable imports. At home, wages, prices, and rents were frozen for ninety days, while both federal taxes and expenditures were cut.[2]

The domestic measures were meant to break the inflationary spiral while giving an additional stimulus to growth. The external measures were supposed to cause a sharp depreciation of the dollar against the currencies of major industrial rivals. Devaluation was intended to produce a major improvement in the US balance of payments, including the trade balance. The import surcharge was to be a bargaining lever against any foreign resistance or retaliation.

In his new Secretary of the Treasury, John Connally, Nixon had found just the kind of figure needed to pull off his coup. Connally demanded a devaluation sufficient to yield a $13 billion surplus in the trade balance, the amount needed, he said, to cover American overseas military burdens and capital investments.[3] Without such a turnaround, the Secretary professed little interest in ever resuming convertibility or removing the import surcharge. Connally's flamboyant pronouncements had an important political aim. They transformed the dollar's retreat into an aggressive attack to improve the American trade balance. The devaluation that could not be avoided was thus made out to be a major American victory.

To be legitimate, however, victory required America's affluent allies to acquiesce formally in a devaluation. Jockeying with the Europeans and Japanese continued throughout the autumn. Foreign and domestic criticism of Connally's "Texas poker" grew intense. Neither he nor Nixon appeared to waver. By December, Nixon and French President Georges Pompidou had worked out a deal in the Azores, which the IMF's "Smithsonian Agreement" formalized shortly thereafter. New parities were established. The dollar was devalued against gold, and nearly all the major industrial currencies were revalued against the dollar — the German mark by 13.58% and the Japanese yen by 16.88%. The United States dropped the import surcharge but pointedly refused to pledge support for the new parities if they again came under pressure.[4]

Nixon's revolution seemed both a diplomatic victory and an economic success. Domestically, the new Economic Policy's package of stimulation and controls appeared to work as hoped. Throughout 1972, the United States enjoyed the largest real growth (5.7%) since 1966 and the lowest rise in consumer prices (3.3%) since 1967. By December, unemployment was down to 5.1%.[5] International success was equally striking. The usual lags delayed an immediate improvement in the trade balance, but capital flows reversed themselves sharply. Foreign portfolio investors developed a new interest in American securities. US net long-term investment abroad dwindled. The overall US balance-of-payments deficit (official reserve transactions) dropped from $29.8 billion in 1971 to $10.4 billion in 1972.[6] With the dollar apparently rejuvenated, America's trading rivals began to hope for a firm restoration of fixed rates, particularly after May 1972, when a conventional liberal, George Schultz, replaced Connally at the Treasury.[7] In other words, the Connally devaluation began to seem a once-for-all cure rather than a fundamental shift toward floating rates. American officials encouraged these hopes with a spate of new proposals for monetary reform, as well as an apparent resumption of normal intervention to support the dollar in exchange markets.[8]

The Permanent Revolution

Contrary to European hopes for a restoration of Bretton Woods, Connally's "shocks" were to prove not an aberration but a formula that was to dominate American economic policy during the rest of the decade. Aside from temporary wage and price controls, the Nixon policy provided no cure for American inflation. On the contrary, by renouncing the commitment to maintain the dollar's convertibility at parity, Nixon swept away a major barrier to that inflation. Thus, the same inflation that prompted the New Economic Policy also sustained its continuation.

Origins of the New Mercantilism

The analysis that lay behind the Nixonian strategy had long been in preparation. Fear of US industrial decline had combined with resentment over America's imperial burdens and handicaps. Floating exchange rates were expected to provide the resolution.

Fears of American industrial decline were long-standing. Kennedy could justify stimulating expansion, for example, by the prospect that Europe and Japan, with their fast rates of growth and rapidly rising productivity, would eventually outstrip a relatively complacent and sluggish United States. The subsequent performance of the American economy had done little to allay these worries. In particular, the decline in the US trade balance in the Johnson years was taken for evidence of America's general economic debility. These fears crystallized in the "Peterson Report" of 1971, the Nixon Administration's high-level study of the country's competitive position. Between 1960 and 1970, the US share of world exports had fallen from 18.2% to 15.4% and the US share of world manufactured exports had dropped from 22.8% to 18.4%. The ratio of US exports to imports of manufactures had been falling since 1964. Together, these trends evidenced America's declining industrial competitiveness.[9]

The significance of such figures could, of course, be questioned. America's "decline" could also be described as the predictable recovery of Europe and Japan. Figures for American productivity were similarly ambiguous. Though America's rate of growth of output per man-hour was not only the lowest among the capitalist countries but slowing down, Europe's and Japan's better figures could be counted merely as an inevitable catching up to American standards. In absolute terms, American unit costs were still competitive, since the rate of increase of both US unit labor costs and US hourly compensation rates were the lowest among advanced industrial countries.[10] Decelerating American productivity might also be tied to a shift in demographic, social, and cultural factors in all industrial societies, a shift occurring earlier in the United States precisely because it was more advanced than the others.[11]

As for trade itself, much of the sharp rise in US imports of manufactures came from two countries, Canada and Japan. Both were special cases, related to balance-of-payments strategy.[12] Canadian trade was much influenced by the automobile agreement of 1965, an arrangement that encouraged the Detroit automakers to manufacture across the border and import into the United States. As a quid pro quo, Canada's central bank was supposed to hold US dollars as if it were a branch of the Federal Reserve. Did the American trade deficit with Canada therefore indicate industrial decline in the United States, or did it merely reflect a deliberate policy to integrate Canada into the US economy?

The Canadian automobile arrangement was a particular case of a more general phenomenon. By the early 1970s, nearly 25% of American trade consisted of exchanges among the various subsidiaries of US multinational corporations.[13] Prices in these intracorporate flows often reflected accounting techniques to minimize taxes rather than actual market values. How then to calculate the true state of the trade balance? Was the American trade decline merely the *Fata Morgana* of corporate accounting?

Japan was also a special case. US policy had deliberately encouraged reconstructing Japanese industry to orient itself toward the American market, presumably as an antidote and compensation for the loss of China and the old "co-prosperity sphere." Japanese trade policy was flagrantly mercantilistic, but the United States had done little to change it or to extract any commercial quid pro quo, aside from vainly trying to open Europe to the "burden" of Japanese trade. Instead, the United States increasingly relied on the Japanese to defend the dollar. Mercantilist Japan safely absorbed an immense quantity of America's exported dollars. Under such circumstances, was the commercial deficit with Japan evidence so much of American industrial decline as of Japanese protectionism, permitted for special reasons?

Though the Peterson Report was sensitive to the ambiguities of American "decline," its general conclusion was unmistakable: "The central assumptions on which our policies had been based had ceased to fit the facts well before August 15. The international measures taken on August 15 marked the first phase of our adjustment to current realities. Had the President chosen to solve the crisis only in terms of its immediate symptoms, he might have acted differently. But then we would have faced yet more crises in the future, and the world economy would have been left in a continuing state of avoidable uncertainty . . .

"Instead, he chose measures which, while protecting our short-term international position, were also designed to encourage the initiation of basic reforms in the international monetary and trading system, and in the distribution of the burdens of leadership among the economically stronger nations . . .

"In response to mounting expressions of American concern and urgings to negotiate corrections to these trends, the reply was too often that international needs or preoccupations precluded meaningful external adjustments. It boiled down to a response of "negotiations later rather than sooner." In the meantime, our own external situation — as measured by mounting balance-of-payments deficits and a rapidly deteriorating trade position — made it increasingly clear to us that this response had to be reversed: we had to convince our partners that negotiations "sooner" were no longer just desirable — they were imperative . . .

"We can no longer assume that every step towards closer ties between certain countries is beneficial to the rest of the world. On the contrary, we must now ask under what conditions we should support integrative efforts and preferential ties among other countries, what the implications are for our competitive position and what other of our attitudes and policies we must alter to protect our own interests, and to advance what the President has called the "world interest."[14]

Allies as Free Riders

For the Nixon Administration, assuming an American decline and blaming it on affluent allies was both congenial and convenient. The Administration lived in a subculture of *Schadenfreude* — a conservative backlash to the youthful rebellion incited by Vietnam, a mood to which its foreign policy wizard, Henry Kissinger, occasionally added a showy Spenglerian gloss. Kissinger's utterances also linked the mood to a growing resentment against

America's rich allies. Europe and Japan, it was felt, had become "free riders," profiting handsomely from the postwar system, but resolutely refusing to share its imperial burdens.[15] As allies, they had not helped but instead criticized the United States in Vietnam. Indeed, they still were not even paying for their own defense.

The economic dimension of this view, outlined in the measured terms of the Peterson Report, was put more bluntly elsewhere. Critics of American foreign policy had long noted the correspondence between the American basic balance-of-payments deficit and the annual exchange outflow for overseas military cost, mostly for troops in Europe. The Nixon Administration, Connally in particular, picked up this point and transformed it into evidence not of America's excessive ambition, but of Europe's geopolitical freeloading. The trade field, above all, was thought to provide the most unequivocal illustration of America's exploitation by its allies. The American government had long complained of European and Japanese mercantilism. The complaints had intensified by Nixon's time. Despite the Kennedy Round, America's partners were still found to be discriminating against American exports, agricultural exports in particular. Hence, it was said, America's generous postwar concessions toward the recovering European and Japanese economies had gradually been transformed into a structural international bias against the American economy. Not only was US trade subject to the usual mercantilist chiseling with taxes and regulations, but the exchange rate itself constituted a major American disability.

Exploitation by Exchange Rate

Pinpointing the exchange rate as the instrument of allied exploitation turned the traditional view on its head. Instead of a weak dollar being blamed on a weak economy, the weak economy was blamed on the weak dollar. In other words, America's trade was said to have been stunted and its economic development distorted by an overvalued dollar. The overvaluation, in turn, was traced to a combination of factors. To domestic inflation and laggard enterprise were added overextended American generosity abroad, foreign mercantilism, and the very structure of the international monetary and trade system. As the Peterson Report concludes: "Some have argued that had we kept our inflation under better control in the '60s, we would have had no or at least insignificant balance-of-payments deficits, and our exports would have continued to exceed imports by a comfortable margin. While inflation has obviously contributed to our problems, this proposition, in my view, goes too far in that direction. No single error or event explains our present difficulties and there is no single panacea for them. Inflation, improved capability of other nations, increased energy needs, obsolete trading and exchange rate adjustment arrangements, less favorable commercial practices — all had their impact."[16]

According to the official view, an overvalued dollar had been part of the discriminatory trade practices initially permitted to Europe and Japan in the interest of their postwar recovery. No appropriate adjustments, however, had marked that recovery. The partners should have revalued but resolutely resisted doing so. Instead, they manipulated their affairs, it was said, to keep the industrial advantages of their own undervaluation in respect to the dollar. Indeed, several countries had increased their advantages by devaluing a number of times after Bretton Woods.[17] But unless the partners would revalue, the system offered no relief to the United States for its overvalued dollar. Under the Bretton Woods structure, the dollar's hegemonic responsibilities as *numeraire* and reserve currency were thought to preclude a devaluation.

The longer the dollar's overvaluation continued unadjusted, the worse the situation became for the structure of American industry. As happens with an overvalued currency, industries producing tradable goods were discouraged, whereas industries producing services were overdeveloped. The same bias that favored foreign over domestic industrial products encouraged foreign over domestic industrial investment. US industry thus grew progressively weaker in the face of its foreign competition. In short, America's obligations to the Bretton Woods regime seemed contrary to its own national economic health, the base upon which American strength in the world ultimately depended.

The conclusion was self-evident. The United States would have to find some way to depreciate the dollar. It could adopt "benign neglect" toward defending parity and urge the dollar's creditors to revalue. If its spoilt allies refused to revalue voluntarily and supported the dollar themselves, the United States would have to find some way to force them to accept a dollar devaluation.[18]

The Liberal Argument for Floating

The case for depreciating the dollar could also be put in less mercantilist terms. An influential school of monetarist economists with impeccable liberal credentials had been favoring not merely devaluation but the end of fixed exchange rates altogether. Their ideas helped legitimize not only the Administration's inability to sustain the dollar's parity in 1971 but also its reluctance to stabilize it thereafter. Within a remarkably short time, the case for floating exchange rates became the conventional orthodoxy among American economists.

The liberal case for floating rested, first of all, on the assertion that, given the nature of modern national economies, a fixed-rate regime had structural biases that favored devaluation over other remedies for disequilibrium. The Bretton Woods rules, contrary to Keynes's wishes, had no serious provision to force surplus countries either to inflate or to revalue their currencies. Instead, surplus countries were permitted to accumulate more reserves without penalty. With no penalties for accumulating surpluses, nothing forced the surplus country to revalue. On the contrary, its interest in retaining a trade surplus reinforced its inertia in keeping its currency undervalued. A deficit country, by contrast, was pushed both by rules and by circumstances toward devaluation. The deficit country ran through its reserves and borrowings until finally, no longer able to support its currency in the exchange market, it was compelled to devalue or withdraw from the system by imposing controls. Hence, though the postwar era saw numerous devaluations, revaluations were infrequent and minimal.[19]

Before devaluing, deficit countries normally sought to deflate their economies, thereby hoping to lower their relative price level, reverse capital flows, and improve trade. But deflationary policies were generally unsucessful, it was believed, because of the behavior of wages. With postwar unions and welfare policies, money wages almost never fell. Instead of lower wage costs, deflation brought higher unemployment. Democratic governments had difficulty in deliberately sustaining such high unemployment long enough to restore the balance of payments. The deficit country thus gave up deflation and devalued. Surplus countries, by contrast, could afford to let wages rise without being forced to do anything about appreciating the currency.

The systemic bias toward devaluation was seen to put the United States in a peculiarly uncomfortable position. Always in deficit, the dollar was supposedly unable to devalue. Deflation was no more successful in the United States then elsewhere. Hence the dollar had grown more and more overvalued, with increasingly deleterious effects on American trade and investment patterns. As foreign holders grew less willing to absorb more surplus dollars, American domestic policy found itself forced more and more often to deflation. Ever more frequent bouts of deflation, while ineffective in curing the dollar's overvaluation, could nevertheless be expected to stunt growth and reinforce the American economy's long-range decline. Liberal analysis thus appeared to arrive at the same conclusion as mercantilist: the United States could no longer tolerate a system that did not allow it to devalue.

Although American liberal analysts found the Bretton Woods system particularly unfortunate for the United States, its defects were also believed harmful to others as well. Fixed rates, for example, were believed highly disruptive for international transactions. Having a fixed-rate system could not prevent changes in parities, but it made the changes unnecessarily violent. Countries invariably tried to defend their unrealistic exchange rates for too long. Stop-go policies distorted economic development and eventually failed. After prolonged artificial support, the exchange rate suddenly collapsed. These sudden shocks were more disruptive, it was argued than the continuous and gradual adjustments that might be expected in a system of floating rates.

Liberal economists also faulted the postwar system for an inherent tendency to transmit inflation. The reasoning was similar to the argument about the fixed-rate system's bias toward devaluation. As long as exchange rates were fixed, whenever one big country followed policies that were inflationary relative to the norm for the system as a whole, the big country's rising prices would naturally, through arbitrage, put upward pressure on prices of traded goods everywhere else. Other countries in chronic deficit would find their own inflationary tendencies reinforced. The inflationary country could be expected to run a balance-of-payments deficit that would swell the money supplies of its creditors. Countries whose domestic policies were relatively less inflationary would thus find themselves importing inflation from their more expansive big neighbor. A less inflationary surplus country could, in theory, revalue. But its path of least resistance lay in absorbing the imported inflation and letting wages rise. As long as they did not rise more than the system's norm, the country's balance of payments would be likely to continue in surplus. Thus, it could be argued, the postwar fixed-rate system imparted to all countries, surplus or deficit, an asymmetrical bias toward inflation.

In a floating-rate system, it was believed, inflation would no longer be transmitted automatically from one country to another. Instead, each country could choose whatever inflation rate best suited its own particular "Phillips Curve." The floating currency would then automatically adjust the national price levels to the international norm. A country with a higher inflation rate would see its currency depreciate. This would automatically lower the domestic prices and wages of that country in world terms. It would no longer export its money and hence its inflation. Similarly, a less inflationary country would see its currency appreciate. This would automatically raise the prices of its domestic goods, services, and wages in world terms, while lowering the price of imports. The less inflationary country would thus start importing goods rather than money. In effect, the system would favor the median inflation rather than the highest inflation rate among the participating countries.[20]

This kind of argument appealed on all sides. Keynesian eco

nomic managers believed their plans for growth would no longer
be frustrated by balance-of-payments constraints.[21] Conservative
monetarists saw floating as the ultimate international triumph of
the free market.[22] Ideas like these from the economists came as
manna to the beleagured Nixon Administration. If nothing else,
they supplied a theoretical gloss for a devaluation that could not
be avoided in any case.

Floating Exchange Rates in Action

In practice, much of the academic theory about floating rates
proved irrelevant. From the start, floating seldom worked in the
fashion prescribed by the theorists. In market parlance, floating
was "dirty" rather than "clean." No country was a "robot," prepared to leave its exchange rate entirely to market forces.[23] Instead, nearly all central banks intervened regularly in the market to
support or depress their own currencies. In theory, regular small
changes in exchange rates were supposed to cure balance-of-payments disequilibria by promoting shifts in trade. In practice, exchange rates dictated by short-term capital movements seemed
notoriously unstable and capricious. The actual thrashings of the
exchange markets made the notion of rational adjustment through
trade seem academic and visionary. Central banks intervened continually to stabilize the price of their own or other currencies. Intervention, however, was hardly limited to "smoothing out" rough
shifts. Instead, exchange-rate policy became an important means
of regulating not only foreign but also domestic economic conditions. Every country tried to calculate its interest and adjust its exchange rate accordingly.

For most countries, however, the new situation decreased
rather than increased the government's control over the economy.
Not only was the offshore capital market immense and uncon-
trolled, with national reserves too small to resist major flows, but
the robot school also proved to have exaggerated expectations
about the rationality of domestic public policy.[24] Expecting nations to "choose" and sustain a particular inflation rate assumed a

degree of settled consensus over the distribution of income and power absent in most advanced industrial countries. It also assumed a degree of mastery over domestic economic conditions rarely vouchsafed to any democratic government. A few countries with low inflation and strong currencies, notably Germany and Switzerland, were able to use appreciation to keep out inflation imported from abroad, although the long-range costs to national economic development worried many of their analysts. For many countries with higher rates of inflation, that is to say most countries, regular automatic depreciation of the currency dangerously exacerbated the inflationary spiral.

Imagining a fixed and stable rate of inflation ignored the volatile and rapidly accumulating effects of inflationary psychology. As the American monetarists themselves had emphasized, in a country seized by inflation, group after group lost its "money illusion" and scrambled not to be left behind. Domestic inflationary pressures thus fed upon themselves and tended to grow progressively. For many countries, fixed parities, with the consequent need to defend the currency, had proved the major check on runaway inflation. By contrast, a floating system not only removed this check but, as the currency depreciated, greatly accelerated the inflationary pressures by raising the price of imports. For inflation-prone countries relying heavily on imports, particularly of food and other primary products, free-floating risked an accelerating spiral of currency depreciation, rising food and raw materials prices, higher wages and domestic prices in consequence, followed by more inflation and further currency depreciation.[25] Under such circumstances, free-floating diminished rather than increased rational control over national economic life.

These consequences, many of which were easily predictable from historical experience or practical knowledge of contemporary political-economic structures, were sadly different from the liberal academic models. Under the circumstances, governments could hardly be expected to leave their exchange rates to the judgement of currency dealers in a "free" market. Instead, governments tried to prevent, as best they could, currency shifts that would upset domestic policies or injure their country's international trade. "Liberal" floating simply removed a major set of constraints on international behavior. In effect, it licensed a more brutal mercantilism than had been seen since the end of World War II.

The United States and Floating Rates

However much the new system belied the expectations of liberal economists, it more than satisfied the immediate aims of American national policy. Devaluation was counted a diplomatic triumph that enhanced rather than diminished American power. Nixon had his boom and won the election handily in 1972, thus providing one of the few examples in modern American politics of a successful "political business cycle."[26]

Devaluation also served the interests of several important domestic constituencies. On the one hand, it improved markedly the competitiveness of domestically produced American products, thus assuaging domestic labor and heavy industry and reducing protectionist pressures on Congress.[27] On the other hand, floating gratified internationalist business by eliminating the danger of serious capital controls, the principal threat to multinational investors, traders, and banks. Thanks to floating, the Republicans were able to dismantle capital controls completely by 1974. American external spending, lending, and borrowing could thus continue without official restraint. The 1970s were to prove the Golden Age of American international banking. For the big banks, profits from foreign operations soon were outstripping those from their domestic operations.[28]

Contrary to the expectations of many theorists, a depreciating dollar did not notably reduce American private foreign investment.[29] On the contrary, American overseas investing continued to grow by leaps and bounds in the seventies. But the depreciated dollar did, as expected, greatly increase private foreign investment in the United States. Many American assets had clearly become a bargain for European investors, particularly those holding currencies that had appreciated so spectacularly against the dollar. In addition, as European and Japanese firms grew larger, they found domestic production increasingly unattractive, in part because of the currency shift. They also observed rising American protectionism and feared military and social instability in Europe. Under these circumstances, investment in discounted American assets made sense. Nevertheless, American foreign investment continued to exceed the reverse flows from abroad.[30]

The Foreign Reaction

Nixon's mercantilist policy was not much appreciated abroad. Foreign unhappiness grew as it became clear that the falling dollar was to be a recurring phenomenon. The end of fixed rates had merely legitimized the dollar's weakness rather than ended it. Against a dollar trending steadily downward, Europeans and Japanese appeared to have three options: to absorb the surplus dollars in their reserves and thus support the dollar's market price; to let their own currencies appreciate and the dollar fall; or if the dollar fell, somehow to protect their markets against the cheapened American goods and money. All three options were unsatisfactory for America's partners. Hoarding dollars boosted inflation; appreciating their own currencies harmed domestic growth and industry; protection was a dangerous game for nations so much more dependent than the United States upon trade. In addition, the relative costs and benefits of these options differed sharply from one country to another. Hence a collective response against the United States was unlikely.

Europeans tried to use the European Community to mount a common response. After their monetary troubles in 1968, European governments began to talk more seriously about a monetary union. A huge international capital market, whose conditions were determined by erratic domestic American monetary policy, disturbed not only European national economies but also intra-European relations generally. Each currency crisis, however, revealed not only Europe's common vulnerability but also its deep divisions. Plans for a monetary union bogged down, for example, over which should come first, integrated exchange rates or integrated national monetary policies, in a familiar rhetorical contest between supranational pretensions and national realities. The theoretical debate reflected, as usual, intractable conflicts of national interest. European states still had wide divergences in economic strategy and practice, particularly in their respective tolerances for inflation. Such differences reflected Western Europe's continuing economic, historical, social, cultural, and political diversity.

Europe's disunity also reflected the unusually low state of Franco-German relations following the Russian invasion of Czechoslovakia in 1968. More fundamentally, France and Germany had not reconciled their differences over the political and economic price Europe needed to pay for its American protectorate. Their disagreements unresolved, the two major European powers could never agree to a coordinated response, either to the franc's weakness in 1969 or to the dollar's collapse in 1971. As the dollar continued to depreciate, a protected bloc was probably the only effective European response. But at least until the later seventies, the Europeans were to prove too disunited, weak, and comfortable to launch so major a challenge to American policy. Nixon's 1971 import surcharge, in fact, highlighted to the Europeans and Japanese their vulnerability to American protectionism, a vulnerability compounded by their own lack of cohesion.[31]

Domestic Criticism

Not all criticism of Nixon's revaluation came from abroad. Some American liberal internationalists sharply attacked the foreign aspect of the New Economic Policy and, in particular, Connally's tactics in implementing it.[32] Much of the criticism was ill-founded and hypocritical, particularly when coming from the more ardent guardians of domestic full employment. The Nixon Administration, after all, could hardly be held solely responsible for the dollar's plight in 1971. Its efforts to control domestic inflation were certainly no less serious than those of its "internationalist" predecessors in the sixties. Those predecessors had themselves never hesitated to abuse the international monetary system in order to pursue domestic economic goals. Thanks to the credit they had already run down, preserving America's economic self-determination required from Nixon a more drastic and obvious breaking away from international constraints.

Internationalists were perhaps justified in condemning Connally's tactics for their gratuitous honesty. Connally's candor made it more difficult for the Europeans to maintain their self-respect. No American interest was served by exposing Europe's weakness so brutally. A mercantilism so self-conscious and self-congratulatory needlessly risked undermining the structure of American hegemony. So long as the general integrating nature of the "affluent alliance" held together, the United States could use its overall political and military weight to sustain its economic advantage. If the pressure grew too great, America's partners might be pushed to more adventurous reactions.

In any event, Connally clearly left himself too exposed at home. He greatly underestimated the power of outmoded ideals. Thirty years of liberal internationalist cant was not an easily disposable waste. In due course, internationalist critics helped ease the Texan out of office. Very little changed. As Kissinger's influence grew in the economic sphere, the same basic foreign economic policy prevailed with, if anything, greater brutality in substance and not much less in form.

5

The Revolution
in Retrospect

NIXON'S REVOLUTIONARY SOLUTION to America's balance-of-payments problem marked the end of one era and the beginning of another. Looking forward as well as backward from 1971, what was the general political and economic significance of America's abandoning the Bretton Woods system? Among other things, how do contemporary explanations and apologies look in retrospect? Is some comprehensive view now possible that fuses and relates in broader perspective the insights of the various approaches of the time?

The Concept of a Balance of Payments

The roots of complex practical problems can often be found growing in the ambiguities of theory. The concept of a balance of payments, for example, carries elusive and contentious economic, political, and even moral assumptions. To begin with, the very notion of balances between countries implies a nationalist definition of the world economy. Each national economy is taken as a discrete entity, a common household whose accounts should be kept in relation to the rest of the world. A more cosmopolitan view might argue that with the world increasingly a "global village" of free men and multinational enterprises, the whole concept of national balances is an impediment to progress. No one, after all, keeps a formal balance between New York and Texas. Flows do occur, but the adjustments take place through the movement of goods, capital, and labor—without anyone reckoning a formal monetary balance that the governments of New York and Texas feel they must somehow act to regulate. Why should the same not be true of monetary flows between the United States and West Germany?

The answer seems obvious. The United States and Germany are sovereign nation-states, whereas New York and Texas are not. Having a balance of payments is an attribute of national sovereignty, for in the present world, sovereignty extends to economic as well as political self-determination. Governments of modern nation-states are expected to regulate their domestic economic environments to provide stable prosperity. They are also expected to do their best to ensure a favorable international context for that domestic prosperity. To meet these expectations, governments normally seek to regulate the national money supply and to promote an exchange rate favorable to domestic development. Economic conditions in New York and Texas, of course, are not deprived of this governmental solicitude. The two states share together the policies set by the US Treasury and Federal Reserve. So, it might also be argued, does the German Federal Republic. In some respects, much of the capitalist world does form an integrated monetary union with a common money supply. With America's special reserve role in the postwar international monetary system, the huge size of its economy, and the growing interdependence of capital markets, monetary conditions in the United States have had a powerful influence on monetary conditions in West Germany. Some find this monetary integration part of a general world progress toward political integration. In this view, the Federal Reserve should quite properly play the role of world central bank.

Again, however, nationalist reality intervenes. American monetary institutions are part of the American political system. American monetary policies are made mainly with American preferences in mind. They reflect the complex conditions of the American economic, social, and political scene. Germans are not willing to hand over the management of their economic environment to Americans. In particular, postwar Germans do not care for American inflation rates. Germans thus insist, as best they can, that their monetary policies be made by institutions that reflect the particular nature of their own economic, political, and social community. Hence the Germans and Americans keep a balance of payments between them.

Not only does the concept of a balance of payments suggest a nationalist international system, but it also traditionally implies a certain balanced relationship among the members of that system. The word *balance* is itself ambivalent. Balance may mean simply a reckoning of pluses and minuses. But it may also mean an equilibrium, as when accounts are "in balance." Such a notion of equilibrium applied to international payments suggests that a country ought ideally to have neither a surplus nor a deficit. Behind this prescription is the vision of a system with a natural law or an inner harmony, attainable if governments behave properly. Liberals, with their faith in free markets, see equilibrium achieved by a "hidden hand," the natural result of unspoilt competition. But not everyone shares such a liberal view of the international order. A Hobbesian view sees instead states in a ceaseless competition where some flourish and others decline. Order is the product not of artless nature but of conscious power. Laws and rules are simply instruments of domination and perhaps exploitation as well. In more strictly economic terms, a traditional mercantilist view sees a payments surplus not as a disequilibrium to be adjusted but as a superior competitive performance to be sustained.[1]

In the postwar world, these rather philosophical questions have been directly embodied in the reserve-currency argument. The issue goes back to the interwar years. During World War I, the European countries had printed money to cover their enormous expenses and, in the process, soon broke the tie between their currencies and gold. The classic gold standard was thus fatally disrupted. For several years thereafter only the dollar remained tied to gold. Moreover, dollar credits to the Allies, and later to the Germans, became increasingly the means by which those countries financed international transactions outside their own imperial sys-

tems. Under these circumstances, the international monetary system became a "gold-exchange standard," with the dollar becoming
a "reserve currency" held by others in place of gold. In due course,
the dollar was joined by the pound, which had always been a reserve currency for countries within the British imperial orbit but
which was now legally acceptable in the national reserves of independent countries.[2]

The arrangement was ripe with possibilities for mutual misun-
derstanding. Under a gold-exchange standard, the country issuing
the reserve currency has a legal obligation to take it back, if requested, and to pay out a set amount of gold in exchange. The reserve-currency country is supposed to regulate its affairs so as to be
able to meet this contractual obligation. As Triffin noted, putting a
reserve currency in the hands of foreigners requires the issuing
country to run a national balance-of-payments deficit. And as
Rueff noted, running that deficit can easily become habitual for the
reserve-currency country. For unlike other countries, when a reserve-currency country sends its money abroad, its domestic
money supply is not thereby correspondingly reduced. Its economy grows addicted to its apparently costless balance-of-payments
deficits, while its foreign recipients turn into increasingly reluctant
holders. Both issuer and recipient become self-righteous and irri-
table. The reserve-currency country sees itself providing "liquidity"
to a world that needs capital to grow. But the neighboring central
banks who increasingly accumulate the reserve currency see themselves making forced loans to cover the profligacy of a country
abusing its reserve-currency status.

Normally, reserve currencies are also widely held in the private
markets. The reserve-currency country thus has not only a large
debt to foreign central banks but also an "overhang" of redeem-
able currency in the hands of private foreigners. This results in the
situation described in "Triffin's Paradox." The more the reserve
currency performs its function of providing liquidity, the less
stable is its value. Balance-of-payments deficits provide the liquidity, but they also undermine parity. Foreigners, official and
private, gradually refuse to hold the reserve currency without a
larger and larger discount. As long as exchange rates are fixed,
they insist on higher and higher interest rates, which means higher

and higher domestic resistance. Hence a growing conflict develops between the reserve country's domestic demands and external obligations. Government policy oscillates between tight money to please its foreign creditors and easy money to satisfy its domestic constituency. Ultimately, a crisis of foreign confidence ensues, confronting the issuing country with demands for gold payments that cannot be met.

Twice in this century these theoretical problems of the gold-exchange standard have led to a serious disruption of the international monetary system. The reserve-currency system broke down with the fall of the pound in 1931 and with the fall of the dollar in 1971. In both cases, the gold-exchange standard was caught in a fatal contradiction. Whereas reserve-currency countries sought to act, in effect, as central banks supplying money for the whole system, the other countries ultimately expected them to act as nations like any other, that is, to keep their external accounts in balance.

In summary, the very concept of a balance of payments is loaded with ambiguous and arguable implications, toward which governments and analysts themselves have shifting and ambivalent views. The lack of real agreement on these fundamental questions is reflected in the inability of states to formulate and sustain any durable international monetary regime. This lack of agreement does not represent merely a perverse incapacity of economic experts from different countries to resolve technical problems. Mercantilists have hold of a fundamental point. In the end, an international monetary regime, like domestic monetary institutions, reflects an overall balance of political and economic power. A monetary system with special rules for one power reflects a group of states dominated by that one power. The system will last as long as the hegemony. A system characterized by equal rules equally obeyed reflects, by contrast, an integrated group of states with a plural diffusion of power among them. Even the biggest states in such a system cannot break the rules with impunity. A pluralistic liberal system of this sort lasts only as long as the political balance that it reflects. Integrated monetary regimes come apart when the member states neither feel constrained to accept hegemony nor share sufficient interests, perceptions, or institutions to consent to common rules. In this situation, a pluralistic international system without consensus, the world's monetary regime tends toward a series of distinct monetary blocs, separated by floating rates and controls.[3]

Not only does an international monetary system reflect the relative power of states, but it also reflects the domestic economic, social, and political character of its principal members. For no international monetary regime is likely to survive unless the domestic economic and social order in each participating country is in harmony with the international regime. The classic gold standard, as Rueff imagined it, needed not only a plural world system in which the major powers were constrained to follow the same rules, but also, within those major powers, domestic societies dominated by social classes interested in monetary stability.[4]

To say that world monetary order must conform to international and domestic political realities is not to say that monetary economics has no laws of its own, or that politics may flout these laws with impunity. The primary function of money, after all, is to serve as the mediator between man's expansive desires and limited resources. When, for one reason or other, money no longer serves as a reliable standard of value, the stability of society itself, domestic and international, is undermined. Inflation, with its disruptiveness and slow growth, is the obvious consequence of monetary mismanagement in our own time. Inflation is, so to speak, the revenge of natural law on political power.[5]

Measuring the Balance of Payments

In addition to the ambiguities in the very concept of balance of payments, ambiguities exist in the way it is measured.[6] American postwar statistics, for example, have used a variety of different official definitions. Any attempt at reckoning an overall balance has had a number of components, each of which is, in turn, a balance of its own. The two basic components are generally "current account" and "capital account." Current account includes the trade balance, net foreign expenditures of the government, and the balance for services or "invisibles" — a figure that encompasses not only freight, insurance, and banking fees but also the return on

overseas investments. Capital account is subdivided into long-term
capital flows, which are funds earmarked for investment of some
duration, including the direct investments of corporations in foreign plant and equipment, and short-term capital flows, which are
liquid funds in search of security and higher interest rates.

Recent years have seen at least three ways of toting up these
components into an overall balance. The most comprehensive is
the "liquidity balance" which includes the current account and all
nonbank capital flows. This measures, in effect, the flow of dollars
between residents and nonresidents of the United States. Since
short-term capital is volatile, sometimes building up for several
years and then flowing in a great rush, it has sometimes been
thought useful to compute a "basic" balance which leaves out
short-term capital and thus presumably gives a more accurate picture of the "real" economy in a given year. This basic balance
therefore includes the entire current account (trade, government,
and services) but only long-term capital flows, presumably because
they represent "real" investment rather than "hot money." A third
computation, the "reserves transaction" or "official settlements"
balance, shows the net change in US monetary reserves. This balance measures only those dollars that end up in foreign central
banks in exchange for local currencies. Unlike the liquidity balance, it leaves out the dollars that nonresidents prefer to accumulate as future claims on the American economy rather than to exchange for local currencies.

Analyzing the American Deficit

The complexities of measuring a balance are amply reflected in
the explanations for a persistent imbalance. Two broad theoretical
approaches are common among policy-makers.[7] One is an item-
by-item approach, the other a monetarist approach. The item-by-
item approach looks at the specific elements in the balance of payments and tries to assign the cause for disequilibrium to some
particular item or group of items. Implied is some notion of a normal set of trade, capital, and governmental flows. Anything that
seems exceptional is suspected. Measures to curb particular out-

flows or augment particular inflows seem the obvious prescription. Mercantilist countries where the banking system is highly integrated and controlled, like Japan or Italy, often have remarkable success in using such specific measures to regulate their balance of payments. Trade, too, can often be manipulated with considerable success by such specific mercantilist measures.[8]

The monetarist approach, by contrast, traces a deficit not to any particular items in the balance of payments but to the management of the domestic economy in general and the management of the money supply in particular. A balance-of-payments deficit is taken as prima facie evidence that the national money supply is expanding too rapidly. Money is being created that cannot be absorbed by growth in real economic activity. Depending on the circumstances, this excessive creation of money will either cause domestic price inflation as too much money chases too few goods, or flow outward and cause a balance-of-payments deficit. Some combination of both external deficits and internal rising prices is normal. In the postwar period, with some degree of inflation nearly everywhere and a high degree of freedom for international capital movements, countries that suffer balance-of-payments deficits are, in effect, those that inflate their money supplies more than the norm. In the monetarist view, a payments deficit will occur from excess money creation regardless of whether the money is needed for either foreign or domestic expenditures. Hence, the item-by-item figures of the basic balance are of no great interest to monetarist analysis. Nor does it matter in what fashion the excess money is created. Central banks may print money to finance government deficits and stimulate the economy, or private banks may pyramid credit in response to demand at home or abroad.

Until the later sixties, official American analysis tended to be item-by-item, whereas foreign critics, like Rueff, tended to be monetarists. In the later sixties, American analysis began to include monetarist elements, but often with very different practical conclusions from the European variety. Surveying this evolution brings into focus the real issues involved in the payments question, as well as the true significance of Nixon's way of resolving these issues.

The Item-by-Item Approach

Official analysis in the Kennedy, Johnson, and even early Nixon Administrations tended to focus on the basic balance, the annual flow in and out of the real economy. Item-by-item analysis of the basic deficits revealed a striking pattern. Despite a regularly positive balance on services and, until 1971, on trade, two large negative items seemed to push the overall basic balance into deficit. These were government transactions (overseas troops and aid) and long-term capital flows (overseas corporate direct investment). This pattern suggested an imperial explanation for America's disequilibrium. The payments deficit seemed the consequence of America's hegemonic role within the international system. The imperial burdens might be military, like keeping troops overseas, or economic, like providing the public and private capital for reconstruction and development.

As the sixties progressed, this imperial explanation seemed increasingly inconvenient and irrelevant. It was inconvenient because, by pinpointing overseas government expenditures and corporate investments as the causes of a weak dollar, it implied these ought to be cut. Balance-of-payments arguments could thus become a pretext for neo-isolationism and protectionism. Apprehensions grew particularly strong when Connally kept noting the rough equivalence, year after year, between the basic US balance-of-payments deficit and the exchange costs of American troops in Europe.[9] To partisans of the *Pax Americana*, an annual outlay of $2 or $3 billion in foreign exchange seemed absurdly insignificant compared to the American geopolitical, and indeed financial, interests involved in Europe's defense. But even the less apocalyptic remedies implied by this approach, like controls on foreign investment or increased European contributions to NATO, all met increasing resistance.

In any event, as the sixties progressed and America's expatriate dollars were collected into an organized offshore capital market, the basic deficits seemed increasingly irrelevant to the dollar's defense, except perhaps as indicators affecting confidence among the holders of the volatile dollar "overhang." In technical terms, attention shifted from the basic balance to the liquidity balance—the flow of "hot money." Ultimately the dollar's fate depended on the reserve transactions balance, the degree to which nonresident holders were going to foreign central banks for exchange, as well as the degree to which the central banks were willing to accept the dollars at the official exchange rate. Under the circumstances, managing the already existing pool of expatriate dollars grew far more significant for the dollar's parity than the "real" flows of the basic balance. With multinational corporations routinely moving several billions of their liquid balances in response to interest rates, the relatively small basic deficits, never more than $3 or $4 billion, were swamped, exacerbated, or multiplied by short-term capital flows of $10 or $20 billion. Abandoning the defense of Europe to save $2 or $3 billion out of deficits running up to $20 billion seemed preposterous.[10] The inconvenient emphasis on overseas military and corporate investments could thus be pushed aside.

In truth, however, the imperial explanation did provide a major insight into the nature of the American predicament. The Vietnam War undoubtedly cost the country's economy a great deal. Enormous defense budgets throughout the postwar era may well have distorted and weakened American economic growth. Steady overseas investment may well have slowed the modernization of domestic industry.[11] Above all, the determination to pursue simultaneously domestic full employment and world leadership was certainly a major cause of inflation. Few of these imperial costs, however, were accurately measured by specific items in the basic balance of payments. To make sense, the imperial explanation of payments deficits had first to be mediated through a more general economic analysis, one that related imperial burdens to the economy's structural weaknesses or persistent monetary inflation.

The SDR Debate

By Johnson's time, official analysis was shifting from item-by-item explanations to what was, in effect, a critique of the institutional structure of the international monetary system itself. Triffin's analysis of the reserve-currency problem reflected a widespread belief that the world was, or would soon be suffering from a "liquidity shortage." National reserves seemed inadequate to cushion growing deficits, particularly as the rising volume of world trade and investment and the inflation of prices made international currency flows larger and larger in relation to national foreign exchange reserves. The shortage appeared particularly acute among the reserve-currency countries, namely Britain and the United States, the developing countries, who were exceptionally prone to deficits, and those international agencies, like the World Bank or the IMF, who were supposed to help reconcile development with world financial order. In effect, all those whose aspirations outran their resources perceived a systemic shortage of liquidity. But there was not a general shortage of money; there was an excess, however maldistributed it may have been. To expect to resolve the world's distributional problems by augmenting its liquidity was, in effect, to practice "money illusion" on a global scale.

The SDR idea was certainly convenient for American policymakers, searching, as they were, for some new source of credit. But the logical link between Triffin's hypothesis about what might happen if the United States should end its deficit and the real problems of actually doing so remained elusive.[12] Seeing the SDR machinery as a solution to the deficit presupposed either that these new IMF credits could shore up the dollar indefinitely or that the dollar deficits really had sprung from an abstract American desire to provide liquidity to the world. According to the latter belief, once the creation of world money was turned over to the IMF, the United States would no longer be forced to run deficits to service the world economy. The dollar's problems would be over. In reality, however, the United States had no real intention of giving up its foreign "burdens," including the tribulations of monetary hegemony. Overseas troops and investments were expressions of American ambition and power as well as idealism. The United States was not running deficits to provide liquidity to others, but as a byproduct of pursuing its domestic and foreign ambitions. As long as the United States held the monetary hegemony involved in the reserve-currency role, it could be certain that ample liquidity would be available to finance its foreign positions. Though the United States was quite happy to use the IMF as a gloss over its monetary hegemony, it had no intention of ceding its real power over the world money supply. The United States was all for supranational government in Europe, but in matters pertaining to their own prerogatives, American statesmen had a firmly nationalist grip on power.

Benign Neglect and Floating

On the whole, American economists seldom lagged behind their statesmen in patriotic bias. By the late sixties, fashionable American economics had taken up a new systemic cause, floating rates. In effect, the academic arguments counseling "benign neglect," devaluation, and floating were rationalizations for a depreciation of the dollar—a mercantilist remedy the Nixon Administration came to believe essential for the rejuvenation of America's faltering domestic economy. The academic rationale for Nixon and Connally's mercantilist offensive based itself on the supposed deficiencies of the Bretton Woods system of fixed rates. Such analyses, to be sure, were not only convenient apologies for American interests but also plausible analyses of the American predicament. By the late sixties, the dollar seemed clearly overvalued, the domestic economic effects deleterious, and America's allies reluctant to give up their advantages. Devaluation was certainly much easier than deflation, a painful and doubtful remedy.

As analysis, however, the academic apologies for benign neglect and floating suffered from a fatal deficiency. Though they gave an accurate enough description of the American predicament after the dollar had become overvalued, they provided, in themselves, a partial explanation at best for why the dollar had become overvalued in the first place. As a result, they could not really provide any policy to keep the dollar from becoming overvalued again. That, however, was the real problem. The 1971 devaluation was not a once-for-all cure but the beginning of chronic depreciation. The reason for the depreciation after 1971 was the same as the reason for the weakness before 1971, namely, accelerating American inflation prompted by relentlessly expansionary fiscal and monetary policies.

By contrast, the reasons assigned in official analyses reflected the endemic tendency among American economists to blame unpleasant facts within the framework of their economic analysis upon "exogenous" disturbances coming from without. Explanations for the overvalued dollar thus typically ignored general economic factors, like inflation, in favor of more specific political factors, like an overly generous American exchange-rate policy at the outset of Bretton Woods or the Machiavellian mercantilism of the allies thereafter. Explanations for inflation showed the same tendency. In the late sixties and early seventies, inflation was blamed on the Vietnam War. A few years later, it was oil prices. Similarly, the failure of floating rates to restore the American balance was blamed on the "dirty floating" of the Europeans and the Japanese. In short, economic analysis was reduced to a series of catastrophes and conspiracies. Not until the late seventies was the role of inflationary domestic management so clear in the dollar's problems that even official economists could no longer ignore it. Even then, American ingenuity was ready with the "locomotive theory," the gist of which blamed the dollar's problems on the "failure" of Europeans to keep up with American inflation.[13]

Unwillingness to face the link between the dollar's weakness and the country's long-range domestic and international policies proved the great failing in American policy itself. On the whole, American academic analysis gave policy little objective guidance. Lack of interest in the whole topic among Keynesians was not surprising. Their prescription, expansion at home in the interest of domestic equity, was, after all, in good part responsible for America's domestic inflation. Understandably, the international inequities and dislocations that resulted were not prime topics for Keynesian analysis. When neo-Keynesians did extend their pattern of thinking to the international political economy, they came up with visionary plans for world-wide equity, like the "Link"—SDR's issued to poor countries to spend on development—or the big-scale world development funds later proposed by the Brandt Report. The latter prescription jarred uncomfortably with the growing awareness of the limits to the world's resources. Keynesians began to rediscover what Keynes had concluded in the thirties, that equity at home required mercantilism abroad. In short, for the Keynesians, examining the consequences of America's inflation was even more embarrassing internationally than domestically.

More puzzling to explain is why American monetarists were generally so diffident about noting the connection between American inflation and the dollar's weakness. The basic monetarist approach explicitly links a balance-of-payments deficit to an inflationary excess of monetary creation. In addition, Friedman's attack on the Phillips Curve had presumably aimed to show how Keynesian demand management was inherently and progressively inflationary. Countries pursuing such policies, according to Friedman, could expect not stable real growth, but inflation with social disruption and economic stagnation. Presumably, countries infected with an excessive Keynesian preference for full employment over monetary stability should also have been told to expect weak currencies.

A monetarist, analyzing the balance-of-payments problem of a country that had been in deficit for two decades, might reasonably be expected to suppose that country to be more inflationary than the norm for the system as a whole, its balance-of-payments deficit being the logical consequence of its higher inflation. That inflation, moreover, might be expected to have some relationship to those analyses of unemployment and inflation that so preoccupied American monetarists in the domestic context. Monetarist analysis logically linked a nation's pursuit of full employment, its inflation rate, and its balance of payments. In an open international system, explaining a deficit in the balance of payments therefore required an international comparison of inflation rates and full-employment goals. The only real cure for a deficit, according to such an analysis, would lie in reducing domestic inflation to a level that did not exceed the norm for the system.[14] From such a perspective the need to defend a fixed-exchange rate should logically have been seen as a major inducement to controlling domestic inflation. Fighting inflation and defending the currency are the same battle.

Exchange Rates and the Limits to Inflation

What stops inflation? Why do democratically elected governments feel constrained to punctuate their excessive stimulation with periodic bouts of restriction, despite the predictable political costs of restraint? For most countries, the reasons are both domestic and foreign. In the long run, inflation tends to grow not only more extreme but also more disruptive. The well-to-do rentier sees his assets deteriorate. In general, as people lose their "money illusion," more and more parts of the society are drawn into a contentious struggle over income shares. Since many of the settled arrangements of an economy can be explained more plausibly by custom rather than by inherent economic logic, this contentiousness grows dangerous for social stability.[15] As prosperity and social peace seem increasingly threatened, a coalition for stability can be expected to increase its political weight in counterpoise to the hitherto dominant coalition for "growth." This internal process, however, may well be lengthy or incomplete. In most societies, dissatisfied interests expecting to profit from growth are always numerous, particularly after a long era habituated to it. Renouncing the dream of even illusory growth is slow and bitter.

For these reasons, inflation in most postwar economies has been curbed less by domestic reactions than by the need to defend the currency internationally. Fixed exchange rates, so to speak, provide a sort of political myth whereby the constraints of international law and national pride can be enlisted in defense of monetary stability.[16]

This being so, the eagerness of American monetarists, Friedman in particular, to establish an international floating-rate system seems odd. Friedman's enthusiasm can presumably be traced to a need to vaunt the advantages of the "market." With floating rates, money would be treated as a commodity, with a "price" like any other. Inflation would be curbed by purely domestic constraints, like the more effective dissemination of Friedman's views on "money illusion."[17] Though no doubt logically defensible, this attitude has greatly weakened the practical effect of monetarist prescriptions for controlling American inflation. Abandoning the Bretton Woods system of fixed exchange rates took away the last major institutional restraint on domestic US inflation. Advocacy of floating rates gave intellectual support to a mercantilist exchange-rate policy, the principal consequence of which was an explosion of inflation, both in the United States and throughout the world. In this respect, conservative French monetarists, like Rueff, might seem somewhat more reliable analysts of the real world, for Rueff's emphasis on the gold standard, whatever its practical defects, was at least logically consistent with his aim of restoring domestic monetary stability.

Aside from its insensitivity to the significance of fixed exchange rates, Friedman's monetarist analysis suffered from another major shortcoming. While his critique of the Phillips Curve explained why all postwar neo-Keynesian economies were inflationary, it did not explain why the United States was so much more inflationary than the norm for others. Why, in fact, was American monetary policy regularly more expansive than the systemic norm? The differing analyses of the payments deficit point to three different causes for America's monetary excess: excessive foreign burdens (the imperial explanation), excessive domestic ambitions (the Phillips-Curve explanation), and the lack of institutional restraints on inflation (the Rueffian explanation). There is no reason why a comprehensive view cannot incorporate all three.

Foreign Burdens

Item-by-item explanations of the balance-of-payments deficit traditionally focused on the foreign-exchange costs of troops abroad. From a monetarist perspective, however, what is important is the overall effect of military costs on the American budget and economy generally. These military costs do, in fact, mark the clearest difference between American fiscal policy and that of its major economic partners. Relative defense expenditures as a percentage of GNP among the United States and its major allies make the point:[18]

Country	1958	1965	1970
United States	11.1	8.0	7.8
West Germany	3.8	4.4	3.3
France	8.0	5.6	4.0
United Kingdom	7.8	6.0	4.9
Japan	–	1.3	0.8

Not only have defense expenditures contributed to America's budgetary deficits, but their very nature, by providing more civilian income without a corresponding increase in civilian goods, is more inflationary than many other forms of government outlay.[19]

America's high military costs were obviously linked to its exceptional foreign obligations. Fully half the annual defense budget was directly tied to America's NATO commitment.[20] This continued to be as true in the seventies as in the sixties and fifties. This huge outlay reflected, in turn, the growing contrast between America's military, political, and economic relationships with Europe and Japan. Though the Western European states had recovered to the point where their collective resources rivaled those of either superpower, the United States continued to assume responsibility not only for Europe's strategic nuclear defense but for leading its ground defense as well. While the NATO allies had regularly failed to put up adequate resources for "burden sharing," American governments had nevertheless clung firmly to their hegemonic military role in NATO. Both the Kennedy and Johnson Administrations had firmly resisted Gaullist initiatives in Europe and what they called neo-isolationism at home. In consequence, America's military role, and the budget to finance it, did not reflect Europe's recovery. Defense expenditures continued to be much higher proportionately in America than among its affluent allies. But while the recovered European states and Japan continued to receive American protection gladly, they grew ever more critical of America's exported inflation.

Domestic Ambitions

Whereas America's military role was clearly an exceptional burden on the economy, the same cannot so easily be said for America's domestic goals. After the war, all advanced industrial democracies practiced some version or other of neo-Keynesian full-employment policy. As Friedman observed, such policies encouraged inflation everywhere. The American version of full-employment policy, however, was not obviously more inflationary than elsewhere. Indeed, the United States had a higher tolerance

for unemployment than several countries that were presumably
less inflationary. Not only were American employment goals not
exceptional, but the proportion of the American GNP devoted to
welfare expenditures was not notably higher than in other advanced industrial states. The government expenditures for social
security programs as a percentage of GNP for selected countries in
1957-1977 support this statement:[21]

Country	1957	1960	1963	1966	1971	1974	1977
Canada	6.5	8.7	9.4	9.0	14.8	13.7	14.6
France	14.3	13.7	15.4	16.6	n.a.	22.4	26.5
West Germany	16.6	16.2	16.9	18.4	18.8	22.5	26.5
Japan	4.3	4.7	5.1	5.6	5.6	6.4	8.7
Sweden	10.5	10.9	12.2	14.5	20.6	24.4	30.7
United Kingdom	10.0	11.0	11.1	12.3	13.5	14.1	17.1
United States	5.0	6.29	6.8	7.7	11.1	12.1	13.7

Broad comparisons of employment goals or domestic fiscal
spending do not, of course, necessarily give a full picture of the
comparative inflationary tendencies of national domestic policies.
One country, for example, may have greater obstacles to full employment than another and may thus require consistently greater
monetary stimulation to achieve the same degree of employment.
How, in fact, can it be explained that countries like the Federal Republic of Germany manage full employment with less inflation
than most of their neighbors? For the monetarist, the answer must
presumably lie in the basic social, economic, and political character of the country, and in particular its structural obstacles to full
employment — in other words, to the same factors that determine
its Phillip's Curve or Friedman's "natural rate of unemployment."
Such factors include capital plant, investment, "entrepreneur-
ship," research, labor organization, education, and social mobility. Among these, the character of the work force itself is particularly significant. Countries with low rates of inflation, like postwar
Germany, tend to have well-trained and homogeneous work
forces. Germany lacks a native *Lumpenproletariat*. Foreign workers of radically different cultural and educational backgrounds are
present in large numbers, but they are not part of the national

community. When unemployment sets in, they are paid off and sent home.[22] What remains, the native German work force, is not itself difficult to employ efficiently. By international standards, relatively little economic stimulation is needed to create enough jobs for these workers. Nor, with such a work force, is it difficult to build political support for stability. The entire society is middle class — employed, affluent, protected, and pensioned. Everyone pays his own way. Inflation is relatively unpopular.

Countries with a relatively high inflation rate have tended to be those with deep social cleavages resulting in a more variegated work force, such as Britain with its class and racial divisions, or Italy with its south. To sustain full employment in such societies requires relatively more stimulation than in Germany. Consequently, Britain and Italy are typically more inflationary than West Germany, and have weaker currencies. Because balance-of-payments difficulties constrain their full-employment policies, they also tend, ironically, to have higher unemployment. In an open international system with fixed parities for currencies, chronically high unemployment and chronic balance-of-payments difficulties go together. A country that needs a higher degree of monetary stimulation to achieve full employment, in other words a country with a relatively high natural rate of unemployment, can expect to be in chronic balance-of-payments difficulties under fixed rates, or to have an habitually depreciating currency under floating rates. International monetary integration thus imposes what might be called a distinctive unemployment quota for each economy, a quota whose size depends on the structural factors that determines the natural rate of unemployment. To deviate from this quota without fundamental structural improvements is to deviate from the international norm for inflation. The result is a chronic balance-of-payments disequilibrium. This whole line of argument is nothing but Friedman's notion of a natural rate of unemployment combined with a monetarist view of the balance of payments. To what extent can such an analysis help explain America's relative high inflation and consequent balance-of-payments deficit?

The reasons for America's deteriorating Phillips Curve date back to the 1930s, when a migration of black rural workers began to flood into American cities.[23] The fifties and sixties saw a major effort to integrate these urban blacks into the work force. By the seventies, the work force was also shifting to include an unprecedented number of women and teenagers. Most advanced societies had a similar shift from rural to urban employment, as well as the same demographic shifts in the composition of the work force. Nearly every country faced complex problems of social integration. But few had complications as daunting as America's race problem. And those that did have significant social "cleavages," like Italy, also tended to have higher inflation rates. In short, America's relatively high rate of inflation among modern industrial states may, to some extent at least, be part of that curse of slavery and racism that has lain so heavily across American history.

Inflation and American Institutions

In theory, efficiency is the enemy of inflation. A more efficient administration could achieve a higher degree of welfare with less cost. Though anything as elusive as comparative governmental "efficiency" seems impossible to measure with any precision, the vast size and diversity of the American system, along with its legal traditions and overlapping federalist structures, make an exceptional degree of administrative efficiency improbable. More specifically, American budgetary procedures scarcely lend themselves to remarkable efficiency by comparison with the more disciplined party or constitutional structures of most West European states. Indeed, even when it wants to, an American Administration cannot control the drafting of its own fiscal budget. Among advanced states, perhaps only Italy has a comparable anarchy. Still, whatever the return on money spent, the United States was not any more addicted to deficits than many other countries in the sixties.[24] Kennedy's full-employment budget idea had its analogue nearly everywhere else.

A country may run substantial budgetary deficits while still avoiding inflation. Budget deficits in themselves do not lead to inflation unless paid for by an easy monetary policy rather than government borrowing of real savings. Italy's fiscal looseness in the sixties, for example, was complemented by strong monetary policy administered by a powerful and relatively independent central bank. Most countries, however, are closer to the American model, where the central bank's nominal independence does not permit it to hold out for long against the political forces bent on inflationary policies.

One exception to both these generalizations is the Federal Republic of Germany. With constitutional barriers to deficits that persisted into the seventies and a powerfully independent *Bundesbank*, West Germany was institutionally as well as otherwise comparatively well-endowed to resist inflation.[25] By contrast, the United States was not endowed with a political system favorable to controlling inflation. America's size, diversity, and overlapping government structure were not conducive either to fiscal control or to administrative efficiency. America's relatively weak central bank made consistent monetary stringency improbable.

The obvious institutional difference between the United States and its major partners was the dollar's reserve-currency role. Thanks to it, as French monetarists like Rueff never tired of pointing out, neither external restraints nor domestic costs limited American capacity to run a balance-of-payments deficit. Others were constrained to hold the deficits, while the expatriate dollars brought no corresponding reduction in domestic American demand. Despite its obvious explanatory strength and monetarist roots, Rueff's view of inflationary dangers accompanying monetary hegemony never gained a serious hearing among American economists, at least before the later seventies. Even monetarists as preoccupied with curbing domestic inflation as Friedman fiercely resisted any external check on America's international monetary hegemony. Among American economists, Keynesian or monetarist, differences over inflation seemed to stop at the water's edge. Why?

Monetary Hegemony and National Power

De Gaulle once described American policy as the will to power cloaked in idealism. A similarly cynical view would find American balance-of-payments policy the will to power cloaked in academic economics. The will to power does seem to provide the one consistent thread to American payments policy and the theories that have informed it since the early sixties. Ignoring the capital markets, harping on the hypothetical liquidity shortage, inflating the International Monetary Fund, demonetizing gold, floating—all have reflected a basic urge to dominate the monetary system so that no external constraint can limit the expansive impulses, at home or abroad, of the American political economy. The upshot has been to make the world subject to American monetary policy and to make that monetary policy, in turn, not subject to any external constraint.

Hegemonic monetary systems are hardly novelties in history.[26] A powerful case can be made for a hegemonic power with a special role in managing a collective system. That role is presumably justified for others by a close and self-evident identity of the hegemon's interest with that of the system as a whole. But since the United States is rather different from most other economies in the system, and far more autarchic, the US Federal Reserve is perhaps not very well suited to be a monetary Vatican City. In the perspective of the other powers, what results from American predominance is less a dutiful management of the collective economic interests than a nationalist exploitation of power. From this perspective, the insensitivities of American academic analysis might, to a foreigner, seem more plausibly explained by nationalism than by ignorance.

An American, of course, might find no lack of national interest in the theories of his European colleagues. The principal intellectual opponents of American policy have been the French. In retrospect, the French monetarists appear more reliable analysts than their American counterparts. Rueff's argument that the use of reserve currencies in the gold-exchange standard was inexorably inflationary seems difficult to fault in the light of subsequent experience. Moreover, since the switch to floating rates in 1971, Rueff's case for some version of a gold standard has certainly not lost its force. The vast increase in dollar credits since the oil crisis, the spread of other reserve currencies, and the liberated credit-creating powers of international banking have all relentlessly assaulted monetary stability. The technical case for gold—for some standard tied to real values and less subject to manipulation—has grown more and more intellectually compelling.

The weakness of the French analysis is the reverse of the American. American analysis is wrong but predominant. French analysis is correct but impractical. For a gold standard, like any other plural but integrated system, ultimately depends upon there being enough power dispersed throughout the system to force even the biggest state to obey the rules. Beyond, it depends upon domestic regimes among the member states willing both to support and to accept for themselves the external restraint. In short, a gold standard rests on politics. It depends upon an international equilibrium of power among the states in the system and a domestic equilibrium favoring monetary stability within each of the major states. Neither condition prevails in the postwar world. In this perspective, Rueffian analysts are no less nationalist than American. But their nationalism is that of a middle power, unable itself to pretend to hegemony but seeking to escape from the unsympathetic hegemony of another.

The problem with the French analysis is that France lacks the power to enforce it. If the American domestic economy exploits Europe as the French maintain, it is because the Americans can get away with it. Europe's monetary weakness stems from its geopolitical weakness—its disunity and hence dependence upon its American protectors. Under these circumstances, American exploitation of the monetary system seems natural. Europeans should blame themselves rather than the Americans. As de Gaulle often noted, those who cannot mobilize their own strength generally suffer the fate they deserve. In view of their temptations—the domestic pressures and foreign ambitions—the Americans could have been a good deal worse. All of this, moreover, needs to be put in its proper geopolitical context. That Americans have so long carried such a disproportionate defense burden is surely a major cause of their inflation. Under the circumstances, it ill behooves the rich protectorates to complain of the monetary hegemony that has made their protection possible. Until the affluent allies can combine the will and resources for a political equilibrium within the capitalist system, they should expect to adjust to policies made for the convenience of others.

But if power has its own rules, economics also has some laws of its own. Key among them is the deleterious effect of bad money.

Thus the triumph of American policy has, more and more, become the ruin of American prosperity. The problem with American economics is not an excessive concern with the national interest but an inability to define that interest properly over the long term. That is the lesson writ large in the decade that followed Nixon's revolution.

T W O

THE NIXON
SOLUTION
1971-1980

6

Shocks at Home and Abroad

IN THE SHORT RUN, Nixon's revolution of August 15, 1971, was a stunning success. And his New Economic Policy remained successful until after the 1972 presidential election. In the election year itself, real GNP rose 5.7% and unemployment dropped to 5.6%. Controls kept price increases to 3.3%.[1] Short-term capital flows reversed, and the balance of payments improved sharply.[2]

Shortly after the election, however, the symptoms of raging inflation reappeared. Government policies had been laying the fire for some time. Fiscal policy had been expansionary, with a deficit of $23 billion in both 1971 and 1972.[3] "Revenue sharing" had encouraged state and local government spending. Tax rebates had spurred the private consumer. Arthur Burns's monetary policy had remained exuberant.[4] The money supply grew by nearly 8% in 1971 and 5.7% throughout 1972.[5] Business borrowing and consumer spending had jumped ahead, but with the memory of the 1969–1970 squeeze still vivid, the savings rate was also high, flooding financial institutions with excess liquidity. The consequence was not only a continuing private housing boom but a proliferation of marginal commercial building projects and speculations, followed eventually by the biggest rash of bankruptcies since the 1930s.[6] By the spring of 1972, the boom had entered a more intensive phase. For the four quarters through the winter of 1972, real GNP increased by 6.1%. Monetary conditions nevertheless were kept easy, with Treasury bill rates falling as low as 3.4%. Controlled prices were relatively steady, although food prices had climbed 4.3% by the year's end.[7]

In January 1973, the Nixon Administration celebrated its reelection by relaxing wage and price controls. After its fling with domestic mercantilism, the Administration was ready to return to liberal orthodoxy. With the economy humming near full capacity, controls were thought to cause too many distortions and bottle-necks. Dropping controls, however, proved the prelude to disaster, hardly a surprising outcome in the hothouse boom that had developed.[8] Farm prices exploded. Rocketing food prices were followed by a general commodities boom, with widespread hoarding and shortages. In no time at all, price inflation began to reach hitherto unimaginable levels. From the fourth quarter of 1972 to the first quarter of 1973, the inflation rate (CPI) jumped from 3.9% to 6.2%. By the second quarter, it was 8.6%. By the fourth, it was 9.8%. By the first quarter of 1974, it was 12.3%. The Federal Reserve nevertheless waited until the spring of 1973 to tighten credit conditions. By the summer, when monetary action finally took hold, interest rates jumped abruptly to record levels. Suddenly, the boom began turning into a crash. Consumer spending began to fall, with food prices squeezing other spending and then inflation in general narrowing consumer choices.[9] As events seemed increasingly out of control, businessmen and consumers grew frightened. OPEC's fourfold raising of oil prices in December 1973 gave another sharp blow to confidence. Higher oil prices promised to augment rampant price inflation still further.[10]

The year 1974 proved the worst for the American economy since World War II. By the time Nixon left office in August, not only was American price inflation at a record height, but the country seemed on its way to a depression. Inflation stayed above a 12% annual rate for most of the year. As prices rose crazily, real income fell. Real GNP declined 2%. Unemployment reached 7.2%, the worst rate in fourteen years. Government policies aggravated the decline as they had previously inflated the boom. Tight money squeezed already beleaguered businesses and consumers. Fiscal policy turned from a stimulus to a "drag," as inflation greatly increased effective tax rates.[11] Stop-go and stagflation returned with a vengeance. The Great Inflation became the Great Recession.

In short, though the New Economic Policy had freed domestic expansion from international constraints, the domestic consequences were disastrous. The shocks, however, were hardly limited to the home economy. Foreign reverberations were to prove no less disruptive, for the United States itself as for the world in general.

The Great World Inflation

America's inflation was matched by an intensification of world inflation unprecedented in the postwar era. After Europe's boom at the end of the sixties, the rate in most industrial countries followed a pattern similar to the American, with a sharp jump from 1972 to 1973, and an even greater leap from 1973 to 1974. By 1974, the ten largest noncommunist industrial economies had reached an aggregate price inflation of 13% for the year. The start of this world peak could be traced to the mid-sixties, when world consumer prices had begun to accelerate from the general rate of 2½% per annum — less than 1½% per annum in the United States. By contrast, in the eight years between the first quarter of 1968 and the fourth quarter of 1975, consumer prices rose 62% in the United States and Canada, 127% in Britain, 85% in France, 92% in Italy, 106% in Japan, and 47% in Germany.[12]

Although rates still differed sharply from country to country, they were nevertheless at an unprecedented high level everywhere. Hence, the "Great World Inflation." General inflation suggested a general explanation. Among conservative intellectuals, it became fashionable to trace inflation to the populist institutions and policies common to all postwar pluralist democracies. Social conditions everywhere in the late sixties and early seventies were seen as particularly conducive to an inflationary explosion, for although growth had been remarkably rapid, economic and social expectations seemed to be rising even faster. Rapid growth spurred intense impatience with any hardship, insecurity, and inequality that remained. But growth also provoked a strong revulsion against its own social and environmental costs. Paradoxically, capitalist prosperity was nourishing the rebirth of socialist ideology and "postindustrial" values. In America, discontent was complicated by the civil-rights and anti-Vietnam movements. In Europe, social unrest was typified by events like the 1968 "May Days" in Paris and the student unrest and wage explosions that followed in nearly every country. The concessions to assuage discontent led not only to higher wage bills but also to a notable growth of government spending. In most countries, Germany included, inflation financed the wage settlements and government expenditures needed to buy social peace.[13] In the aftermath, all countries enjoyed an artificial boom simultaneously. High demand and shortages became world-wide. International conditions thus reinforced the domestic inflation in each country. "Ungovernability" was becoming universal.

This conservative sociological perspective, blaming inflation on the simultaneous rise of domestic dissatisfaction in rich industrial societies, contained large elements of truth. It was an interpretation, moreover, especially congenial to the Nixon and Kissinger world view. Protracted prosperity, it was thought, had led to self-indulgent socialism and restless activism. America had caught this alien disease from the more decadent societies of Europe. To Kissinger, it was all Weimar and Spengler. The "ungovernability thesis" was not only congenial to American policy-makers but highly convenient, for its sociological analysis of world inflation distracted attention from the rather special economic responsibility of the United States.

A more embarrassing view of world inflation, developed not only in Europe but among more cosmopolitan American monetarists, found inflation's cause primarily in American policy, Nixon's domestic economic policies above all. According to this view, the nature of the world monetary system meant that America's domestic inflation was rapidly exported to the world at large, with powerful reinforcement to all the inflationary tendencies in other countries.[14] American inflation was transmitted through America's soaring balance-of-payments deficits. With the dollar as a reserve currency, US balance-of-payments deficits had no restraining consequences for the domestic American money supply. By a similar process, private banking flows were creating liquidity in Europe without reducing it in America.[15] Even countries strongly resistant to inflation could not keep it out. Under the Bretton Woods arrangements, countries might try to use "open market operations" to reduce their national money supplies in compensation for the dollar inflows. But the techniques for reducing the money supply almost invariably raised domestic interest rates and thereby attracted still larger inflows.[16] Thus, even large countries, unusually determined to resist inflation, found the "sterilization" of dollars increasingly difficult without exchange controls. Foreign governments therefore found themselves with two options. They could align their monetary conditions with the dollar inflow, that is, inflate. Otherwise, they could revalue their currencies, a step believed harmful for foreign trade and domestic employment.

Nixon's August revolution raised the stakes. With the Americans inflating wildly and actively seeking depreciation, the pressure was much greater on surplus countries to appreciate. Those that did so were able to keep their inflation rates lower than the systemic average. But with the dollar falling sharply and recurrently, appreciation carried ever more serious risks for a country's international competitiveness and domestic employment. Countries that did appreciate, like Germany and Switzerland, had highly competitive Phillips Curves and hence had comparatively less difficulty avoiding serious unemployment. In particular, both Germany and Switzerland had a high proportion of immigrant workers who could be sent home. But even such countries could not avoid inflation. Germany, which appreciated the German mark against the dollar nearly 75% between 1968 and 1975, still endured an inflation of 42%.[17]

Countries less favorably situated to endure the deflationary consequences of appreciation relied heavily on "dirty" floating. They absorbed their dollar inflows and thereby expanded their domestic money supplies. Sometimes they actively intervened to support the dollar in currency markets. Thus their currencies depreciated along with the dollar. Some, like England and Italy, followed an even more inflationary policy than the United States and let their currencies float downward against the dollar. Such countries soon found themselves in a vicious spiral of anticipatory depreciations that augmented their inflation still further.[18]

In short, under floating rates either depreciation or appreciation against the dollar carried serious costs. Hence American domestic policy continued after 1971 to exercise a decisive influence on world monetary conditions. Just as the high rate of American monetary inflation from the mid-sixties stimulated inflation everywhere, Nixon's own extraordinary monetary explosion in the early seventies gave another powerful boost to inflationary forces already thoroughly aroused. Even if most countries did have ample domestic causes for inflation, these were powerfully and continuously reinforced by the American money machine.

Revolt of the Primary Products

Just as American domestic inflation reinforced inflation throughout the world, so world inflation returned to plague the United States. As American domestic inflation reverberated into world inflation, among the most notable consequences were abrupt increases in world prices for primary products. These world increases were then felt on American domestic prices. In 1973, for example, American food prices climbed nearly 14.5%, thanks in great part to international demand. Several other commodities also enjoyed a sharp boom.[19] In December 1973, international oil prices increased fourfold. To many economists these price increases seemed "exogenous variables" or fortuitous "shocks," in other words, catastrophic acts of God, man, or nature from outside the economic system itself.[20] Here, as elsewhere, the widespread tendency toward catastrophism seriously distorted economic analysis.

Primary products, like other products, have their own cyclical price movements. The same process of over- and underinvestment exists in these industries as in others. The time scale, however, is noticeably longer. The most celebrated attempt to codify price movements for primary products is the forty-year "Kondratieff Cycle," observed and promulgated by a Russian economist of the interwar period. Kondratieff's pattern fits the postwar era remarkably well. Before 1970, the Korean War in the early fifties provided the last occasion for a major boom in primary products. Thereafter, prices of raw materials fell steadily against prices of manufactures. The next boom arrived promptly on schedule in the early seventies. Signs of a shift began to be visible in the late sixties. The Great Inflation's superheated demand and general explosion of industrial prices provided a trigger.[21]

In a market economy, such a major upswing in raw-material prices is expected to promote a major shift to new investment in industries connected with procuring raw products or finding their substitutes. After 1973, however, the adaptations to compensate for high oil prices were impeded by the inflationary conditions resulting from years of pumped-up consumer demand. To channel resources out of consumption into new investment meant a major reversal of the whole postwar Keynesian pattern. Many economists, having failed to forecast the shift in prices, also did their best to impede any remedy. The OECD economists, for example, counseled governments to react to the oil crisis by stimulating general consumption further, lest higher prices in food and fuel suck away buying power and, by lowering consumer demand, result in unemployment. Though prudence may have counseled some such policy as a way of preventing abrupt dislocations, simply continuing traditional full-employment policies meant, in effect, making no real adjustment at all.[22]

Not only was adjustment to a Kondratieff upswing made all the more difficult by long-standing macro-economic policies geared to full employment, but certain American policies hastened and amplified the shortages themselves. While the explosion in agricultural prices, for example, was triggered by a series of natural disasters from 1972 to 1974, long-range trends, bolstered by various national policies, had been setting the conditions for chronic international shortages. On the one hand, burgeoning prosperity and shifting diets among industrial states, plus huge population growth among developing countries, had been pushing up the world's demand for food. On the other hand, world agricultural price increases had remained notably below the upward trend of industrial prices, particularly in periods of rapid inflation like the late sixties and early seventies.[23] The logical consequence was a chronic world food shortage and, ultimately, an explosion in prices. The early signs began to appear in Asian markets during the 1960s.

Among the various national policies contributing to this fateful paradox of rising demand and lagging prices, the American was pre-eminent. During the sixties, for example, various American aid programs subsidized nearly half of US wheat exports. The effect was to make the world, and developing countries particularly, more and more dependent upon American grain. The subsidized exports made dependence economically feasible for Third World countries and discouraged investment in their own domestic agriculture. America's dumping abroad was matched, moreover, by its running down of buffer stocks at home. Thus, by the time world trends were making shortages increasingly likely, stocks were finally exhausted. In summary, the explosion in food prices was not merely the consequence of a few temporary crop failures. Crops are always failing. Rather, predictable long-range trends, plus long-standing policies that constrained supply and augmented demand, helped created a context in which sudden shortages and price explosions became nearly inevitable.[24]

In many respects, the explosion in petroleum prices repeated a similar pattern. Throughout the fifties and sixties, oil prices fell absolutely, as well as relative to industrial prices. Huge new discoveries were regularly coming into production. By setting production quotas for the largest fields of Texas, Louisiana, and Oklahoma, the United States, or rather the Texas Railroad Commission, effectively controlled world oil prices.[25] If world prices rose to what was judged an excessive level, increased US domestic production could drive them down. These conditions also protected international oil companies from the demands of producing countries for higher royalties. As long as American fields had enough slack to meet shortfalls from abroad, an effective cartel of foreign producers was impossible.

American fields, however, were gradually growing less competitive, and domestic production began to fall. In the late fifties, a new American system of quotas on imports subsidized domestic oil exploration and thus propped up domestic production. But while the import quotas kept prices of American crude higher than world prices, tax policies also kept domestic retail petroleum prices far lower than abroad.[26] In effect, the government's policy encouraged both high domestic production and high domestic consumption.

Cheap energy had predictable consequences. By the mid-sixties the United States was beginning to increase sharply the proportion of energy use to its GNP, thus diverging sharply from a trend common to most advanced economies since the war. By world standards, energy use per capita in the United States began to reach astonishing levels.[27] By the early seventies, the raging US appetite for oil began to make itself felt more and more strongly on the world market. US domestic production was continuing to fall, despite the import quotas, while the Alaskan fields were being blocked by environmentalists. The growing domestic appetite combined with the declining domestic production had an obvious consequence. Even with full production most of the time, American fields were increasingly inadequate for domestic demand. Under these circumstances, the United States could no longer control the world oil market by regulating its own domestic production.

By 1973, these long-range trends, encouraged by domestic American oil policy, finally shifted world market conditions drastically enough to permit an effective international cartel. OPEC had formed itself in 1960, after the international oil companies had unilaterally cut royalties to the producing countries. Not until 1973, however, were conditions ripe for the producing countries to turn the tables.

In this perspective, the events of 1973 hardly seem an unforeseeable catastrophe. Deliberate policies had encouraged high consumption in the United States. Predictably, the United States grew increasingly dependent on the world market. US dependence greatly increased demand pressures in that world market.[28] Under these conditions, world oil prices could hardly be expected to remain frozen throughout the 1970s as they had in the fifties and sixties, particularly with inflation rapidly pushing up other prices and undermining monetary assets. Again, adventitious events provided the trigger. American support for Israel in the Yom Kippur War no doubt provided a useful occasion to crystallize OPEC solidarity. But the general evolution to much higher oil prices should have surprised no one.

Lessons from the Shocks

Broad shifts in the terms of trade have generally occurred regularly in the past and doubtless will not be unknown in the future. Future economic historians will look at the postwar era's thirty years of unprecedented industrial growth and note how it was based increasingly on a raw material whose price remained fixed while industrial prices continued to rise. They are unlikely to be astonished by the eventual shift to high oil prices. Harder for them to fathom will be the contemporary economists who apparently saw postwar rates of industrial growth and price inflation as indefinitely sustainable without some such revolt in primary prices.

Those who manage economies, it seems, are seldom good at foreseeing long-range developments. Their models are designed for short-range predictions and manipulations. The less hectic variables are simply assumed. Relationships on a different time-scale thus tend to be ignored, only to reappear as "catastrophes" inflicted by vengeful gods or fickle politicians.

Not only is it wrong to see the oil-price explosion as an unpredictable catastrophe, unrelated to deliberate and long-standing public policies, but it is also mistaken to overrate its effects on the basic course of economic events in 1974. The oil crisis did not cause the Great Recession of 1974–1975, any more than it caused the Great Inflation that preceded it. Doubtless the sharp rise in fuel prices, coming on top of the food explosion, exacerbated inflation and deepened the subsequent recession. But the Great Inflation was already rampant before the oil crisis, and the seeds of the Great Recession were already planted and nourished. As early as the fall of 1973, severe monetary restraint was in force and the runaway boom collapsing from accumulating inflation and shortages.[29] Like Vietnam in the sixties, the oil crisis was a special event with far-reaching consequences. In both cases, and most certainly with the oil crisis, neither the event nor its consequence was unpredictable. Moreover, neither Vietnam nor the oil crisis was necessary to explain stagflation in general or the short-term oscillations of the business cycle in particular. For Nixon's boom, the oil crisis of 1974 was not even the last straw. The camel was already heavily laden and sinking fast.

The Rejuvenation of America's Foreign Economic Position

Although the United States was not spared at home from the consequences of the disruption it had exported abroad, most other countries were affected worse. In particular, Nixon's mercantilism did, as hoped, strengthen American trade against its major partners. The new monetary system performed especially well. After the initial devaluation in late 1971, the dollar continued depreciating until late 1973.[30] After the usual lags, depreciation sharply improved American trade. Even the "catastrophes" had favorable effects. The food price explosion greatly increased American export earnings, and the oil crisis strengthened America's geopolitical position vis-à-vis the other major capitalist industrial powers.

Trade figures revealed the new strength. The year 1973 saw a small surplus. And even with the fourfold increase in the oil price, the 1974 trade balance was in deficit by only $5.3 billion. Despite oil, that year's overall imports in constant dollars actually declined 4%, reflecting not only a recessing US economy but also the continuing improvement of American competitiveness in the home market. Exports showed a comparable improvement. The US merchandise surplus with the European Community tripled, and the net surplus in manufactures rose to $9 billion. Exports of capital goods remained high despite the world-wide recession. Income on American investments abroad also rose sharply, from oil companies in particular.[31]

The year 1974 also opened a profitable new era for the big American banks. The oil crisis greatly augmented the level of world indebtedness while also generating a vast pool of savings from OPEC states. Renouncing Bretton Woods had, as promised, permitted the end of US capital controls. With no commitment to defend the dollar's parity, funds could flow in and out without impediment. The United States, with its huge open markets, big banks, and ample supply of investment instruments, seemed the natural entrepôt between new OPEC money and the world's greatly expanded need for finance. The Eurodollar market continued to be the physical locus of much of international banking, but American banks themselves occupied a major position in the offshore market. With no capital controls, domestic and offshore operations blended easily together.[32]

America's new competitive strength in international trade and finance illustrated a shift in America's political terms of trade. As the international economic system grew more disorderly and "mercantilistic," with rules eroded and power more significant, the United States seemed well able to take care of itself. The events of 1973, including the Arab-Israeli War, with its threat of Russian intervention, or the oil crisis, with its twin threats of strangulation and bankruptcy, drove home the significance of American military power. Western Europe and Japan depended upon the international framework sustained by that power. By themselves, they lacked the military means to sustain the international environment upon which they depended. The Americans, moreover, were far less immediately dependent economically upon the rest of the world and hence less easily held to ransom.

Nixon's United States was not slow to take advantage. Kissinger immediately sought to manage the oil crisis in such a way as to reestablish America's faltering hegemony over Europe and Japan. Hence his proposals for an International Energy Agency. Oil consumers were to be tied to a collective strategy managed by the Americans, complete with a financial safety net to put European financial needs under American tutelage.[33] The Washington Energy Conference of February 1974, called to lay down the common Western line, was notable for the extraordinarily ill-tempered exchanges between Kissinger and the French Foreign Minister, Michel Jobert. The French refused to acknowledge a common interest with the Americans sufficient to justify a unified trans-Atlantic policy. The other allies accepted the American proposals in form but adroitly avoided the substance, a common confrontation with OPEC. Instead, Europeans and Japanese began a long-range campaign to bolster their own political and economic influence in the Middle East. Americans did the same, and with conspicuous success. Indeed, under Kissinger's energetic diplomacy, the United States achieved what seemed an unprecedented mastery over the entire Middle East, OPEC notwithstanding. Thanks to Nixon and then Kissinger, political success abroad was soon able, once more, to underwrite economic success at home.

7

The Nixon-Kissinger
World System

W HATEVER THE DOMESTIC WRECKAGE left behind by the Nixon
Administration, its foreign policy achieved a major restoration of American external power. And after Nixon's own demise, this power was to underwrite still another domestic American boom. Nixon's foreign success was not a fortuitous accident. He had long been brooding over foreign policy. He was determined to confirm America's pre-eminent international position, badly shaken by the disastrous war in Vietnam. In due course, he did extricate the United States from Vietnam, perhaps with less damage to its international position than might have been expected. And he also seemed to manage skillfully the other major historic failure of American foreign policy, the fall of the dollar. The dollar's defeat was transformed into a successful mercantilist counterattack to rebuild American trade.

Re-elected by an overwhelming majority, Nixon could have expected to consolidate these external victories into a new era of American world power. In Henry Kissinger, he had found a Secretary of State with the historical vision and diplomatic skill that seemed required. Not the least of Kissinger's talents was his articulateness and ability to conceptualize on a large scale, thanks to which American policy acquired coherence and comprehensiveness, absent since the breakdown of the Kennedy-Johnson

Grand Design. But after having skillfully avoided disaster for his country abroad, Nixon was destroyed by his own bizarre and sordid indiscretions at home. Nevertheless, Kissinger was able, under Ford, to fill out the Nixon foreign policy. His diplomatic achievements provided the context for a Nixon economic policy that was to last until the end of the decade.

The Kissinger World View

In obvious ways, Kissinger was a conservative. He had little sympathy with idealistic schemes for social transformation or international income redistribution. He wished to preserve the postwar international system as it was before Vietnam, and he wished to restore, indeed to extend, America's position within that system. To do so without causing domestic exhaustion and revolt would, he realized, require a more careful use of American strength. He entered office arguing that the United States was overstretched in its commitments and should practice selective devolution of its world burdens. By devolution, he meant not that the United States should abdicate its leadership, but that others should bear more of the costs. Hence, he was always on the lookout for regional surrogates—the Shah's Iran being the most notorious example. An unsympathetic characterization of this strategy is "hegemony on the cheap."[1]

Not only did the United States need to find worthy deputies to share its burdens, Kissinger believed, but it needed to restore its own domestic strength and freedom of action. The official apology for the 1971 devaluation matched Kissinger's general perspectives very well. According to that apology, the United States, as architect and leader of the postwar order, had submitted to economic discrimination favoring the recovery of the other capitalist powers. The result had been an overvalued dollar that, after more than twenty years, was undermining the economic base of American power. US policy had to restore that base by recovering the freedom to adjust its exchange rates and protect its industries against unfair competition. Hence the new monetary order of 1971, confirmed in Jamaica. Hence, too, the Administration embarked upon a new wave of trade negotiations, including, most notably, the Tokyo Round of GATT agreements. In the official perspective, these new monetary and trade policies were counted as overdue adjustments in the world economy rather than as American withdrawals from responsibility. In particular, they were seen as an overdue adjustment in America's relations with its pusillanimous European and Japanese allies — reluctant surrogates and "free-riders" who had long been living off American geopolitical exertions.

The conventional view about the "shocks" that followed in the early seventies also suited Kissinger's perspectives. The explosions in food and oil prices that shook the world economy were seen not so much as the sign of some fundamental malfunctioning of the international economic system, let alone as reactions to American economic policy, but as adventitious natural or political catastrophes provoked or exacerbated by a revolutionary restlessness in both developed countries and the Third World. Kissinger inclined toward that conservative sociological view, according to which the West's widespread inflation was the symptom of a long-gestating social, political, and moral crisis. The affluent Western public, spoilt with prosperity, detente, and leisure, was increasingly resisting all economic and political discipline. Hence, cost-push inflation, chaotic universities, and the rejuvenation of the radical left. A childhood refugee from Hitler, Kissinger was contemptuous, suspicious, and tough toward Western Europe, to a degree seldom seen among America's home-grown Europeanists. Without American hegemony, Kissinger appeared to believe a decadent Europe would soon again become a menace to itself and the world, and an easy prey to Russian domination.[2]

Kissinger inclined toward a similarly unsentimental and conservative view of the militant demands put forward by states in the Third World.[3] In the early seventies, Third World demands for international income redistribution constituted a sort of moral offensive. A great many European and American scholars took claims for a "New International Economic Order" seriously. Many American liberal intellectuals suffered considerable discomfort. Third World claims inconveniently pushed certain liberal ideals to their logical conclusions. An integrating liberal world, like an integrating liberal nation and state, presumably implied a bond of brother-hood and, somewhere in the distance, a common standard of wel-fare. As an outrageously rich society in a hungry, restless, and straitened world, practical American interests hardly lay with radical world-income redistribution. Postwar liberals, counting on limitless growth to resolve all problems, had yet to face this issue, either at home or abroad. But as expectations of unlimited growth began to recede before Malthusian analysis, Americans who took these kinds of liberal egalitarian ideas seriously grew increasingly disabled.[4]

Kissinger was better endowed. Metternich and Bismarck were his political mentors, not Jefferson and Wilson. Kissinger's vision was "One World," but with the parts remaining distinctly unequal. Like other academic analysts with essentially geopolitical perspec-tives, Kissinger accepted, without anguish, that America's interest lay in preserving inequality. Nor was Kissinger bashful about ac-knowledging the vital role of power in preserving American and Western interests. Much of the world's restlessness, Kissinger be-lieved, came from Vietnam's devaluing of Western military pres-tige. OPEC's forcible redistribution of power had inflamed radical expectations still further, while seriously undermining the actual economic situation in developed and developing countries alike. It was not the moment for America to retreat any further, Kissinger believed. It was not that the United States wished to ignore or alienate the Third World. On the contrary, America's postwar strategy for development had looked to the incorporation of these formerly colonized regions into an integrated world economy. That strategy should not now be abandoned, but instead should be pressed to fulfillment, particularly as it was becoming important to the growth of many American enterprises.[5]

American national interest, however, did not lie with a Third World of mercantilist socialist states. On the contrary, to survive at home, liberal capitalism needed a congenial open environment abroad. That environment, moreover, was in the true interest of the peoples of the Third World themselves. Lessening world in-equality, or at least raising the unequal poor to a more prosperous level, was to be accomplished not by despoiling rich countries, but by developing the economic possibilities of poor countries. An open world economy, with a large role for private capital and enterprise, domestic and foreign, meant more rapid growth and freer, more dynamic social and political systems in the Third World. Development required open and responsive markets, private capital, and private enterprise generally. Preposterous claims for some sweeping New International Economic Order would therefore have to be met with a supple policy of constraints and blandishments aimed at keeping Third World development within America's postwar world system.[6]

The Contradictions of American Hegemony

The claims of the Third World absorbed a great deal of attention among Kissinger's fellow intellectuals. But the more immediate economic threat to Kissinger's refurbished *Pax Americana* came not from the claims of poor developing countries or their academic supporters but from the general drift toward mercantilism among the powerful industrial nations. For all Kissinger's contempt for their "provincial" perspectives, the Europeans and Japanese were using their growing economic power to reshape the postwar order. The Common Market had steadily extended its regional arrangements into the Mediterranean, Africa, the Middle East, indeed into Eastern Europe and the Soviet Union itself. Japan was again cultivating special relations in the Far East but also extending its reach into Africa and the Middle East. European and Japanese interests were growing powerful even in Latin America.

Many observers saw this expansion of European and Japanese influence, as well as their increasingly tense relations with the United States, as leading the world away from the integrated economic order of the *Pax Americana* and toward a looser system of blocs. Like every American leader since the war, Kissinger resisted such an evolution. But general world economic conditions seemed to be turning against him. Free trade had flourished in the great postwar boom, where expanding prosperity had permitted a game with many winners and few losers. As growth slowed, free trade was hurting more and more domestic interests everywhere, and the essentially mercantilist character of modern states was reasserting itself. The United States could hardly claim to be lagging behind the general trend, as the whole drift of Nixon's foreign economic policy reflected it. Thus, while US policy in general strove to sustain the postwar liberal order, US economic policy was steadily undermining the constituent principles of that order.

The contradiction hardly began with Nixon. American policy in the sixties was bedeviled by a similar tension between domestic aspirations and the pretension to shape and lead an orderly international system. By the late sixties, the dollar's weakness, itself the consequence of conflicting ambitions at home and abroad, threatened to force either an unacceptable restriction on American domestic prosperity or else a major retreat from international leadership. Nixon's solution, perennial devaluation, used political hegemony over the system to escape from the economic restraints the system was meant to impose. Political hegemony precluded serious foreign economic retaliation against what foreigners could hardly help but see as a series of American "beggar-thy-neighbor" devaluations. In effect, US policy sought to combine the benefits of liberal internationalism and mercantilist advantage. As still the most powerful economy, the United States expected to benefit from a liberal world system that provided all the usual advantages of integration, including the ability of the powerful to penetrate other economies. At the same time, the United States expected to use its hegemony within the system to claim special advantages and exemptions from discipline. Paradoxically, the United States was driven to these expedients by its own weakness, a debility that had begun, in turn, to threaten its hegemony.

In the short run at least, the contradiction in logic was not disabling in practice. On the contrary, lingering international hegemony gave special leverage for asserting national interest. That was the key to the Nixon-Connally strategy in 1971. Geopolitics came to the rescue of economics. The real weakness of American policy, as it happened, was that it did little to cure America's domestic economic decline.

The New International Monetary System

After Nixon abandoned the dollar's parity in August 1971, flexible exchange rates had become essential to America's foreign and domestic economic policy. Given America's chronic monetary inflation, the devaluation of 1971 could not be a once-for-all remedy. New parities could not be sustained and a fixed-rate system could not be restored. American policy therefore needed a continuing freedom from fixed exchange rates. In the absence of any serious will to root out inflation, the dollar had to be free to depreciate whenever pursuit of full-employment policies proved incompatible with defending the exchange rates. After 1973, chronic depreciation became essential to another imperative of American policy, the ability to go on importing oil without stint. In short, the flexible international monetary system was the substitute for curing the domestic economy of inflation or adjusting it to higher oil prices. Chronic depreciation also served a broad spectrum of particular American interests. It gave relief to domestic American producers from foreign competition. It also permitted the extraordinary overseas expansion of the banking industry to go forward unhampered by restraints on the free movement of money abroad. As a result, within a remarkably short time, chronic dollar depreciation became embedded in the very structure of the American economy. For all these reasons, American policy's first aim was to retain the ability to depreciate freely and, if possible, to persuade its partners to legitimate the new arrangements.

In this aim, American diplomacy was brilliantly successful. The major capitalist states solemnly subscribed to Nixon's recasting of the new international monetary order, first at the Rambouillet summit in late 1975, and then formally at the Jamaican IMF meeting in February 1976.[7] By this time, the advantages of floating rates with "orderly marketing arrangements" had become conventional economic wisdom. General international conditions made the American formula almost inevitable in any event. The universal balance-of-payments disequilibruim following the oil crisis made restoring fixed parities even more quixotic than formerly. Most European states were themselves still heavily in deficit. European monetary solidarity was disintegrating as the French were about to be constrained, once again, to join the errant British and Italians outside the perpetually embryonic European Monetary Union.[8]

Not only were the Europeans weak, but the dollar was exceptionally strong. Throughout 1975, with the recession and the effects of the 1971–1973 dollar depreciation, the United States enjoyed a trade surplus, and the dollar acutally appreciated against major European currencies. The situation, however, returned to normal in 1976. As the American domestic recovery gathered steam, the trade surplus turned into an accelerating deficit.[9] Capital outflows jumped sharply, and the dollar resumed its decline for the rest of the decade. With the end of this interlude of dollar strength, the real test of the new international monetary structure began, a test that fell primarily on the Carter Administration. The policy to be defended, however, remained Nixon's.

When the international monetary struggle renewed, American policy was ready with a full complement of ideological armaments evolved from the new orthodoxy of 1971. As the United States returned to even bigger trade deficits than before, Europeans were criticized for "dirty floating," or not letting the dollar depreciate enough against their currencies. No sooner did the dollar begin to stabilize and appreciate in 1974 and 1975, for example, than American officials called it "overvalued" and an unfair burden to American products. When Europeans complained of America's "beggar-thy-neighbor" dollar depreciations, the United States unveiled its "locomotive" theory of international equilibrium.

The locomotive argument reflected the unwillingness of economists to abandon their Keynesian formulas in the face of the oil crisis. Thus, the United States was said to be running a trade and payments deficit not because its economy was too expansive, but because the economies of others were not expansive enough. The oil price revolution, it was said, had sucked purchasing power from national economies and thereby caused a world-wide recession. Governments, preoccupied with restoring their trade balances, had suppressed domestic demand further. If everyone followed such a policy, the world recession would be deep and protracted. Fortunately, it was argued, America's enlightened domestic management had reflated instead. Naturally, with America's the only expanding economy, the United States would pull in imports and its money would flow outward toward Europe's restrictive interest rates. The consequent trade deficit and declining dollar, however, were badges of American virtue, not signs of excess.

General world equilibrim should be restored not by dragging everyone down to Europe's recession, but by having everyone join the United States in expansion. Others who could afford a trade deficit, in particular Germany and Japan, should strongly reflate along with the United States. Their trade deficits, like the American, would permit genuinely poor countries to return to balance.[10] Europe's fears of inflation were dismissed as ideological gloss — camouflage for habitually mercantilist policies favoring export industries over domestic consumption.

The rhetorical battle heated up along with the Carter boom and the consequent new American payments and trade deficits. Germans ridiculed economic forecasts professing to see the world pulled from recession if only the Federal Republic would reflate still more. Pushing everyone up to the same inflation rate was not the proper cure for international disequilibrium, in the German view.[11] Nothing was to be gained by ruining those few economies whose inflation was not as bad as the rest. Stable growth would not resume, the Germans argued, until national economies were put on a sound basis. Real adjustment to higher oil prices required a structural shift toward exports in all manufacturing countries. Nevertheless, the Germans did reflate more aggressively, and in due course their own growth and inflation rates began to climb. By 1979, the *Bundesbank* grew alarmed and began raising the discount rate, whereupon it was promptly accused of undermining the dollar.[12]

In a sense, all these trans-Atlantic quarrels merely demonstrated the continuing success of the Nixon monetary strategy. Through periodic depreciations of the dollar, the United States was able to pursue its domestic and foreign goals without serious hindrance. The world had accepted Nixon's international monetary system and was being forced to live with it.

The Trade Offensive

Nixon's monetary strategy was part of a comprehensive policy to arrest America's alleged industrial decline and restore the competitiveness of its industry. Dollar depreciation was linked to a trade offensive. "Locomotive" and "dirty floating" arguments were weapons in the American mercantilist arsenal.

The trade offensive, like dollar depreciation, stemmed from domestic necessity. Throughout the 1970s, deterioration in some industries and regions was arousing powerful political forces favoring protection. Labor's drift manifested itself early in the notorious Burke-Hartke Bill.[13] The American government grew increasingly responsive. Even fervent free-traders could see that, if American industrial deterioration were not ameliorated, the result might well be barriers so severe that liberal world trade would collapse. Though a large segment of American business depended upon an open international environment, and protectionists by no means controlled business associations, the internationalist interests began to see discretion as the better part of valor. Timely special concessions for the disadvantaged segments of American industry were preferable to a general breakdown of free trade. Protectionist rancor was better directed against unfair competition from abroad than against internationally oriented firms at home. Fashionable enthusiasm for a "product cycle" leading the United States into a "high technology" and "service economy" at the expense of its "low order technology," like textiles, metal-working, chemicals, and presumably automobiles, began to give way to a serious campaign to resuscitate the country's basic industries.

In 1970, Congress passed a new trade bill with a fresh armory of threats against the protectionist gimmicks of America's trading partners.[14] Thus endowed, the United States entered the new Tokyo Round of GATT negotiations, as well as a whole series of bilateral deals. As usual in such negotiations, Congress proved an especially convenient institution. Just as the forever imminent Mansfield Amendment could be used in the 1960s to pry troop offset payments from the Germans, so Congress's perennial "protectionist sentiment" could be used to extract trade concessions in the 1970s.

Trade negotiations grew acerbic with the Common Market and especially with the Japanese. Under floating rates, Japan was no longer a "black hole" absorbing countless American dollars off the exchange markets. Japan's dollar absorption had become "dirty floating." The Japanese home market, meanwhile, remained as impenetrable as ever. The continuing competitiveness of Japanese products in the American market, despite the rising yen, strongly suggested dumping. A series of tough bilateral negotiations culminated in "orderly marketing agreements," namely import quotas for Japanese products. Japan was also strongly pressured to open its capital markets to American funds; thus it was hoped the government's iron grip might be broken and the economy opened to American enterprise.[15]

America's mercantilist trade offensive lasted throughout the decade. Many concessions were won by negotiation. Unquestionably, the dollar's depreciations improved the competitiveness of American products at home and abroad. From 1970 to 1975, for example, US exports rose from 14.4% to 24.1% of the total production of all goods produced domestically.[16] Around 1976, however, the rapid improvement slowed, even if the new ratio was nevertheless sustained. Despite the obvious advantages won by these tactics, by 1977 the United States was once more running large trade deficits. Studies of the trade balance from 1975 to 1977 attribute about half the decline to rising oil imports, a quarter to "the failure of cyclical recovery abroad," namely the stalled European locomotive, and roughly a fifth to "competitive deterioration."[17] What American analysts counted as "failure of cyclical recovery abroad" was, however, regarded as sound policy by the Europeans. It meant, in effect, that their economies had a lower rate of inflation and were making a more successful adaptation to the new oil prices. In other words, "failure" to recover abroad, as well as "competitive deterioration" at home, were in effect direct consequences of America's relatively higher domestic inflation. And the third negative factor — oil — reflected America's reliance on inflation in place of a structural energy policy.

Once the dollar resumed its depreciation in 1977, the American trade balance could be expected at least to stop its rapid deterioration, as happened selectively in 1978 and globally in 1979. By the late seventies, however, foreign resistance to more dollar depreciation was finally forcing an American retreat from the monetary side of its mercantilist strategy. But even with an almost unfettered capacity for depreciating the dollar throughout most of the decade, the overall results of the mercantilist strategy were disquieting. Despite several bouts of sharp depreciation, much of America's domestic industry seemed to be growing weaker in the face of foreign competition.[18] If so, an immediate explanation seemed obvious. The United States continued to lag well behind most other industrial countries in its ratio of capital formation to GNP. The United States was not investing and hence not growing. Americans were not saving either. By the later seventies, the US ratio of savings to disposable personal income was roughly a quarter of Japan's, a third of France's, and well below half of Germany's.[19] While economists and politicians could provide innumerable special reasons for these figures, low saving and investment were in fact the familiar and predictable consequences of prolonged inflation. In short, Nixon's mercantilist strategy was not achieving its broader goal. Dollar depreciation had not cured the American malaise. It had merely relieved some of the major symptoms. The American economy, meanwhile, had grown even more addicted to inflation.

Oil

The self-defeating character of American mercantilism in the seventies reveals itself most clearly in the country's adaptation to the oil crisis. Oil became a major preoccupation of domestic and foreign policy. The United States had for several years artificially structured its domestic oil market to encourage both high production and high consumption. After OPEC's price revolution, the existing structure, by keeping US prices well below world prices, continued to promote high consumption but perversely discouraged domestic production. Nixon proposed a new energy policy to eliminate the bias favoring oil consumption and to encourage oil substitutes as well as domestic oil production. Nixon's "Project Independence" failed in Congress, and he left the Presidency before OPEC's price effects began to be felt. Ford's domestic energy policy was similar and also failed in Congress.[20]

Accordingly, the oil problem resolved itself in the same fashion as the dollar problem: America's international power underwrote its domestic maladjustment. Fundamental structural issues were evaded at home and resolved by manipulation abroad. The manipulation depended on that structure of American power so carefully nurtured by Nixon and Kissinger, which included not only the new monetary system, but a broad geopolitical relationship with the Middle East, Europe, and the Soviet Union. Unlike domestic energy policy, foreign energy policy succeeded. Thanks to it, the US domestic economy could put off the oil problem for the rest of the decade. The details of this pattern are not only interesting in themselves, but furnish a microcosmic view of how the Nixonian formula continued to be applied through the decade.

Adjusting the Real Economy

Broadly speaking, the United States had three possibilities for coping with OPEC's raising of oil prices. The first lay in asserting American political power to reverse the oil price increases; the second in making compensating adjustments in the country's real economy; and the third in monetary manipulation. The possibilities were not mutually exclusive. Any option, for example, required exerting political power at home or abroad. But reversing the price increase by direct force was soon rejected. Practical difficulties, hopeful expectations about the alternatives, European opposition, and American recollections of Vietnam together inhibited so straightforward a geopolitical response.

The second option, adjusting the real economy, meant either increasing America's foreign earnings enough to compensate for the increased cost of oil imports, or reducing consumption of imported oil enough to bring the current account back into balance. Obviously, the two courses could be complementary. Conditions in 1974 were propitious for increased foreign earnings. Income from foreign investments jumped sharply as American oil companies began repatriating some of their vast windfall profits.[21] Servicing the oil producers' unspent earnings also proved a lucrative source of new income for financial institutions. America's big banks and huge capital market were well able to compete with the Europeans as an entrepôt for surplus oil dollars in search of investments. Besides the greatly augmented American income from ser vices to the oil-rich countries, huge new markets were developing for certain products, arms and capital goods in particular. The United States was the world's largest producer of both. American diplomacy and business exploited the possibilities with alacrity. The 1971–1973 devaluations had helped make American export prices extremely competitive. Domestic recession encouraged firms to look to foreign markets. American exports to the OPEC oil producers thus jumped from $3.6 billion in 1973 to $10.8 billion in 1975. Partly in consequence, the United States suffered only a small trade deficit in 1974 and enjoyed a sizable surplus in 1975, the oil price rise notwithstanding.

Unfortunately, America's apparently successful adjustment of 1974 and 1975 was an illusion. All depended upon recession. As long as the slump continued, domestic demand for oil stayed flat and exports of manufactures increased. But as the economy climbed out of its trough in 1976, the steady rise in American oil imports resumed as if the OPEC price revolution had never occurred. Hence, the volume of US crude petroleum imports jumped over 20% in 1976 alone. Exports and foreign earnings failed to grow fast enough to compensate, particularly as the new boom expanded domestic demand. Hence, 1976 saw a $14.7 billion trade deficit (f.a.s.), which then rose to an unprecedented $36.4 billion in 1977 and remained at roughly the same level into 1980.[22] This collapse of the trade balance was highly predictable. Although exports and foreign earnings had grown, little had occurred to promote the structural changes needed to control the American economy's vaulting demand for imported petroleum. Again and again, Congress refused the legislation.

On the face of it, prospects for American structural adaptations were not unpromising, particularly when the American situation was compared to that of most other industrial countries. Substitution for imported oil seemed relatively easy. The United States had considerable untapped petroleum, colossal coal reserves, and an advanced nuclear power industry, not to mention the possibilities for the more exotic sources like shale and tar sands.[23] As for conservation, American energy use per capita was substantially higher than in other countries at comparable stages of development. Though some differences might be explained by size and climate,

American energy waste was notorious.[24] America's relative profligacy could, moreover, be laid to the years of relatively subsidized consumption that had kept American gasoline prices much lower than in nearly all other industrialized countries.[25] Government intervention had similarly kept down natural gas prices. Such policies, manifestly artificial under existing circumstances, could presumably have been reversed without imposing burdens greater than those long ago absorbed by other affluent economies.

The American government had little difficulty imagining the required plans. Policies for conservation called for sharp price increases or gasoline rationing. Policies to develop substitutes for imported oil called for subsidized investments and tolerance for greater environmental damage. At the very least, in a market economy, the artificial subsidy to consumption should have been ended by allowing domestic oil prices to rise to world levels. Sharply higher domestic oil prices could be expected, in themselves, to promote energy saving and import substitution. What was wanted was an increase in the *relative* price of oil, not a general increase in all prices with oil leading the way. Thus, to be effective, the raising or "decontrol" of oil prices would presumably have to be combined with generally restrictive economic policies, very possibly reinforced by wage and price controls. Otherwise inflation, triggered by oil's price increases, would soon raise all other prices to the same level and hence erode the new differential for oil that was meant to promote conservation.

Though both Nixon and Ford Administrations proposed policies to promote the needed price changes, neither could prevail over a heterogeneous political coalition opposed, in effect, to any domestic adjustment at all. Opposition to "decontrol" was widespread in domestic American politics. The poor would suffer disproportionately, it was noted, and exorbitant profits would accrue to the rich oil companies, often believed in collusion with OPEC. Without decontrol, market pressure for conserving oil, finding new domestic sources, or developing substitutes was predictably insufficient to have any serious effect. Even if fuel prices did rise somewhat, the general progress of inflation soon eroded their relative gain.

In short, no real adjustment was made in the structure of the

American domestic economy. Naturally, when the recession ended, the accelerating demand for oil of the preceding years resumed and, along with it, the American trade deficit.

Monetary Adjustment

Since the United States was willing neither to remain in permanent recession nor to make adequate structural adjustments within its real economy, actual adjustment came mostly in the monetary sphere. Though recession had brought down American inflation from a year-long high of 11% in 1974 to 5.8% by 1976, thereafter, as the boom gathered force, the annual rate rose every year and reached 13.5% (CPI) by 1980. As inflation pushed up the overall price level at so rapid a rate, the 1973 price increases of imported oil within the American economy were gradually dissipated. Subsequent increases in petroleum prices did not catch up with the US inflation rate until 1979. Rising US inflation also helped start the dollar on another round of drastic depreciation against the stronger foreign currencies. Thus, from mid-1976 to December 1979, the dollar fell 48% against the German mark. Since oil prices were traditionally factored in dollars, dollar depreciation on such a scale in itself greatly reduced the real price of crude petroleum in markets outside the dollar zone. In other words, petroleum prices were falling not only in relation to other prices factored in dollars but even more to prices factored in stronger currencies. Oil producers thus received less in real terms for their oil and paid more for inflating industrial products, with an additional premium for products factored in stronger currencies. Inflation plus depreciation also steadily depreciated the producers' liquid dollar assets. In exchanging oil for dollar securities, producers were thus giving up a reserve that could appreciate for one that steadily declined.[26]

The depreciating dollar naturally favored American industrial producers by keeping their inflating domestic prices internationally competitive at the expense of the Europeans and the Japanese. But since oil was factored in dollars, those countries whose currencies were appreciating against the dollar were also paying less for their imported petroleum. Lower energy costs helped keep down their export prices, despite their appreciating currencies. In other words, part of the American advantage was shared with its more affluent allies. In summary, for the United States in particular and to a considerable extent for the industrial world in general, inflation became the principal means of adjustment to the oil price explosion.

The durability of such an adjustment depended upon the oil producers' not raising their dollar oil prices to compensate for US inflation, or not factoring their oil prices in some medium other than the falling dollar. Their forbearance, in turn, depended upon a number of conditions—in particular, the temporary oil glut in the recessionary years of 1974–1975 and the divergent interests within OPEC.[27] But bearing heavily on these more economic considerations was the weight of America's political and military position in the Middle East, a position Kissinger brilliantly cultivated in the aftermath of the 1973 Arab-Israeli War. The critical importance of American power in the Middle East made the adjustment to higher oil prices through inflation and depreciation not unlike the international monetary mechanism that made the monetary policy possible. Both monetary and oil policies depended heavily upon American power.

Political Adjustment

Since World War II, the United States had clearly been the dominant diplomatic force in the Middle East. In 1956, our prewar rivals, the British and the French, were decisively humiliated. Though the Russians established themselves in Egypt in the 1950s, Egypt quarrelled with the Soviets before the 1973 Arab-Israeli War and subsequently reversed its alliances. The Soviets were thus excluded from active participation in the regional balance. The United States was left to preside exclusively over an Arab-Israeli settlement.[28] For the time being, this role gave the United States extraordinary leverage. Israel was America's client, and only America, presumably, could deliver the concessions needed not only to satisfy the Egyptians but also to pacify the Palestinians, whose radical dissatisfaction increasingly threatened stability within the conservative Arab states.

In addition to supplanting the Russians in Egypt, Kissinger as-
siduously promoted a special military relationship with the two
major conservative oil states in the region, Iran and Saudi Arabia.
These were to become not only American protectorates vis-à-vis
the Soviet Union but also surrogates policing regional stability.[29]
Such a role called for massive arms purchases, in themselves of
great assistance to American trade and industry. By making the
Saudi monarchy its client, American diplomacy gained not only
considerable commercial advantage but a certain containing influence over the rest of OPEC. With its huge spare capacity, Saudi
Arabia became a reincarnation of the Texas Railroad Commission, able to thwart attempts by others to raise oil prices further.[30]
The Saudis used their power on several occasions after 1973.
Thanks in good part to that power, world oil price increases remained below the dollar's real depreciation, at least until 1979.

In the end, the whole arrangement depended upon American
power — power to keep OPEC divided, power to keep the Russians
out of the Middle East, power to keep the Europeans, Japanese,
and Arabs from revolting against the falling dollar. Thanks to
Nixon and Kissinger, the United States enjoyed that power until
the last years of the decade.

Unforeseen International Consequences

For better or worse, economics has some rules of its own, which
power is not always able to suppress. America's continual currency
debasement and the international mechanism needed to effect it
had general consequences for the international system as a whole.
Just as dollar inflation in the early seventies led to world-wide inflation and hastened and intensified the explosion of oil prices, so
America's inflationary solution to the oil crisis led to a new explosion of world inflation. Other debtor countries similarly disinclined to make real adjustments also began to use the inflationary
international monetary mechanisms created and employed by
American policy, in particular, the rapidly expanding international
private banking system.

As an immediate result of 1973's huge increase in oil prices,
nearly every non-OPEC country began running a large balance-of-

payments deficit. Overall, OPEC purchases of goods and services could not possibly rise quickly enough to compensate for the four-fold oil-price increase. Thus the OPEC countries had huge surplus funds that needed to be kept in some relatively safe, accessible, and profitable medium. The greatest demand for short-term funds came from OPEC's customers, who needed loans to finance their huge payments deficits, at least until their economies could adjust to the new prices. OPEC's money, it was said, had to be "recycled" back to the oil importers. Various multilateral agencies sought to assist and control this recycling. But official arrangements, multilateral or national, came with the usual strings, involving various forms of economic probity and political deference. Both the oil-importing borrowers and their OPEC lenders came to prefer the huge Eurodollar market. International banking profits grew very large as a result.[31]

The whole mechanism of "recycling" through the banking system became in itself a major new source of world inflation. In effect, this Eurodollar mechanism repeated, in the private sphere, the same process of credit creation that characterized relations among central banks in the gold-exchange standard. A non-US bank in the Eurodollar market, including any offshore branch of a US bank, stood to a big New York bank in much the same relationship as a European central bank stood to the Federal Reserve under the gold-exchange standard. Since the dollar deposit base in an offshore Eurodollar bank perforce corresponded to a dollar deposit in some domestic American bank, the increase in the Eurodollar bank's deposit base required no compensatory reduction in the deposit base of the domestic US bank. Dollars that went to work in Europe also stayed home to work in America. In other words, just as nothing automatically limited the credit foreign central banks could make available to the US central bank under the gold-exchange standard, so nothing automatically limited the credit the Eurobanking system could extend to the domestic American banking system.[32] Until 1974, US capital controls placed some limit on the flow of funds that might be exported. With floating, the barrier was gradually swept away.

Spurred by the oil crisis, the private mechanism of credit creation began immediately to run at high speed. With a banking system capable of extending infinite credit, any "credit-worthy" firm or state could borrow whatever was necessary to carry on its oil imports as before. The world economy thus avoided the sharp decline in transactions that higher oil prices would otherwise have compelled.[33]

Swelling international credit creation was also fed from a new source. With the steady depreciation of the dollar, the market began to prefer other currencies, particularly for long-term transactions. Initially, countries like Germany had strongly resisted letting their currencies become public and private reserves for foreigners. They thus hoped to avoid the disruptive consequences for domestic management illustrated so vividly in the British and American examples before them. But as American inflation continued its relentless upward pressure on the German mark, its development into an international reserve currency grew more and more difficult to resist. For as the deutsche mark became increasingly "overvalued," market pressure naturally encouraged Germans to invest abroad rather than at home. A large outflow for foreign investment, moreover, helped reduce pressure for appreciation, thus limiting the competitive damage to domestic industry and employment.[34] Under these pressures, the deutsche mark increasingly became an international currency, held in large quantities by nonresidents. The same process worked to a lesser degree on other major European currencies. By the end of the seventies, as Europeans began to put together their European Monetary System, they were talking of "multilateralizing" their growing reserve role by allowing the European Currency Unit (ECU), the new system's unit of account, to become a reserve currency.[35]

In any event, new reserve currencies, multilateral or national, had the same inflationary effects as old reserve currencies. Deutsche marks held in foreign central banks were also deutsche marks held as part of the *Bundesbank*'s monetary base. Credit was created abroad but not reduced at home. The same inflationary process worked for private holdings in the international capital market. The deposit base in a Eurobank was also part of a deposit base in a German bank.

The proliferation of these mechanisms of public and private monetary creation marked a profound change in the international monetary system. Formerly, countries other than the United States had to keep their balance of payments in some sort of equilibrium.

They had to "earn" the money they wished to spend abroad. Now they could borrow it. With liquidity apparently capable of infinite expansion, countries deemed credit-worthy no longer had any external check on foreign spending. Several countries, in fact, while running large current-account deficits, nevertheless greatly increased their official monetary reserves by borrowing from the Eurodollar market.[36] Under such circumstances, a balance-of-payments deficit no longer provided, in itself, an automatic check to domestic inflation. Countries in deficit could borrow indefinitely from the magic liquidity machine. Many countries, in particular, some of the poorest developing countries, thus joined the United States in avoiding any real adjustment to higher oil prices. Not surprisingly, world inflation continued accelerating throughout the decade, and fears of collapse in the private banking system grew increasingly vivid. More and more debts were "rescheduled," and a number of poor countries grew flagrantly insolvent. Schemes proliferated for unloading bad bank loans on the IMF or the OPEC countries themselves.[37]

Where this whole process might end, no one could say. If history were any guide, a serious financial crash would be followed by a new era of tight national control over banking and trade. In such a catastrophe, the United States would have a special responsibility. It would have exported not only its inflation, but its mercantilist nationalism. The world system that might be expected to result from such dramatic events would presumably be rather different from the postwar *Pax Americana*. The contradictions between America's hegemony and the liberal international system it had created would finally destroy both the hegemony and the system.

Although the international system was still to show great resilience throughout the seventies, the growing weakness of the American real economy, together with the increasing reliance on power to compensate, created a progressively unstable condition. The more often American external power was used to compensate for internal weakness, the more rapidly the power eroded. Thus, by the end of the seventies, both the Nixon *Pax Americana* and the Nixon domestic economic policy were apparently coming to an end. As Nixon had inherited the bankruptcy of the Kennedy-Johnson policies, so Carter was to inherit the breakdown of the Nixon.

8

The Carter Cycle

IN 1974, the year Nixon departed from office, the domestic economy was left even more disrupted than at the finish of Johnson's administration. The troubles lasted for at least a year thereafter. The record postwar inflation continued into 1975. By then the country seemed well into a depression. But before 1975 was half over, the American economy started on a new boom that was to continue through Carter's election in 1976 and to last until 1980. It proved to be one of the longer upswings in postwar American history, all the more remarkable since the rest of the world economy was still slowed by the effects of the energy crisis.[1] Like the Nixon boom, the Carter boom was to accumulate the familiar symptoms of America's economic disorder: record inflation, huge trade deficits, a deteriorating dollar, abrupt and rigorous monetary restraint, bounding oil prices, and finally a severe recession.

From an historical perspective, the Ford-Carter cycle provided few novelties. Domestic expansion was fueled by the familiar combination of fiscal deficits and monetary accommodation. Equally familiar were the inflationary consequences. As before, Kissinger's refurbished *Pax Americana* was manipulated to fend off restraint from abroad. By 1979, however, foreign reactions were seriously qualifying America's capacity for external manipulation. The reactions reflected not only growing resistance abroad to specific consequences of America's economic indiscipline, but also a more general decline in America's geopolitical power. Economic resentments contributed to that political decline. And along with growing external resistance, strong reactions against inflation began to affect domestic credit markets, with important consequences for monetary and even fiscal policy. These domestic and foreign reactions reflected significant changes in America's political and economic environment, changes that began to force Carter toward fundamental revisions in the policies inherited from Nixon. The Ford-Carter period reveals not only how purblind, distracted, and contradictory government policy had become, but also what halting early steps were taken toward a new American economic policy.

Ford's Recovery

Ford came into office during one of those particularly unhappy periods when a collapsing boom left behind it a still record inflation rate, while several other signs pointed to a bad recession. The annual inflation rate for 1975 was 9.1%. The year nevertheless started off with a spiral of falling purchasing power, sales, and employment that rivaled the beginnings of the Great Depression of the 1930s. Unemployment rose from 5.5% in the third quarter of 1974 to 9.0% by the following May. In roughly the same period, real business fixed investment was declining at an annual rate of 16.5%. New housing starts, 2.057 million in 1973, had plunged to a one million rate by late 1975.[2]

Analogies with the 1930s proved premature, however. By the summer of 1975, expansive policies, built-in "stabilizers," and good luck pulled the economy back from its downward slide. Fiscal policy turned highly stimulative, with Congress passing on May 1, 1975, the largest tax reduction in its history, thereby injecting some $22.8 billion into the economy. Automatic stabilizers braked the decline in consumer spending while augmenting the government deficit. Unemployment insurance, for example, jumped from $8.5 billion to $18.1 billion in two quarters. Overall federal spending increased 19%, and federal deficits reached $71.2 billion for fiscal 1975.[3] Monetary conditions also grew easy, with the federal funds rate dropping from 12.9% in July 1974 to 5.2% in May 1975.[4] Mercifully, no further "shocks" jolted the fragile confidence. A reasonable harvest meant no renewed explosions in agricultural prices. Oil prices increased only moderately. New York City steered around bankruptcy. By the third quarter of 1975, recovery was under way. GNP was growing at an annual rate of 12%, and the Dow Jones stock market average rose 65 points from December 1974 to June 1975, for the largest six-months' point gain in its history.[5]

Momentum continued into early 1976, with the first quarter showing a 9.2% rate of growth. By the second quarter, however, growth slowed sharply. The unemployment rate remained particularly high, at 7.7%, although some 2.7 million workers were added to the labor force.[6] Congressional pressure mounted for more stimulation. By the end of 1976, economists professed to see a 10% gap between actual and potential output.[7] But Ford, worried about an inflation rate still at 5% after two years of recession, struggled to contain tax cutting and vetoed a record number of congressional appropriations bills. As a result, the Ford Administration, despite its 1976 fiscal deficit of $66.4 billion, was widely blamed for the slowdown and continually reproached for the unemployment rate. The economy became the featured issue in the election campaign, with Carter severely criticizing the Ford Administration for excessive timidity. An output that could be reckoned at 10% below potential and an unemployment rate averaging 7.7% were, Carter professed, intolerable social burdens, falling mainly on those disadvantaged citizens least able to bear them. Ford defended himself by stressing the importance of combatting inflation. Ford lost.[8]

Carter's Domestic Economic Policy

From the start, the Carter Administration's economic policies followed an annual cycle of their own. The new Administration arrived in an expansive mood. Congress immediately received an amended budget, with tax reductions, rebates, and increased ex penditures. Spending was to increase 12.2% in fiscal 1977 and 7% in fiscal 1978, with projected budget deficits of $57.2 billion and $47 billion respectively.[9]

By the end of the first quarter, however, the new Administration abruptly shifted its rhetoric and, to some extent, its policies as well. Inflation had jumped back to an annual rate of 8.8%. The stimulative package of January was accordingly revised in April. The President, moreover, solemnly promised to balance the budget by fiscal 1981 and announced studies and consultations to see how to reduce inflation to a 6% per-annum rate by the end of 1979.[10] The Administration also persuaded Congress to schedule major increases in social security taxes, a reform that, if actually carried out, could be expected to improve greatly the prospects for balancing future budgets.[11]

While in its stern April mood, the Administration also unveiled its first energy program. A federal tax at the wellhead was to raise domestic oil prices to world levels. A discretionary excise tax on gasoline of as much as fifty cents a gallon was to cut any persisting excessive consumption. Like the Nixon and Ford proposals, however, Carter's energy plan was soon stalled in Congress, not to be rescued until the last year of his term.[12]

Meanwhile, as estimates for the actual government balance in fiscal 1977 became available at midyear, the deficit looked to be only $45 billion rather than the $57.2 billion originally estimated, in part because the government was unable to spend all the money appropriated. Since a $45 billion deficit was a considerable improvement over the previous year's $66.4 billion, the Administration congratulated itself on moving toward fiscal "restraint."[13]

Midsummer saw a new shift. The Administration's springtime preoccupation with inflation was being displaced by its summertime disappointment over flagging growth and employment figures. GNP, which had expanded 7.5% in the first quarter of 1977, slowed sharply for the rest of the year. The overall 1977 figures were nevertheless far from desperate. Real GNP and per-capita income both expanded by 4.9%; employment rose by 4.1 million workers, with the jobless rate dropping to 6.4%. Industrial productivity rose by 5.6% and corporate profits by 9.5%. The Administration, however, was again determined to press for expansion.[14]

The January 1978 budget accordingly called for cuts and reforms to produce a $25 billion net reduction of taxes and an estimated fiscal deficit of $60.6 billion.[15] Once again, the holiday boom in January was followed by a Lenten repentance. April 1978, like April 1977, saw the President trimming and delaying his tax proposals and announcing a new anti-inflation program. Business and labor were presented with "guidelines," and federal pay raises were cut.[16]

April's restraint notwithstanding, 1978 proved the country's fourth straight year of boom. Output and employment continued to rise, although more slowly. The growth rate dropped from 5½% to 4½%. Employment nevertheless grew by 3.3 million, and the unemployment rate fell to 5.8% by the last quarter. Signs of excess were not difficult to perceive. Production began to reach full capacity, and productivity growth dropped significantly. The rate of consumer-price increases jumped from 6.5% to 7.7%, and the GNP deflator rose from 6.0% to 7.3%.[17]

The year 1978 also saw the first signs of effective foreign anger at American inflation and currency depreciation. All through the Carter boom, the United States ran record trade and current-account deficits. The dollar steadily declined against the mark, the Swiss franc, and the yen, despite a large influx of foreign investment capital into the United States.[18] The quarrels over benign neglect and the locomotive theory grew more intense. By the fall of 1978, the Administration was pressing a new anti-inflation campaign partly in response to foreign pressure. By November, the dollar's rapid depreciation led to a much-publicized "rescue package" of domestic monetary measures and foreign credits to stabilize the currency markets.[19]

The budget presented in January 1979 was meant to reflect the same chastened mood. The projected dificit for fiscal 1980 was $29 billion, down from the $37.4 billion projected for the previous fiscal year. The Administration congratulated itself on a "lean but merciful" budget, although numerous commentators found the forecast for the reduced deficit absurdly optimistic.[20] By the middle of 1979, however, the Administration's mood had shifted once more. Recession and unemployment were widely predicted. Proposals for stimulatory spending and tax cuts sprouted on all sides.[21] These were soon to be blighted, however, by a new dollar crisis and monetary squeeze in the autumn.[22]

All these abrupt but regular shifts in economic policy reflected the Administration's internal ambivalence. The President was worried and threatened politically by the high and rising level of inflation. At the same time, he continued to fret over the remaining jobless workers and to fear the onset of a recession and higher unemployment. The oscillation between these concerns produced a policy that, on balance, inched toward fiscal restraint too slowly to arrest inflation or achieve budgetary equilibrium. As a result, the huge deficits of Ford's recession and recovery continued throughout the three succeeding years of Carter's upswing. Rising tax revenues generated from continuing prosperity, plus the fiscal drag from inflation, were regularly dissipated by tax cuts and new expenditures. Thus, the actual federal deficit for fiscal 1978 was nearly $49 billion, for fiscal 1979 nearly $28 billion, and for fiscal 1980 some $60 billion — surprising figures for the fourth, fifth, and sixth years of an upswing, with an economy near full employment.

Yet the President had pledged to balance the budget by fiscal 1981. This was a dubious promise even from the start, since the business cycle could have been expected by then to have turned downward. It seemed a curious Keynesianism that would not balance the budget over the longest recovery in the postwar era, but planned to do so after the probable onset of a recession.

Monetary Policy

With the federal budget regularly in heavy deficit, the task of containing inflation fell to the Federal Reserve. In the early Carter period, the Chairman was still Arthur Burns, Nixon's old friend who had presided over the monetary binge and crash of the earlier 1970s. In March 1977, Burns was replaced by William Miller, an intelligent businessman, but without deep experience in either public or private banking.

In 1975 and 1976, economic slack left over from the recession had kept down the demand for credit. The money supply remained steady and interest rates moderate. By 1977, monetary bases began expanding rapidly. The Federal Reserve, fearing renewed price inflation, regularly lowered its targets, and just as regularly the money supply exceeded them. Interest rates moved steadily upward, but so did the rate of monetary growth.[23] The Fed's real control over the money supply seemed increasingly uncertain, as a series of institutional changes had greatly increased the mobility of domestic capital in the banking system.[24] Whatever the causes, monetary targets continued to be exceeded until the third quarter of 1978, when the gathering dollar crisis led to a sharp rise in US interest rates, along with the Treasury's "rescue package" of loans from foreign central banks. These "November measures" were widely perceived as the consequence of foreign pressure, a significant portent both of growing foreign opposition to American policy and of American vulnerability to that opposition. For a few months thereafter, from October 1978 to March 1979, the monetary base (M1) actually fell slightly. Restraint, however, was short-lived. From March to June 1979, the money supply grew at an annual rate of nearly 12%. Not surprisingly, the inflation rate eventually began to climb and the dollar to slip.[25]

In August 1979, the Administration's internal tensions over economic policy broke into the open. Treasury Secretary Michael Blumenthal was fired, along with Energy Secretary James Schlesinger and HEW Secretary Joseph Califano. Miller went from the Federal Reserve to become Secretary of the Treasury. His replacement at the Fed was Paul Volcker, Chairman of the New York Federal Reserve Bank, an experienced central banker, in and out of the Treasury since the early sixties, and the principal architect of the Jamaica Agreements to legitimize floating rates.[26] Volcker immediately faced a renewed dollar crisis. On October 6 he introduced a package of radical new measures to restrict monetary growth. These included a number of significant technical innovations, which were reactions, in part, to a large downward shift in the public demand for money. The shift was, in turn, a consequence both of changes in banking procedures and the general rise in inflationary expectations. Henceforth, Volcker announced, the

Board would concentrate upon the monetary aggregates themselves and let interest rates fluctuate as the market indicated.[27]

Volcker's measures were widely heralded as a revolution in American economic policy. The immediate effects were striking. Prime interest rates rose quickly to over 15%, and the dollar's fall was arrested and sharply reversed.[28] Not everyone was pleased. As interest rates rose to historic highs, Volcker seemed in danger of losing majority support at the Fed itself. The President had supported the new measures, but in a fashion that lacked conviction. Volcker tenaciously defended his position.[29] In an Administration without clear economic direction, he became a symbol of competence and integrity. For the moment, he was also indispensable. By the fall of 1979, the dollar's weakness was threatening the exchange markets with a genuine panic. Foreign governments were both frightened and outraged. By the end of the year, gold prices had exploded, and the domestic bond market came to the verge of collapse. Currency and credit markets were together mounting a major foreign and domestic revolt against American inflation. In the gold market, the dollar price per ounce rose from $431 on December 10 to $850 on January 21, 1980. Arabs and Europeans were rumored to be dumping dollars wholesale. The dramatic fall of the dollar against gold raised fears of a catastrophic liquidation of the dollar's role as reserve currency, and even of a general stampede away from paper money.[30]

In Europe, a renewed Franco-German entente revived the continental monetary union and implied a new international reserve currency, the ECU. Even if European solidarity was as ambiguous as ever, structures were nevertheless being put into place that would permit a radical revolt against the postwar monetary system. By mid-1979, the oil market was joining the currency market in reaction against the depreciated dollar. From December 1978 to April 1980, dollar prices of oil jumped 120%, the first significant increase since the explosion of 1973.[31] These dramatic developments in the currency and oil markets represented a sort of European-Arab revolt against further dollar depreciation. Under these circumstances, more benign neglect became a serious threat to that international order from which a mercantilist United States had been deriving so much apparent tribute. America's foreign geese were suddenly and effectively demanding respect for their golden eggs. Volcker was needed to keep the geese pacified.

Volcker's Strategy

Although some foreigners may have seen Volcker as the instrument for a long overdue retribution, his own view of economic prospects was essentially optimistic. Several months of genuine monetary restraint would, he hoped, bring down inflation, allow domestic interest rates to fall of their own accord, and result in an environment more conducive to investment and growth.[32] In other words, Volcker hoped a more responsible government policy could return the business cycle to manageable limits typical of the earlier postwar era.

Success, Volcker believed, depended upon sustaining monetary restraint long enough to lower inflationary expectations. That would be much easier if fiscal policy could be brought into harmony with monetary restraint. To do so, however, meant drastically scaling down the fiscal deficits of the middle to late seventies. Technically, prospects were not unpromising.[33] The year 1980, however, was an election year, not the best setting for a policy whose predictable effects would be high unemployment and a more severe recession. Moreover, just as "exogenous" events in the foreign exchange market had reinforced Volcker's anti-inflationary program, other exogenous events, both economic and political, kept upsetting his calculations. The sharp rise in oil prices in December 1979, while reinforcing the need to stabilize the dollar, also augmented domestic inflation, hence lengthening and deepening the prescribed monetary cure.[34] The taking of American hostages in Iran, the Soviet invasion of Afghanistan, and the broad deterioration of detente also fed the Administration's growing enthusiasm for military spending, while election-year politics made compensatory cuts in civilian spending unlikely.[35]

The Boom Ends

The year 1980 was one of great confusion, not least because of the intersection and confrontation of the conflicting directions in government policy. For a start, experts disagreed widely over actual economic conditions. At the beginning of the year, signs of a serious downturn were easily found. A considerable number of commentators nevertheless remained skeptical that the long boom had ended. By midyear, official statistics confirmed a recession, but government officials claimed a new upturn had already begun. Modest increases in GNP were recorded for July and August. The inflation rate was meanwhile meant to be falling, but nevertheless the Consumer Price Index remained stubbornly in place, held up, it was said, by "special" factors. Unemployment, at a record 7.5%, appeared to have stopped increasing, although it was ultimately expected to rise above 8%.[36]

Government policies reflected and exacerbated the confusion over actual trends. Early 1980 provided a repetition of the familiar Carter budgetary cycle. Once again, the Administration presented an expansive budget in January and was busy cutting it in March. The January version raised military expenditures 14.2% and projected a deficit of $16 billion, a sharp decrease from fiscal 1980's deficit, then estimated at $40 billion.[37] With the recession widely expected, few took the budgetary projections seriously. In a recession, revenues would obviously fall and welfare costs balloon. Refusing to cut taxes would not only be politically improbable but economically imprudent. Congressional economists were already predicting a $25 billion deficit in fiscal 1981.[38] In short, instead of reducing inflationary expectations, Carter's January budget confirmed them. Few, moreover, expected the Federal Reserve to offset such pressures successfully. Indeed, a number of signs suggested that the Fed was already loosening its tight monetary policy as early as the end of 1979. A strong inflationary spurt in 1980's first quarter left the annual Consumer Price Index reaching toward 17%. The accumulating fear over inflation prompted a new collapse in the already depressed bond market. By March, the Fed had reacted by a savage new tightening of monetary and credit conditions that sent prime interest rates close to 20%.[39]

Spring once more brought Carter to repentance. The President revealed on March 14 that he intended to balance the 1981 fiscal budget after all. By this time, almost everyone believed the recession was at hand, although expert opinion was still sharply divided as to whether it would be mild or severe. Not surprisingly, analysts began wondering whether a balanced budget was the proper way to offset a downturn. Fiscal austerity might bring an unnecessarily severe recession. Carter's presidential opponents — Kennedy on the left and Reagan on the right — began calling for a tax cut. But Congress, prodded by Carter, went through an elaborate springtime exercise to balance the 1981 fiscal budget, a forlorn hope, since a recession, with falling revenues and rising welfare, could be expected to unbalance the budget whatever Congress did. More significantly, Congress finally passed an energy bill, with gradual "decontrol" of domestic prices, a step which promised to accelerate considerably the country's long-delayed adaptation to world energy costs.[40]

By early summer, the technical argument over the recession was finally settled officially. The GNP had been shrinking for two quarters. Interest rates had been falling rapidly, credit restrictions were eased, money was abundant, and the dollar was once more feeble. Cynics suspected the Federal Reserve of boosting the Carter campaign.[41] By the end of the summer, expectations of a quick recovery were widespread. July and August showed a modest growth of GNP.[42] The stock market boomed, and Carter, although still opposing an election-year tax cut, began outlining grand schemes for the country's economic "revitalization."[43] His Republican opponent, meanwhile, went on calling for a major "supply-side" tax cut, although the Republican platform was also demanding a return to the gold standard.[44] By the fall, the rapidly growing money supply was pushing the Fed back to a tight monetary policy, despite the election, high unemployment, and depressed business profits. The outbreak of war between Iran and Iraq doubtlessly strengthened resolve at the Fed by increasing the prospect that a new burst of inflation would provoke a new round of oil price increases or an explosion in the gold market. Chances for a quick and strong domestic recovery thus grew dimmer. Carter began attacking the Fed for its "overreaction."[45] Toward the year's end, interest rates rebounded beyond 20%. The postelectoral boom in the stock market receded, along with the price of gold. With such high interest rates, the dollar seemed on an upward course, while the year-end economic figures suggested a renewed downturn for the economy.

Prospect for the New Decade

No one could say with much conviction what gyrations the eco nomy might take in the rest of the new decade, nor what broad government policies might emerge. The most probable future seemed some extrapolation of the immediate past. The recession that began in 1980, like that of 1974–1975, would have some severe aspects, particularly in industries with long-term problems, but would be less dire overall than suggested by its early signs. The recession would also give more support to the dollar and the trade balance, as well as supplement the real economy's slow adaptation to high energy prices. The inflation rate would recede for a time, but to a higher basic level than before the cycle began. With inflation persisting, so would its consequences: America's characteristically low saving, investment, and productivity rates. Long-range prospects for the real economy would remain discouraging. Recovery, when it came, would be hobbled by stop-go monetary policies. Any boom that might be provoked by the Reagan Administration's "supply side" tax cuts would soon be throttled to prevent a new collapse of the dollar. In other words, Nixon's revolution would have failed in its larger object. Despite the freedom of action floating had given American domestic economic policy, a freedom energetically exploited by nearly a decade of mercantilist international policies, the real American economy would continue to grow weaker.

More optimistic observers could place their hopes in what might appropriately be called the Volcker variation. The Federal Reserve, bolstered at home and abroad, would persevere in the more resolute application of conventional monetary restraint. And more conservative congresses or administrations would return to balancing budgets in boom times. These practices might turn back the clock to the healthier cycles of the early 1960s, with their greater price stability, saving, investment, and growth. Such a re turn would reverse a twenty-year inflationary trend with its wider and wider cyclical oscillations.

This twenty-year trend, however, resulted not from fortuitous mistakes and coincidences, but from basic economic policies and expectations now deeply rooted in the structure of American government, business, and society. Perpetually unbalanced budgets, ratified by easy monetary policy, accurately reflected the broad excess of American expectations over American resources. In a democratic system, restoring balance would not prove easy or popular. Cutting back expectations nourished for two decades would very likely precipitate powerful social unrest. Returning to equilibrium would mean a great weeding out of marginal business activities nourished by a policy of perpetual boom.

Political leaders in the new decade might therefore be expected to search for some other resolution than prolonged austerity. It would certainly be attractive politically to promote growing resources rather than shrinking expectations. The old Keynesian formula of social peace through growth, whatever its economic flaws, would remain almost irresistible politically. Nor would its practical appeal be limited to the left, as the infatuation of conservatives with supply-side economics in the 1980 campaign amply demonstrated. But whatever its appeal, in the conditions of the 1960s and 1970s, growth through stimulation had invariably also meant more inflation. By the end of the 1970s inflation seemed to have reached the stage where it was strangling growth. Real growth could not resume, it seemed, until inflation was reversed.[46] Austerity would have to precede prosperity. This would be a harsh truth for American democracy to accept. Any serious amelioration of the prevailing inflationary trend was likely to require a fundamental change in mentality and institutions, a change that still seemed far from the agenda of practical politics.

Events, however, might not permit leisurely adaptations. If the trend of two decades continued to accelerate in the 1980s, the increasing violence of the cycles might lead to more adventurous outcomes than either slow deterioration or gradual improvement. If the hectic pattern of the 1970s continued through the 1980s, what was to keep the accelerating inflation rate from jumping to

Latin American levels? How many cycles were left before some overextended and collapsing boom required monetary restraint so severe that a deep cyclical recession would be combined with a severe financial crash? How solid was the world's financial structure in any event?

The deterioration of financial conditions was a particularly worrisome trend. International finance in the seventies had organized itself around a magic money machine of ceaseless credit. Big banks had granted developing countries huge loans, often for current expenses. Many of these countries seemed hopelessly overextended. Attempts to unload these debts on the IMF or OPEC countries predictably met with only limited success. Meanwhile, fear of inflation had undermined credit markets everywhere, and proper long-range finance was growing more and more difficult to arrange, not only for states but for business firms as well. Knowledgeable analysts were alarmed at the debt structure of many domestic American corporations.[47] In short, if a major financial breakdown occurred in the eighties, no one would have any trouble explaining it afterward. Nor was fear of some general breakdown limited to visionaries and cranks. On the contrary, predictions of catastrophe were becoming the new conventional wisdom.

An heroic optimist could, of course, take comfort from the general trends that had emerged in the Carter era. Both the chaotic events and the gloomy climate at the end of 1980 might presage healthier conditions in the future. For 1980 saw, in effect, the apparent demise of the Nixon strategy that had linked inflation at home to dollar depreciation abroad. A growing domestic American reaction against inflation was decisively reinforced by a marked increase in foreign resistance to depreciation. These increasingly effective foreign reactions reflected the unraveling of Nixon and Kissinger's *Pax Americana*. Ironically, the deterioration in external hegemony provoked the first serious steps toward domestic reformation. Thanks to Khomeini, America got Volcker's monetary policy and Carter's first real efforts to balance the budget.

However salutary the novel domestic discipline, no American administration was likely to view the shifting geopolitical balance with complacency. America's world decline was a major theme in the electoral campaign that ended the Carter Administration. The Reagan Administration came to office pledged to restore not only domestic equilibrium but also foreign power. The new Administration, it soon became clear, had never thought through the relationship between the two. Only time would tell whether Reagan was a conservative genuinely devoted to equilibrium or a Nixon reborn.

9

Reagan's
Temptation

TO SUCCEED AT HOME, Nixonian economic policies required freedom from foreign retaliation. America's economic invulner-
ability depended, in turn, upon its political power within the postwar international order. Three dimensions of America's
geopolitical primacy were particularly critical: primacy over Western Europe and Japan to prevent serious retaliation against exported inflation and a continually declining dollar; primacy over
the Middle East to restrain OPEC from raising oil prices to compensate adequately for America's inflation and declining dollar;
and detente with the Soviet Union sufficient to inhibit direct Soviet
challenges or Soviet support for others inclined to challenge American influence and power in the Middle East or among the non-
communist industrialized countries.

All three conditions were principal objects of foreign policy in
the Nixon and Ford Administrations. And all three deteriorated
markedly during the Carter Administration. Indeed, by the end of
the decade, bipolar detente was a shambles, American predominance in the Middle East had collapsed, and relations with Europe
were worse than at any time since the war. Among its other effects,
this geopolitical deterioration spelled the beginning of the end for
the Nixon economic strategy. After mid-1979, the Federal Reserve, faced with tumultuous conditions in currency and gold mar-

kets, along with bolting oil prices, began a policy of unprecedented restraint over the money supply; the President, within a few months, started calling for a balanced federal budget. By April 1980, interest rates had reached 20%, and the long-delayed cyclical downturn finally hit with exceptional severity. The second quarter saw a decline in industrial production even worse than in the recession of 1974–1975. Although economic prospects brightened over the summer of 1980, particularly as money grew less tight before the election, the start of a new and sustained Nixonian boom in 1981 seemed unlikely, whatever the predispositions of the Reagan Administration. The continued virulence of American price inflation, combined with the heightened dangers of foreign retaliation, seemed to preclude a return to the old pattern. A new round of inflation and dollar depreciation would risk not only runaway inflation at home, but rapid deterioration of the international system, with incalculable political repercussions. Under such conditions, the necessity for tight money was likely to keep the economy on a very short tether. In sum, by 1980 the country was back to Nixon's original dilemma at the start of the seventies, but with the apparent difference that international conditions precluded the Nixon solution.

Prosperity Without Power

If the new Reagan Administration was to be so constrained, how could it avoid the monetary restraint of Carter's last years, that is to say, a continuation of stop-go policy and stagflation? In other words, can some fundamental new economic formula be found for the 1980s that will permit domestic prosperity without generating inflation? Is there any cure for inflation that does not preclude prosperity?

The question can only be answered by the future course of events. In theory, inflation may be cured either by reducing demand or by increasing supply. The latter method, curing inflation through growth, is understandably preferred by governments and their electorates. Supposedly conservative governments are generally not any different in this respect, as the new Reagan Administration's enthusiasm for supply-side economics illustrated. Supply-side economics can be seen as the most recent version of the hope that inflation can be cured through rapid growth. Unlike the neo-Keynesians, who seek growth by stimulating demand, supply-siders seek growth by stimulating supply. Many of their recommendations are praiseworthy. A sensible revision of tax law to encourage saving and investment is doubtless long overdue, and the government's mania for regulation badly needs curbing. In due course, such policies may well increase efficiency and production and thus provide more supply to satisfy a level of demand that is now inflationary.

The problem of inflation in the 1980s, however, is not only long-range but also immediate. Deregulation and tax changes are unlikely, in themselves, to generate at once the magical flood of new resources needed to eliminate current inflation. And unless inflation can be curbed in the short run, it is unlikely to be curbed in the long run. A good case can be made, after all, that America's high and accelerating inflation has itself become the principal drag on long-range investment and growth. As long as inflation is rampant, unsettled economic and social conditions themselves profoundly discourage personal saving and long-range business investment. But how is inflation to be held in check long enough for long-range policies to work?

Analysts who cannot agree on the causes of inflation are unlikely to agree on the cure. Inflation obviously has deep roots in the structure of our whole political economy. But in the cure as in the cause, government policy is the critical checkpoint. Long-range remedies cannot be expected to make progress in the face of persistent, relentless inflationary stimulus from the government's own spending and finance. Whatever else may be needed, inflation is unlikely to end until the government stops running large fiscal deficits through all phases of the business cycle and financing them with easy money. Ending inflation has to start, therefore, with ending those government policies that have been fueling it. Moreover, as recent years ought to have made clear, not to mention Prime Minister Margaret Thatcher's experiment in Britain, tight money is not enough.[1] Controlling the money supply alone cannot be efficacious without concurrent budgetary constraint. Tight money and loose budgets mean inflation and slow growth.

Bringing American budget deficits under control, however, will require an extremely bitter and divisive struggle within the political system. One can expect not only an intense battle over the domestic component of the budget but, inevitably, a struggle for priority between domestic and foreign goals. The task is complicated in the 1980s by strong pressure for a major American rearmament. To put its fiscal affairs in order, the United States will have to sacrifice more at home to pay for its international position, or it will have to scale down its world commitments.

The Unacceptable Dilemma

However conventional and commonsensical such an analysis may be, its conclusion is highly unsatisfactory politically. Indeed, over the past two decades a great deal of economic talent has been devoted to avoiding just that conclusion. For neither the domestic nor the foreign components of the budget offer easy targets for serious cutting. On the one hand, demands for domestic American spending are urgent for all the reasons common to advanced societies everywhere. America's domestic outlay, moreover, does not seem excessive by comparison with other industrial societies. On the other hand, though American military spending is in fact much higher than that of its allies, America's security is plausibly linked to international stability, and that stability is linked to a wide range of American military commitments. The United States has also grown deeply habituated to both the pleasures and the pains of world responsibility, as well as to the convenient foreign escapes that the world role provides for domestic economic and social disequilibria. Resistance to change in what might be described as the imperial status quo is thus structured all across the American political spectrum. Nor is resistance confined to the United States. Though America's rich allies and OPEC would doubtless welcome an end to American inflation, most, even in OPEC, would not like a corresponding American withdrawal from international burdens.

Rather than face such divisive and dangerous choices, any administration in the eighties will naturally hope to sustain the juggling act of the sixties and seventies. Some new infusion of "will" and competence, or some magic new economic formula, will be preferred to the domestic discord or foreign retreat involved in serious budgetary retrenchment. In the sixties and seventies, the success of the juggling act depended upon America's power over the international system. Thus inflation could be exported and the dollar could be regularly depreciated. Any administration that wishes to return to the old policies will have to restore the old power.

Prospects for Geopolitical Restoration

If the 1980 campaign was any indication, the Reagan Administration was strongly predisposed to foreign-policy activism for its own sake. Like the Kennedy Administration, the Reagan Administration looked to growth at home and a renewal of power abroad. The prospects for foreign renewal, however, depended upon a certain view of why America's external position had so precipitously declined.

The new Administration arrived in power with two broad theories about the foreign decline and how, therefore, to reverse it. What might be called the Administration's "literary" right saw the decline under Carter as a pusillanimous failure of will to compete with the Soviets, a diffidence combined with wishful thinking about Soviet intentions and an excessive tenderness toward the outrageous claims of the Third World. The other major theory, popular in Kissingerian circles, blamed American decline on a radical falling-off of competence in the management of foreign policy after 1976.[2] Hopes for a quick restoration of American power rose from these analyses of the decline. Moral and military rearmament, it was believed, could restore American primacy.

A link could easily be imagined between the Administration's foreign policy objectives and its search for a new economic prosperity without inflation. With the restoration of geopolitical primacy, Nixon foreign economic policies could also presumably be revived. OPEC could be intimidated and Europeans overawed. Time would be made available for expansive supply-side economics to bring about structural improvements. Inflation could be cured through abundance rather than restraint. Foreign power would once again come to the aid of domestic economics. In short, with geopolitical power restored, Reagan could enjoy America's traditional capacity to export its disequilibrium. Reagan's chances for an even cosmetic success, however, were much reduced.

To begin with, it bears remembering that while the Nixon economic policy helped several sectors, it also encouraged inflation and thus throttled growth and productivity. But quite apart from its questionable economic expectations, the case for a restoration of American global predominance depends upon an unrealistic and excessively partisan view of why American power has declined. Although the Carter Administration, like most others, doubtless had its inadequacies, the geopolitical decline that underlay the end of Nixon policy was not the consequence of accidents, tactical mistakes, or a pusillanimous disposition in high places. The contradictions manifest in Carter's foreign policy were long-standing. They reflected a persisting American failure to develop a basic strategy appropriate to the logical evolution of the postwar world. Why, in fact, did the American external position deteriorate so rapidly under Carter? Was the deterioration necessary? Might a new administration restore the former position, and with it the old Nixon policy of the seventies?

Carter's Geopolitical Failure

The most spectacular "loss" for American power in the Carter Administration was the collapse of the Shah's regime in Iran, a profound social and cultural upheaval full of implications for the Moslem world as a whole. The United States was singled out as the revolution's principal enemy, partly because it was seen as incurably pro-Israeli, but more because it had taken such an extended, visible, and direct role in the Shah's domestic system. The United States became the scapegoat for a century or more of accumulated Persian resentments against the West. Khomeini's revolution raised disturbing questions about the dangers of imposed technocratic "development" either for the domestic stability of an developing country or for world order in general. Iran also revealed the

vulnerabilities of American "hegemony on the cheap," with "surrogates" substituting for direct American power. And as the subsequent war between Iran and Iraq threatened chaos and destruction
to the entire oil region, the dangers of dumping arms in unstable
parts of the world grew increasingly vivid.

America's detente policy with the Soviet Union also proved
highly vulnerable. Although detente, stretching back to the late
fifties, had seemingly reached its apogee under Kissinger, its foun-
dations had been eroding since Kissinger's later years. The first
SALT agreement outraged congressional conservatives.[3] Anger
multiplied as Russian military strength was seen to be growing
and, with it, Russian assertiveness in the Third World. Insatiable
Soviet imperialism, it was thought, was mocking the premises of
detente. Kissinger himself had complained bitterly over the incursions of Russia and its Cuban surrogate into Angola.[4]

The Carter Administration, despite its eccentric early disarmament proposals and its awkward preoccupation with human rights
in the Soviet Union, made a major diplomatic effort to follow the
logic of bipolar detente through SALT II negotiations.[5] But the
steady growth of anti-Soviet opinion made ratification of any
SALT II treaty increasingly improbable. To save the treaty, the
Carter Administration felt constrained to appease the forces hostile to it. To seem legitimate before these forces, SALT II had to be
presented as a victory over the Soviets rather than as a new step
toward mutual accommodation. Since nothing could compel the
Russians to accept terms sufficiently unbalanced to be presented as
an American "victory," the Carter Administration put itself hopelessly on the defensive before its domestic critics.

The self-defeating contradictions of Carter's policies became
painfully obvious during the Afghan crisis in late 1979. The Administration took the invasion as an aggressive challenge to America's Middle East position and a general betrayal of detente. To
show strength and punish the Russians, several years of Western
"bridge-building" were to be dismantled in short order. Though
the Administration's conservative domestic critics were thus pre-
empted, the SALT II treaty was doomed.

Predictably, the United States also put itself sharply at odds
with its European allies. As unenthusiastic about Soviet incursions

into vital oil regions as the Americans, the Europeans were prepared to condemn the Afghan invasion, warn the Russians about Pakistan and the Persian Gulf, and make matters in the region itself as difficult for the Soviets as possible. Europeans also hoped to take advantage of Moslem outrage over Afghanistan to deflect the Iranian revolution from its anti-Western preoccupation. They were thus disinclined to join America in sanctions against Iran. Above all, Europeans were not willing to let the United States make Afghanistan the occasion for a return to the Cold War in Europe itself.[6] Rightly or wrongly, the Europeans felt they had more to lose than to gain from an end to detente in their own region. Thus, whereas the United States saw Europe as a place to put pressure on the Russians as part of a global game, Europeans believed Europe should, if at all possible, remain a safe zone insulated from the confrontations inevitable elsewhere.

In effect, the Europeans had their own distinct interests in detente. From de Gaulle's time onward, they had done their best to prevent Western-Soviet relations from being managed exclusively by the Americans. Among other things, a detente policy of their own gave Europeans room for maneuver against too much American domination, in the economic sphere particularly. To be sure, European diplomacy toward the Russians took place within the context of their fundamental "Western" orientation. Not even de Gaulle ever intended some dramatic reversal of alliances.[7] Militarily, the states of Europe remained American protectorates, but they were nevertheless determined to keep the price for that protection within reasonable bounds. No one familiar with European views of American foreign economic policy could find that determination altogether surprising, particularly in a period of extreme trans-Atlantic tension over what was judged America's ceaseless exploitation of dollar hegemony. Keeping down the price for their American protection required maintaining "normal," if wary, relations with the Russians within Europe itself. In addition to this broad geopolitical imperative, detente brought Western Europe numerous commercial advantages, made life easier for East European states, and had many human benefits. Thus, to have expected the Europeans to jump to the new tune, to break their carefully cultivated regional relations with the Soviets, was to court a rebuff. Indeed, a certain degree of heightened Soviet-American tension outside Europe was not altogether unwelcome to the Europeans. It seemed to give them leverage for a more independent position, insofar as amateurish American diplomacy and aggressive Soviet adventurism did not plunge the world into a war.

In summary, American relations with the Middle East, the Soviets, and Europe seemed caught in a spiral of mutual deterioration. The economic consequences were not long delayed. The three international conditions for maintaining the Nixon economic policy — conditions carefully cultivated in the Nixon-Kissinger era — eroded together. The public soon came to doubt Carter's competence in foreign policy. In longer perspective, however, Carter's failings came less from what was new in his foreign policy than from what was old. For many of Carter's awkward tergiversations reflected the effort to sustain already obsolescent American perspectives of the 1960s, carried over in Kissinger's flashy reconstruction of the 1970s. These views had become "mother errors" in American foreign policy. They included not only the inadequate foreign and domestic economic policies but also an unrealistic view of detente and an unrealistic view of trans-Atlantic relations.

Detente Oversold

Neither Carter, nor Kissinger before him, thought through adequately the consequences of a detente policy toward the Soviet Union. Just as Kissinger wanted hegemony on the cheap in the Middle East, so he expected detente on the cheap in the world at large. Both expectations represented wishful thinking doomed to disappointment.

Ever since the 1960s, detente had rested upon America's increasing acceptance of Soviet nuclear parity. Predictably, nuclear parity would alter decisively the American capacity to deny the Soviets influence in the world beyond their home sphere. Since the growth of Soviet strategic nuclear power had manifestly been accompanied by expanding Soviet conventional capabilities for intervention far from home, strategic parity pointed toward a troubled period of local challenges and negotiations. It was unreasonable to acknowledge the Soviets as America's strategic equals without expecting them to demand a greater influence in local affairs throughout the world. But in regions of vital interest to the West, like the Persian Gulf, Soviet adventurism could easily deteriorate into direct superpower confrontation. Under these circumstances, it was essential for the United States to do its best to limit the opportunities and raise the costs of Soviet meddling. In a world of rampant nationalism, much of the effort, to be effective, would have to be diplomatic, economic, and political. But there was also an inescapable military dimension. The Russians were particularly apt to lose their heads in a world where the conventional military balance was shifting decisively against the United States. It was hardly the time for a drastic drawing down of conventional American military strength. Since, with parity, neither side could credibly resort to strategic threats over peripheral challenges, local military and political power would logically grow more decisive. But Nixon and Ford, caught in the backlash of the Vietnam War, gradually cut real military spending, particularly after 1972. Most cuts fell on conventional arms, particularly after the end of the draft in 1973.[8] Carter tried to reverse the trend, but still without the draft. As Carter's budgets illustrated all too clearly, major additions to defense expenditures could not easily be reconciled with the fiscal discipline needed to control inflation.[9] No amount of patriotic rhetoric or fiscal legerdemain could make the dilemma disappear.

Carter's political problems were compounded by the general overselling of detente, typical perhaps of all postwar administrations but particularly egregious in the Nixon-Ford era. Nixon and Kissinger, like Kennedy and Johnson before them, had a strong tendency to talk as if detente would resolve the world's problems. Such expectations not only belied the probable effects of parity on Soviet-American competition throughout the world but also exaggerated the capacity of either Russia or the United States to influence global events. In reality, both superpowers were growing relatively less important among states. Even had they wished it, they could not have run the world between them. Their diminishing power, moreover, while not diminishing their competition, changed its context and form. As the superpowers declined, the international system of Cold War blocs gradually gave way to an arena of volatile nationalist states. Alignments grew more conditional and wary. Double-dealing was to be expected.

No administration in the 1970s took on the task of giving the Congress or the public at large a proper set of expectations about Soviet-American relations. No one provided a new strategic idea to replace the bipolar containment of the Acheson-Dulles era. Hence a new consensus was never created around a realistic view of America's diplomatic and strategic position following strategic parity. The United States was thus doubly unprepared for parity. The public had unrealistic expectations from bipolar negotiations, while the military was woefully unadapted to cope with the new situation. As the public inevitably felt deceived in its expectations about the Russians and outraged at American weakness, it turned against SALT and detente itself. Foreign policy without a firm base in public support gradually lost its legitimacy. An increasingly confused and unpredictable public opinion oscillated between impossible expectations and unreasonable anger. With political leaders providing no clear and realistic conception of national interest, foreign policy soon became captive to vigorous special interests.

This inability to lead the American political system toward accepting a more complex world must be counted as the major failing of American foreign policy in the 1970s. Like the failure in America's foreign economic policy, it was a failure at home rather than abroad. The fault lay not with the Russians, who on the whole behaved as might have been expected: they kept their strategic agreements without ceasing to be as cautiously aggressive as they have always been. The fault lay with an American leadership that, expecting more from superpower detente than it could reasonably deliver, therefore failed to endow Congress or the public with a realistic view of the world and, finally, failed to equip American forces properly to deal with that world.

The Unreformed Alliance

The consequences were by no means limited to Soviet-American relations. The same inability to grasp the evolving character of interstate relations began to poison trans-Atlantic relations as well. Superpower detente based on nuclear parity called for a basic rethinking of the constituent strategic principles within the Atlantic Alliance. Soviet-American nuclear parity would inevitably put in question the credibility of the American deterrent for Western Europe. A new American attitude toward independent European deterrents was in order, along with a corresponding reshaping of NATO.

Reshaping, however, hardly meant ending the Alliance. Under almost any conceivable circumstances, European deterrence is greatly reinforced by its American connection. But it meant recognizing that the American deterrent would no longer be considered, in itself, sufficient for European security. Increasingly, collective nuclear security based on American power would have to be supplemented by European national strength. Kissinger, while talking a good deal about adjusting to a more plural world, had in fact done his best to sustain America's European hegemony in its most traditional form. The Carter Administration, in the same vein, had actually reinforced American opposition to nuclear "proliferation" and thereby come perilously close to a major quarrel with the European allies over commercial nuclear development.[10] In short, America's European policy revealed the same inner contradiction as its detente policy. A strategic policy with the Soviets that inevitably lessened the value of the American nuclear protectorate for Europe was combined with a strategic policy in Europe that presupposed its undiminished continuation.

American hegemony was acceptable to Europe because it provided security not only for Europe's own territory but also for Europe's access to raw materials and markets in the Third World. At the same time, as America's combination of inflation, dollar depreciation, and failure to adjust to high energy prices increasingly offended the interests of both the Europeans and the oil producers, Europeans also grew increasingly skeptical of America's ability to defend their interests in the Third World. Instead, American policy seemed bent on destroying detente in Europe to compensate for America's weakness in the world at large. Thus, as American relations deteriorated with Russia and the Middle East, they also deteriorated with Europe itself. The causes were not only the long-standing economic frictions but a growing divergence of security interests as well.

Success Abandoned

Carter's diplomatic troubles need to be seen in a larger perspective. The crisis in American foreign policy at the end of the seventies, like the crisis in domestic economic policy, had been gathering through several administrations. The failures were not merely tactical, but strategic. As Europe and Japan had revived and the Third World developed, the international system had grown more plural. With nuclear parity, the superpowers themselves grew more equal. These changes inevitably affected America's world position. They represented not so much the decline of America as the revival of the world.

They did not, moreover, represent the defeat of America's fundamental postwar policy. On the contrary, with its goals of European recovery, superpower detente, and Third World development, American world leadership had encouraged the very evolution that led to its own relative decline. While, from one perspective, such a policy may seem to have been foolish or irresponsible, from another, it seems to have been not only generous but also eminently practical. The United States, it may be argued, lacked the temperament and institutions to impose a permanent imperial order. And despite America's continuing vast resources, a reviving world was unlikely to tolerate any imperial system for more than a few decades. To have based America's future as a nation upon its episodic career as the dominant world power would thus have been a very bad bet historically.

Nixon economics, to be sure, was a mutation in the postwar policy. With Nixon, America's domestic prosperity came to depend upon the exploitation of its geopolitical primacy. By 1980, a predictable evolution of events had shaken that primacy, with a resultant discomfort to domestic prosperity. To try to restore primacy would be, in effect, to try to reverse the geopolitical trend of the past two decades. Such a policy, if pursued seriously, would carry great risks for the United States and for the world. Among the greatest and most immediate risks was the predictable effect of such a foreign policy on domestic American inflation, as a look at the first Reagan budget made clear.

Foreign Policy and the Reagan Budget

Reagan came to office in 1981 pledged to end Carter's inflation and stagnation. By early March, the outlines of the new program had been sketched.[11] Along with supply-side tax cuts to induce investment and growth, the Reagan proposals demanded drastic reductions in domestic spending and sizable increases in military spending. In effect, the burden of fiscal adjustment was to fall on domestic programs. Among the advanced industrial democracies, however, the United States was not exceptionally profligate in the sums devoted to domestic purposes.[12] To expect to balance budgets largely by deep cuts in domestic programs therefore presupposed either that the American government could provide services more efficiently than other governments or that the American people were less demanding than those of Europe. Neither presupposition was well founded. The country's size and diversity, reflected in its constitution and general political and economic culture, made an exceptional degree of bureaucratic efficiency improbable. And without the violent shock of a major war, the American public was more likely to resemble its European cousins than the disciplined and downtrodden Russians.

America's comparative military spending was another matter, as shown by the defense expenditures as a percentage of GNP in six countries in 1980:[13]

United States	5.5
United Kingdom	5.1
France	3.9
West Germany	3.2
Italy	2.4
Japan	0.9

If the American defense budget seemed outsized in Carter's time, Reagan's plans would make it far more so. The new Administration projected a series of annual increases over five years that would raise the annual defense expenditure from $162 billion in fiscal 1981 to $343 billion in fiscal 1986—a gradual increase of the annual defense budget to a level $181 billion higher. If actually carried out, the increase would represent a military build-up three times as large, in constant dollars, as the one that took place during the Vietnam War.[14]

Why was the Reagan defense budget to be so large? Different foreign policies obviously require different military resources. The Reagan Administration's proposals and pronouncements suggested it was flirting with restoring America's world primacy. Such a policy, turning back the geopolitical clock to the mid-1960s, would be very expensive and altogether incompatible with ending inflation without putting the economy on a wartime footing. Reagan's defense budget seemed surprising in view of his commitment to end inflation. It also appeared to ignore completely the unhappy experience of the previous Administration. Rising military expenditures were a major obstacle to Carter's efforts to achieve fiscal balance. Carter's Administration, presumably devoted to detente and a more relaxed international view, nevertheless felt America's present international role and commitments required augmenting military expenditures substantially. Most of Carter's increases went for conventional forces.[15] Behind the increases lay the Carter Administration's perception that, in a world with strategic parity, so many new powers, greater Soviet conventional reach, and an American volunteer army, the United States could not hold its traditional positions without substantial increases in its military budget. Few at home or abroad felt the United States too well armed for its commitments. In short, Carter faced the same dilemma that has faced every American administration since the war. Like Kennedy after Eisenhower, he believed America's world position required a sizable rearmament. And like Kennedy and all the others, he could not fit the costs of America's world role and domestic aspirations together within a balanced budget. Is there any hope for a future reconciliation?

The European Commitment

Saving money on defense, to occur rationally, will require some new formulation of national interest which reduces American commitments themselves and not merely the forces used to meet them. To reduce spending in a world where power is increasingly widespread, the United States will have to concentrate its own military responsibilities while relying on a more effective diplomacy to seize the advantages of leverage. Such a course assumes the existence of regions where American interests are no longer worth the resources needed to underwrite their security, or where indigenous forces are themselves able to take a significantly larger share.

Any inventory of American world commitments at the start of the 1980s cannot fail to note the central place of European defense and the anomalous relationship between the United States and the West European states. Since the 1950s, from a third to a half of the entire American defense budget had been devoted, directly or indirectly, to forces to defend Western Europe in a massive conventional war. In the 1981 fiscal budget, the cost was reckoned at some $81 billion.[16] In effect, the United States was still assuming the primary responsibility for managing the continent's conventional defense. Hence, America provided the commander for NATO, a fleet in the Mediterranean, large tactical air units, and ten divisions either stationed in Europe or able to get there in time for the decisive battles.

America's commitment to manage Europe's ground defense was undertaken in 1950, when American strategic superiority made a European land war improbable. At the same time, the weakness of the European states made their own self-defense problematical and American reassurance essential to their recovery. By 1980, the American commitment to a mass army for Europe had continued for over thirty years, with little or no account taken of Europe's economic and political recovery. Although the reasons for America's profound interest in Europe's fate may not have changed since 1950, by any objective measurement of relative resources the United States was playing a disproportionate role in European defense. Meanwhile, the Soviet Union had achieved nuclear parity, which inevitably undermined the credibility of America's foreign commitments. And the United States itself had given up the draft in the face of a deep public anti-pathy to military service, a development that limited its ability to provide a reliable mass army for a continental war.

America's huge annual bill for NATO reflected a fundamental political problem within the world political economy. The major countries of Western Europe were once more among the world's half-dozen richest and most powerful states. But NATO's struc-ture still suggested a relationship appropriate to the Romans and their auxiliaries, or Napoleon and his satellites. This Napolenic model meant that the United States actively managed Europe's forces and hence was constrained to keep a preponderant conven-tional force of its own for the European theater.

If the Reagan Administration, or some successor in the eighties, were seriously concerned with balancing American budgets, parti-cularly if new resources were needed for countering the Soviets in the Third World, a more traditional balance-of-power alliance with Europe would seem a more promising arrangement than con-tinuing the postwar Napoleonic structure. Shifting responsibility for managing European ground defense to the Europeans could, in theory, save the United States a substantial budgetary sum. It can be estimated, for example, that disbanding six of the existing ten US-NATO divisions in 1981 would alone have brought, within three years, an annual saving to the defense budget of some $30 billion.[17] Saving on any such scale would have gone a long way toward ending America's regular fiscal deficits. For the years 1977, 1978, and 1979, for example, the annual deficits were $45 billion, $49 billion, and $28 billion, respectively. In the budgetary struggle required for any serious attempt to control inflation, possible sav ings of this magnitude would be unlikely to escape notice.

Successive American administrations had, of course, tried to shift NATO burdens to the Europeans since the early days of the Alliance. Their poor record pointed to the need for a new ap-proach. A shift in the balance of military forces within the Alliance would undoubtedly call for a shift in the political balance as well. While some American divisions and substantial air and naval power would presumably remain in Europe, the Supreme Allied Commander could no longer be an American general, if the major European states were expected to take primary responsibility for managing their own collective defense. New provisions for nuclear defense would also logically follow.

The political problems in any such transformation would be formidable. France and Germany would constitute the necessary core of any European construction. Over the sixties and seventies they learned to harmonize their efforts over a wide range of vexatious domestic economic concerns. They, along with the British, had large and efficient military forces, flourishing arms industries, and formidable military experience.[18] Nevertheless, the French, as well as the Germans and British, would be loath to trade arrangements giving them American-subsidized security for a more responsible, expensive, and constraining role in managing European defense. And Europe's smaller countries would prefer a distant and distracted America to the more active leadership of their own big neighbors. Under the circumstances, for Washington to use evidence of disunity as an excuse for preserving the status quo would always be plausible, and playing countries off against each other all too easy. If serious about transforming NATO, the United States would have to stop using Europe's hesitations and divisions as a pretext for its own inaction. Washington would have to assume that Europe's big powers would act as responsible states, and not try to prevent them from doing so.

An American administration that genuinely faced the true costs of inflation would also be aware of how limited its choices had grown. Alliance questions would continue to grow more and more entangled with America's economic predicament. Against the risks of change in NATO would have to be weighed the certain international deterioration implicit in a continuing American inflation. Reforming America's European commitment would be only a step toward curing America's inflation, certainly not a panacea. But without some such major breakthrough in military spending, prospects for real improvement would remain improbable. For no amount of military spending would be likely to restore America's political hegemony of the seventies, or the Nixon economic policy that accompanied it. In the absence of a domestic budgetary equilibrium, the frustration of America's domestic and foreign policy could be expected to continue, and trans-Atlantic relations to grow ever more acrimonious. Should the Reagan Administration persist in the course it set for itself upon entering office, such seems its most probable fate.

Economic Equilibrium and the Balance of Power

Intuitively, many people have come to see American inflation as the manifestation of a long-standing national hubris. This way of thinking grew popular in the late 1960s when the explosion of inflation and the agony of Vietnam were sensed as symptoms of a sort of national disequilibrium, of an ambition for leadership and benevolence grown extravagant and wanton.

In 1968, Americans elected an avowedly conservative government. The Nixon Administration spent its early years trying to restore economic balance at home while talking of a more realistic disposition of American power abroad. But it lacked the political strength, and perhaps the moral stamina, to persevere. It abandoned domestic economic restraint and used American power abroad to permit a seemingly painless inflation at home. In the face of growing Soviet power, it abandoned its half-hearted attempts to coax Europe into a new role and, instead, relied more and more exclusively upon superpower detente. An adventitious and unstable supremacy in the Middle East underwrote a shameful delay in facing the energy crisis at home.

Seen in this historical perspective, Nixon and Kissinger's apparent foreign successes of the early 1970s take on a different look. Their *Pax Americana* appears less a firm restoration than a nostalgic fantasy. Worse, it represents a false turning and a missed opportunity. Although the old predominance was superficially confirmed in Europe and extended to the Middle East, the United States lacked the resources to sustain its positions. This lack of resources to meet all domestic and foreign ambitions led, in turn, to an exploitation of the international economic system increasingly intolerable to America's allies and of questionable benefit for the United States. Manipulating the international system became the substitute for painful adjustments at home. Instead of domestic strength being the foundation of overseas power, diplomacy subsidized domestic prosperity.

Sadly, the breakdown in American foreign policy could be traced not to a failure of America's long-range strategy but to a failure to exploit its success. America's historic policy was to restore Europe, not to conquer it. By the 1970s, European power had, in fact, recovered to the point where the United States should have played its "European card" in the interests of a new world balance. Unhappily, at a critical historical moment, American statecraft proved unable to press its own historic policies to successful completion. Instead, it wandered into a cul-de-sac of unsustainable geopolitical pretensions and wanton domestic inflation. Not until the external system began to unravel in the late 1970s was there much support for domestic regeneration. Thanks to Khomeini, there was Volcker. But as the past decade ought to have made clear, equilibrium will not return to the economy at home without a more realistic balance of power abroad.

Conclusion

The American Disease and Its Cures

AFTER TWENTY YEARS, inflation has grown deeply rooted in America's society, political system, and world role. A return toward equilibrium will not be easy to achieve, and the dangers of a serious breakdown are not so remote as they once seemed. An historical survey perhaps has something to contribute to the regaining of health. For while historical analysis cannot offer the conceptual clarity of economic models, it is more attuned to the complexities of the real world. The historian's long perspective seems particularly useful in analyzing economic policy, for probably no other major subject of general public discussion is more regularly distorted by partial views and sectarian obfuscation.

The Age of Gimmicks

Throughout the postwar era of economic policy-making, pedantic mystification has served, again and again, to bemuse common sense. It thus seems an age of economic gimcrackery, in which governments have trifled with the country's basic problems, inflation above all. Policy has been a restless search for magic tricks and formulas. No sooner is one fashionable remedy discredited than another replaces it. Perhaps the major precondition for real progress is a general purge of ancient remedies. Here, history can help.

To succeed in gaining public support, gimmicks require plausibility. Characteristically, therefore, the more popular gimmicks are never entirely wrong, but merely half-right. Invariably, a gimmick is based on too partial a view of economic and political realities.

The first and most durably popular of the postwar economic elixirs has been the neo-Keynesian full-employment budget. It represents an extended formulation of Keynes's preoccupation with underemployment, the prevailing economic reality during England's interwar years. In the postwar era, conditions in most industrial countries have been radically different. Meanwhile, however, Keynes's grand theories have been turned into a bag of tricks, applied indiscriminately by economists lacking Keynes's own sense of history and politics. Several decades of postwar history now reveal what perhaps should have been obvious from the start. This is no longer an age of underconsumption, but of inflation. In retrospect, the full-employment neo-Keynesian budget stands unmasked as a learned justification for inflation. The subsequent decorating of the full-employment budget with the Phillips Curve further reinforced the notion that inflation could be stabilized and traded off for more employment. Again, the record suggests otherwise. Inflation unleashed grows from one cycle to the next, according to a self-generating logic of its own. In due course, the policies needed to check the acceleration mean diminishing growth. Stagflation becomes endemic as government policy oscillates between concern for unemployment and concern for inflation.

As the Keynesian sixties gave way to the monetarist seventies, tight monetary policy became the new magic formula. Since inflation was too much money chasing too few goods, restricting the money supply seemed, by definition, the logical cure. At its most simple-minded, the monetarist approach blames inflation essentially on incompetence at the Federal Reserve. More worldly monetarists do admit further complications. The same political pressures that do not permit governments to control their budgets, for example, may also force monetary authorities to accommodate the deficits with easy money. The problem, it seems, is not technical but political. But the notion that the proper monetary policies could control inflation if only democracies ordered their ambitions and ignored their private interest groups, or if only enlightened dictatorships were not obliged to heed public discontent, even though true by definition, suggests a political program considerably beyond the intellectual and moral scope of monetarist analysis.

Perhaps even more damaging to the intellectual pretension of the monetarists than their political naivety has been their technical incapacity, once in power, to control or even define the money supply. With banking ingenuity in one of its periods of cyclical efflorescence, the nature of money itself has become particularly protean and elusive. To reduce it to the simple substance needed for the monetarist model would require draconian controls over the world's banks — a program unlikely to appeal to the libertarian enthusiasms of most monetarist economists. Aside from an inability to define money itself, the other great obstacle to controlling the money supply lies in the internationalization of capital markets. Since monetarists have been among the principal enthusiasts for dismantling obstacles to a world money market, they are understandably reluctant to acknowledge financial autarchy as the precondition for applying their remedies. A floating international exchange-rate system was once their preferred resolution. Its shortcomings are now manifest. After a decade's experience, floating must be counted, at best, a necessary evil; at worst, a major symptom of disease.

Logic has seduced more consistent theorists to embrace the ultimate monetarist gimmick, the gold standard. In theory, with the money supply in each country tied to gold, and all countries regularly and automatically settling their debts in gold, inflation would vanish. Again, the cure is by definition. If the political system would permit, doubtless the rules of the gold standard would reinforce domestic equilibrium. Power, ambition, and greed would submit themselves to the Golden Mean. But the political requirements for such a transformation markedly outrun the scope of the technical analysis.

With the shortcomings of monetarist gimmicks increasingly exposed, fashion may well swing back to controls, a more appealing solution to economists of the left. According to controllers, with the economy dominated by firms and unions large enough to impose inflationary prices on the market, stemming inflation requires the state to exert its power directly. The general will has to replace the sham market. But like the gold standard, the controller's cure begins by assuming away the disease. No reasonable person denies that state policy must shape and influence the market. Controls over wages and prices, moreover, could doubtless be useful in breaking the public's inflationary expectations. But only on condition that a change in basic policies made inflationary expectations unrealistic. Otherwise, controlling wages and prices to stop inflation is analogous to expecting to cure a fever by forbidding the mercury to rise in the thermometer. To be a serious remedy, controls require a system of rational planning—with the government allocating resources and rewards in a fashion adequate to satisfy not only the economic requirements of stability and growth, but also the political demands for progress and equity. Once more, this is a program rather more ambitious than economists generally have in mind. In any event, it is a task for which their own discipline does not necessarily provide an adequate moral, cultural, or political endowment.

The principal problem with the fashionable postwar gimmicks is their too partial view of economic, social, and political reality. As they stand displayed in history, they are not so much false as simple-minded. They ignore politics and human nature. As Burke once said of earlier and similarly pretentious groups of "captivating" theories: "their abstract perfection is their practical defect. The nature of man is intricate; the objects of society are of the greatest possible complexity . . . When I hear the simplicity of contrivance aimed at and boasted of in any new political constitutions, I am at no loss to decide that the artificers are grossly ignorant of their trade or totally negligent of their duty."[1]

Restraining Policy

If gimmicks provide no easy cures, what are the more general approaches that at least face the American economic malaise in all its complexity? Broadly speaking, inflation can be approached from two sides. The problem, presumably, is too much demand and too few goods. Policy can therefore aim to reduce demand to fit supply or endeavor to make supply adequate to demand. In other words, inflation can be resolved either through more restraint or more growth. In fact, both policies must proceed in tandem. Obviously, growth is the more attractive option politically. Restraint is not a viable long-range solution, particularly for democracies. But spurring growth cannot resolve the immediate problems of acute inflation. Unfortunately for democracies, the dynamics of inflation dictate that, after a certain point, restraint must be achieved before growth can resume. For the threat of severe inflation, in highly developed economies at least, is itself a major impediment to growth.

In most countries, restraining demand to control inflation needs to begin with government policy itself. Restraint requires curbing the government's own overspending, as well as the complaisant monetary policies needed to finance it. In most countries, neither fiscal nor monetary restraint will work by itself. In particular, monetary policy will not work alone, for experience shows that tight money without budgetary discipline means endemic stagflation, particularly whenever the inflation cannot be exported. To be at all effective, restraint based on tight money alone results in an increasingly unacceptable degree of stagnation and unemployment. But initially, at least, restraint through fiscal policy seems even more difficult. Budget pruning to achieve fiscal restraint means reversing practices enshrined in several years of full-employment budgets, which is extremely difficult politically. A budget is a mirror of the political system's aspirations and balances of power. Reducing any significant "entitlement" or tax advantage invariably requires a major political battle. Changing the flow of resources disrupts the nation's political and social balance and perhaps its foreign engagements as well. To escape facing these issues directly, administrations prefer to rely on gimmicks, trying either to produce by magic the missing resources, or to reduce demand indirectly and thus without the direct political confrontations involved in budget-cutting. Hence governments prefer monetary policy, where restraint can be treated as a technical matter, managed by a secretive central bank, and dressed up in opaque abracadabra. Where budgets do have to be curbed directly, governments generally prefer to disguise their aim as providing "efficiency" in services rather than as significantly shifting the economic share enjoyed by one entrenched interest over another.

Restraint Through Efficiency

Every administration comes to power pledging more efficiency. And more efficiency in administration could in fact reduce costs without reducing benefits. But while the struggle is worthy and never-ending, and the waste doubtless prodigious, durable improvement decisive enough to affect inflation has proved extremely difficult to achieve. The waste of the American political system is not only endemic but organic. It reflects pluralist political structures rooted in the country's vast size and diversity.

A major improvement in governmental administration is not likely to come from minor tinkering or earnest exhortation, but will require a major revamping of relations among the Congress, the bureaucracy, the Presidency, and the courts. Ubiquitous court interference with the details of administration and regulation is, for example, a major impediment to coherent administration. So is the prevailing adversary relationship between government and business, and a legal system that perpetuates and feasts off that antagonism. Federal and state jurisdictions, moreover, overlap in a fashion hardly conducive to responsible or efficient government. But bringing real efficiency to local and regional government seems improbable in many parts of the country without a major redrawing of political jurisdictions to correspond to economic and social realities. In short, a radical improvement in efficiency would require a major overhaul of constitutional structures, practices, and attitudes.

Restraint and Political Priority

If efficiency is unlikely to obviate the struggle over political priority, the problem of restraint returns to budgetary politics. A budget to break inflation requires a new ranking and trimming of political goals to fit the resources available. For a start, foreign goals and strategies have to be brought into harmony with the real resources the political system is willing to provide. The United States should rethink not only the sort of military establishment it maintains, but also its established security commitments and relationships, with Europe in particular. The traditional conservative attitude that no sacrifice is too great for defense is, like the full-employment budget among liberals, a license for fiscal irresponsibility and inflation. Indeed, defense outlays, which tend to increase demand in the economy without providing corresponding civilian goods, are a particularly inflationary form of public spending. America's outsized world role, involving as it does an unnatural, one-sided dependency between the United States and its rich allies, not only is a major cause of America's domestic fiscal imbalance, but also is a major impediment to the proper functioning of the international system. American power and European dependency have allowed the United States to escape from the normal international constraints against inflation, to the profit neither of the American domestic economy nor of the rest of the world.

Nevertheless, cutting American military expenditures cannot be easy. The mood of the early eighties, in fact, calls for sharp increases. The Reagan Administration apparently expects civilian welfare spending to bear the burden of fiscal retrenchment. Actual US expenditures for welfare, however, are not excessive by the standards common to other advanced democracies.

Inflation and the Deteriorating Labor Force

Comparisons with Europe might be counted irrelevant. For one thing, European states may themselves be overextended in welfare spending. For another, the goal of full employment in the United States perhaps requires more monetary stimulus than in other countries with more homogeneous work forces. Hence, it could be argued, if the United States wishes to control its inflation, it cannot afford European standards of welfare and full employment. As far as inflation is concerned, the United States suffers from a comparative disadvantage.

To reverse this comparative inflationary disadvantage and thus avoid a lower target for welfare would require a substantial improvement in the overall productivity of the American labor force. Unfortunately, however, the American labor force and its productivity appear, in recent years, to have been evolving in a contrary direction. Achieving noninflationary full employment in America thus seems to have grown more rather than less difficult. While total employment expanded rapidly in the 1970s, even as the rates of unemployment also rose, the character of the work force also altered radically. By the later seventies, the proportion of American labor in services had passed one-half and exceeded that of any comparable country. Although an increasing ratio of employment in services as opposed to manufacturing is characteristic of the more advanced industrial societies, historically the trend has nevertheless coincided with an increasing productivity in manufacturing. In other words, that part of the economy subject to international competition, the industrial sector above all, has remained competitive. In the 1970s, however, growing services combined with a faltering growth of productivity in manufacturing. This declining productivity, in turn, was presumably not unrelated to the consequences for investment of America's accelerating inflation. And that inflation, in turn, was presumably not unrelated to the rapidly growing government spending, in good part on civilian welfare. Government welfare spending, in turn, was given powerful impetus by the shifts in the work force to services.

The connection between welfare spending and the growth of services is suggested by a closer look at the growth of the service sector in the seventies. The category "services" is notoriously vague, including everyone from bank presidents to janitors. Three industries were particularly prominent in the rapid growth of the seventies: health care, eating and drinking places, and business services. The first encompasses hospitals and nursing homes; fast-food chains are prominent in the second; data processing, secretarial services, building maintenance, and similar services characterize the third. More new jobs were created in these three industries than existed absolutely in the entire industrial sector.

This trend in the character of employment reflected major changes in American society, in particular the gradual disintegration of the traditional extended family. Such a social evolution seems mutually reinforcing with the further growth of services. Employment, in services or elsewhere, that draws women out of their traditional family role, for example, increases corresponding demands for public and private care for children, the sick, and the old. Government expenditure to provide this care, directly or indirectly, is not so much a benevolent extension of largesse as an essential collective response to the changing family structure. In the face of such rapid social change, the growth and cost of government services may be expected to grow harder to control.

At the same time, full-employment policies themselves are likely to grow more inflationary. Drawing increasing number of women and youngsters into the labor force more or less automatically raises the "normal" level of unemployment. In the new service economy, with the Phillips Curve thus "shifting to the left," macroeconomic stimulation to meet traditional full-employment quotas will presumably be increasingly inflationary.

Restoring a less inflationary degree of thrift and rationality to burgeoning social services and full-employment policies generally will go hand in hand with formulating more coherent governmental strategies and organization. Otherwise, excessive government spending and monetary stimulation, with the consequent inflation, will continue to erode productivity. If government spending is to be controlled, however, the question of priority between domestic and foreign goals will grow all the more urgent. Full-employment goals themselves will have to be redefined. In short, providing full employment and social peace without inflationary fiscal and monetary policy, the problem America has not been able to resolve in the past, will grow even more difficult in the future. In view of the evolution of the work force, however, it does not seem realistic to expect to achieve restraint by deep cuts in social services accompanied by steep rises in military spending. In its expectations of welfare, the American public is more likely to resemble its European cousins than its Soviet rivals.

Fighting Inflation Through Growth

Policies of restraint, with their political difficulties and scant prospects for success, seldom remain popular. Even among sup-

posed conservatives, the ascetic monetarism fashionable in the
1970s was already making way for supply-side theories in the early
eighties. That politicians should prefer growth over austerity is
hardly surprising. Why, however, should Reagan's supply-side
growth be less inflationary in the eighties than Kennedy's neo-Keynesian demand management in the sixties?

According to the fashionable apology, supply-side tax cuts
stimulate production and productivity directly, whereas neo-Keynesian policies, by increasing general demand, stimulate supply
only indirectly. Skepticism is understandable. Direct stimuli to
production are hardly novel. The early Kennedy policies, for example, placed heavy emphasis on investment tax credits and accelerated depreciation allowances. The Carter Administration, in its
last months, talked grandly of a new system of incentives to promote the "reindustrialization" of America. No doubt, supply-side
changes in tax codes have a beneficial effect, all other things being
equal. If nothing else, they remove some of the needless hin-
drances to growth and efficiency imposed by government itself.
Tax laws, for example, that prevent depreciation rates from
matching inflating replacement costs may discourage adequate expenditures to renew plant and equipment. Discriminating tax rates
on "unearned" investment income hardly encourage saving and
capital accumulation. Indeed, more radical tax changes than Reagan's early proposals may long be overdue.[2] But while changes in
tax policies may remove the more obvious government-imposed
barriers to growth, America's reindustrialization will not necessarily follow. More fundamental obstacles stand in the way.

International Obstacles to American Growth

Over the long run, the decline of American industry will have
less to do with unwise taxes than with the competition implicit in a
rapidly developing world economy. As industrial technology
spreads beyond the Western or "Westernized" welfare states, it will
be difficult to change domestic American tax and depreciation policy sufficiently to counterbalance the advantages for manufacturing offered by countries with cheap and disciplined labor, lower so-

cial and environmental charges, and governments more eager to oblige. This is a reality particularly difficult for orthodox economists to acknowledge.

American economists, left and right, have tended to be fierce partisans of international integration. In the orthodox vision, a "product-cycle theory" explains how free international competition leads to progress on all sides. A country like America is supposed to compensate for the demise of its labor-intensive manufacturing of old products by developing either new products that are capital-intensive and reflect high technology, or else new services that reflect its work force's high level of education and expertise. Both high-technology products and services have, in fact, grown at a rapid pace in recent years. But it remains far from certain that their growth can compensate for the concurrent competitive decline of such basic industries as automobiles, metals, chemicals, and rubber. And though some of the expansion in services has provided new opportunities for trained expertise, the great bulk of the new employment in this category lies in industries that are neither advanced nor internationally salable. The growth of service employment has, in reality, created a vast new American subproletariat — personnel working short hours at low pay in fast-food chains, hospitals, nursing homes, and discount retail outlets, or for clerical, cleaning, and maintenance contractors. In effect, the replacement of jobs in industry by jobs in services has meant that workers with high pay and high productivity in manufacturing are being replaced by women, teenagers, and Latin American immigrants in services. Although it may be argued that the shift to services is a traditional pattern for most, if not all, advanced economies, the concomitant decline in industrial productivity is something rather less common.

Such a general evolution for the American economy, among other things, clouds liberal hopes for a benevolent international repartition of comparative advantage. Alongside blithe liberal visions of ever-greater prosperity through international specialization is a grimmer prospect, not unlike the famous prophecy that the economic writer J. A. Hobson painted for the British at the beginning of this century.[3] Hobson saw the British bemused by an archaic liberalism that no longer suited their national interest. As a result, they were sacrificing their national manufacturing in favor of cosmopolitan finance. Their industrial capital was emigrating along with their working population. In the end, Hobson suggested, the population of Britain would consist of retired imperial administrators, bankers, and those in related commercial enterprises, along with symbiotic artists, educators, purveyors of luxuries, and an imported mongrel proletariat to support domestic amenities and country gardens. Hobson's predictions seem, unfortunately, not as inapplicable to contemporary Britain as might be wished. In any event, a free-trade policy with such consequences — however appropriate for Britain, the island center of a world network — seems less obviously suited to a vast continental confederation like the United States. Before America reaches the British condition, domestically rooted industrial corporations, and particularly their workers, may be expected to generate intense pressure for protectionism. Greater and greater tension within the American political economy will result.

World economic integration and its protectionist backlash bear heavily upon the prospects for America's reindustrialization through supply-side economics. In themselves, positive tax incentives are unlikely to reverse the competitive decline of older industries or provide new domestic industries on the needed scale. Nor can the compensating growth of services be expected to restore productivity and industrial competitiveness to the American economy of the future.

Rejuvenation of American industry within an integrating world is likely to require not only a reassessment of traditional liberal views about the world economy but also a more far-reaching and comprehensive alteration in industrial policy than a package of investment tax incentives. Without confronting the basic issues, supply-side economics will prove just one more gimmick. Like the others, it will produce more inflation than growth.

Growth Through Market Liberalization

In the political culture of the early 1980s, supply-side economics is closely related to a broadly based drive toward market "liberalization." Liberalization appeals to both restrainers and supply-siders. In a market unclogged of hidden and direct subsidies, it is believed, economic conditions would respond more quickly to restraining monetary and fiscal policy. At the same time, lightening the load of government regulation and interference would eliminate a good deal of wasted effort in business and would promote, it is expected, a vigorous upsurge of creative enterprise.

Many arguments for liberalizing the market are mirror images of arguments for controlling it. Like the controllers, the liberalizers focus on the contemporary market's unresponsive nature. According to the controllers, so many aspects of the economy are dominated by oligopolistic business and labor, or are mingled so intimately with political subsidies and regulations, that the market cannot be expected to correct its own maladjustments. The liberal decontrollers agree, but would solve the problem by restoring the market's "freedom." Instead of capping business and labor oligopoly by a coherently authoritarian government, they favor a radical decrease in governmental regulation and subsidy of industry, and a more active enforcement of regulations to liberate competition. Thus, economic liberals have tried in recent years to "deregulate" everything from airlines to municipal garbage collection. How realistic are their prescriptions?

Though doubtless much might be done to prune excessive regulation and make markets more effective, the basic structural reforms needed to break oligopoly in business and labor seem no less politically difficult than the imposition of comprehensive governmental controls, and are a good deal less in keeping with the general evolution of modern societies. The evolution toward business oligopoly and state intervention proceeds not so much from the influence of an anticapitalist left as from the development of capitalist enterprise itself. As John Kenneth Galbraith has argued ceaselessly over the years, a classic free market long ago became incompatible with modern capitalist business organization itself, let alone with the rest of modern Western society.[4]

Today's big business corporation is unable and indeed unwilling to operate within genuinely free market conditions. Modern industry requires huge long-range investments. These cannot be mustered without a reasonably stable and hence predictable environment. A genuinely free market would be too volatile a guide for pricing and production policies. The same resistance to market signals characterizes labor unions. Wages are pushed up in defiance of high rates of unemployment. This is not to say that market conditions have no influence on those who set prices and wages. But the most powerful actors in our economy—big business, labor, government, and even the affluent consumer—all have the political power and financial cushion to resist immediate market forces for considerable periods of time.[5] In other words, business can set higher prices despite falling demand; labor can achieve higher wages despite rising unemployment; governments can sustain and increase expenditures despite falling revenues; and the general public can sustain demand in the face of falling income. Hence, monetary restraint has so much difficulty curbing inflation. Too many actors have the ability to ignore high interest rates or falling demand to permit either prices or wages to fall.

All these conditions, these market "imperfections," are common to any advanced and plural industrial society. Nowhere is big labor or big business at the mercy of immediate market forces. Both reckon long-term trends and pace their demands accordingly. Both have substantial influence over supply in markets, and both have the resources to finance a long-range view. In every country, both also have substantial political power, enough generally to reverse in time the policies they are resisting.

The government's own tendency to resist the market lies in those countercyclical stabilizers that increase expenditures at the same time as revenues shrink. This tendency, too, clearly reflects the general evolution of modern industrial societies. The Keynesian "fiscal revolution" has legitimated the use of deficits for economic stabilization. The beneficent stabilizers that prevent deep recessions are also the deficits that counterbalance recessionary effects on demand. Although this relieves the distress of the unemployed and limits the dangers to business of falling demand, it also impedes a definitive "cure" of the underlying inflation. Moreover, it soon forces a retreat from monetary restraint. Fiscal deficits, after all, have to be financed, generally through monetary expansion which, in itself, acts as a ratchet on inflation. Meanwhile, governmental bureaucracies have grown to satisfy demands at every level of modern society. In many respects, central economic policy-makers have no more control over the growth of these "entitled" expenditures than over the behavior of corporations, labor unions, or the general consumer. The imperviousness of government expenditure to government income is particularly significant during periods when monetary policy is trying to induce deflation. As unemployment rises and government revenues decline, government welfare expenditures increase dramatically.

Although these market imperfections doubtless encourage inflation and impede its restraint, attempting to break up big business, labor, and government in order to restore the market mechanism is not a policy that commends itself to common sense. The growth of "bigness" is not a fall from innocence but part of the inevitable evolution of the modern capitalist system. In a complicated modern society, a market economy is not more spontaneous or "natural" than a command economy. Government and politics inevitably are mingled with all aspects of modern life. Governments must provide for the common defense, protect the consumer and the environment, encourage prosperity and growth, regulate traffic, stabilize the money supply, and punish law-breakers. At this stage of economic development, to eject public authority from the marketplace is no less political an act than to insert it. Thus, for example, to outlaw federal deficits by a constitutional amendment is as much a "control" as putting a ceiling on food prices. Any serious attempt to reverse this direction would require a major use of power to reverse the domestic status quo, in much the same way as restoring the gold standard would require a major use of power to change international relations.

If the truth be admitted, market "freedom" is all too often a euphemism for a radical devaluation of one kind of power at the expense of another. Insofar as the countervailing power of the government is removed from markets, oligopolistic wealth remains on the field; democratic number does not. But America's present mixed market economic structures and arrangements represent not the ascendancy of mistaken economic theories but the balance of political and social forces. Within the secure and predictable environment provided by the democratic welfare state, business has profited no less than labor, the middle class no less than the poor.

Significantly altering that balance would reverse the socioeconomic trend of several decades and constitute, in effect, a political revolution.

Such an effort might risk a great deal. Though big business has as much right to assert its claims to power as any other element in the political economy, the notion that business corporations are more legitimate exercisers of power than the state is not an ideology likely to carry the day. The demands of consumers for protection or residents for a safe environment are not a passing public fancy. Anything more than a selective dismantling of the web of state controls is unlikely to be politically viable or, for that matter, in the interests of business itself. Any excessive flaunting of business power is likely, sooner or later, to provoke a vigorous counterattack. To tilt the balance a bit within the American system is part of the game. To change the rules drastically will launch a political adventure from which neither business in particular, nor economic growth in general, is likely to profit. Instead of a burst of renewed economic growth, the United States can expect unprecedented social conflict. In short, to promote some greater measure of economic competition, choice, and room for initiative is admirable. To expect to dismantle public power and thus resolve the inflationary scramble for resources is both unrealistic and dangerous, a policy that undermines the very springs of the nation's prosperity and power.

Toward a Broader Vision

To note the shortcomings of the "conservative" reaction at the start of the eighties is not to deny either the legitimacy of the feelings or the necessity for broad changes. If the postwar welfare state reflects the demands both of a modern society and of America's world role, it also embodies a way of responding that has produced a gathering inflationary crisis. The crisis is both immediate, with accelerating prices and increasing international tension, and long-range, with declining domestic productivity and growth. If the clock cannot be turned back to some imaginary liberal past, neither can it be stopped where it is. In short, the argument here is not against change, but against simple-minded formulas that frustrate reform by gravely underestimating its difficulty.

Real improvement in America's condition is likely to depend upon two broad changes in the political culture and institutions. On the one hand, a greater sense of measure must discipline national aims; on the other, the state must acquire a greater capacity to formulate coherent policies and persevere in them. Restored discipline is needed, above all, in economic policy itself. Inflation represents the revenge of economics on politics. If inflation is to stop, America's persistent overextension at home and abroad, legitimized by neo-Keynesian or supply-side budgetary policies, must cease. Not only do such policies produce inflation now but, by discouraging growth, they guarantee inflation in the future.

The aspect of the Keynesian welfare state most particularly damaging to growth is its tendency to subsidize failure. Keynesian demand-management that smoothes out the business cycle removes not only much of the misery and disruption of a recessionary downturn, but also its cleansing effect on unviable enterprises. As the economist Joseph Schumpeter observed early in the century, capitalism thrives on "creative destruction."[6] The business cycle prunes away those firms that have lost their vitality and creates conditions that prompt new growth and general efficiency. An economic policy that mitigates the effects of the cycle must also reduce its benefits. Not surprisingly, a modern welfare economy gradually loses it productivity as it accumulates a growing inventory of weak firms. As the process continues, weakness accelerates. As more and more marginal firms survive, demands that political power prop them up become more and more insistent. Labor joins business in pressing for subsidy to rescue jobs and capital. Ultimately, subsidy is often succeeded by nationalization. In many instances, the troubled firms are the giants of a previous era. Their very size and inherited comfort inhibit their adaptation to new technologies and demands. The size that makes them commercially sluggish also gives them political power. With so much money and employment at stake, the state is hard put to leave the aging giants to their fate. The indirect protection of sustaining demand in general gives way to particular subsidies, tariffs, and nationalization.

Such an evolution of policy scarcely encourages growth. But it does reflect political necessities in a way that some heroic neoliberal return to creative destruction does not. Neither the society in general, nor business in particular, is willing to tolerate the disruption and suffering of the unregulated business cycle. Moreover, much of the destruction was not very creative. In the good old days, as Schumpeter himself observed, recession's financial crush carried away not only the unfit but also large numbers of small but otherwise viable firms, leaving entrepreneurs ruined and workers jobless through no fault of their own.

Schumpeter himself imagined a solution, although he wondered if states would ever be capable of it. Business cycles should not be blocked, he argued, but mitigated by selective aid favoring long-range growth. Promising adolescent firms should be shielded from the gale of market forces. By a similar reasoning, fading enterprises should be protected only long enough either to permit rejuvenation, where possible, or to allow shifts in employment and capital without traumatuc shocks unacceptable to the political system.

Schumpeter's solution raises the specter of "planning," still proscribed from the American political lexicon. Since Schumpeter wrote, however, most other modern states have had ample experience with government attempts at industrial planning. Indeed, in almost any other country, planning would join this chapter's introductory list of postwar economic gimmicks. Much of the current liberal nostalgia throughout the world is an angry reaction against what seems an endlessly meddling and increasingly politicized bureaucracy. But planning, in the sense of some reasonably coherent general economic strategy for the state, does not necessarily mean detailed interference in the actual management of firms. Political discourse in this country might be considerably more productive if the public imagination could entertain a distinction between the strong state that America needs and the bloated state from which it suffers.[7] All the phobia against planning, after all, has not saved Americans from high taxes, excessive regulation, inflation, and foreign excess. In the real world, these afflictions can be cured not by abolishing the state, but by endowing it with a greater degree of measured discipline, a discipline that might be ex-

expected to help generate and mobilize a greater sense of cooperation and responsibility in the community at large.

At the very least, the political system must somewhere have the capacity to formulate a long-range national economic strategy. Such a capacity does not imply an increasingly direct government intervention in the management of the economy. Quite the contrary. Widespread deregulation might well be an early fruit of a more comprehensive and coherent state policy. With settled long-range goals rather than a disconnected series of adventitious remedies, government might be able not only to coordinate intelligently its own myriad interventions, but also to reduce them. Nor does a strong state have to be authoritarian in the way it formulates policy. To succeed, any strategy for reindustrialization, for example, would have to engage business and labor in a context that promoted long-range views and emphasized the overriding general interest in steady growth and prosperity.

Economics and Politics

In a world where people's infinite desires must come to terms with the earth's limited resources, society requires institutions capable of making intelligent choices and convincing people to honor them. Democracy depends upon sustaining some reasonable balance between demand that must be disciplined and supply that must be augmented. America's inflation reflects the failure to maintain that balance at home, as well as an unhealthy absence of political balance within the world economy at large.

It is not hard to conceive of a government policy more informed, deliberate, disciplined, and economical than that of American administrations in the sixties and seventies. But more serious policies seem unlikely without a broad reform of American political institutions. Disciplined long-range policy seems improbable within the present American political environment, with its institutionalized adversarial relationships and its fragmentation of governmental authority—both within the federal government and among federal, state, and local governments. As many knowledgeable Europeans have observed privately, the United States is too big to be governed. The traditional sprawling incoherence of the American political system has been further exaggerated in recent years by the decline of presidential power after Watergate. Traditionally, the Presidency has been the "national" institution in the system, the place to aggregate and harmonize. Whatever the faults of presidential leadership, nothing has been found to replace it.

What are the prospects for serious political reform? Great transformations in political culture and institutions do not simply follow the tune of fashionable theory but somehow reflect the agreement of ideas with the play of forces and circumstances. Any society, let alone a "world system," is such a copious scheme of elements that no formula can hope to grasp its entirety. Political-economic systems are not cast from the mold of theory; they grow out of the soil of history. Theory, however, can help. Too often, in this postwar era, economics has not so much summoned society to its duty as provided learned apologies for its vices. The penchant for gimmickry has reflected not only a populist faith that future growth will bail out present extravagance, but also an elitist intellectual conviction that technocratic manipulation can substitute indefinitely for genuine equilibrium. Thanks to its clever economists, society was supposed to be able to avoid choices forever.

The same presumption has been equally fashionable among professional students of politics. The dominant model among American political scientists has been the interest-group society, where "bargaining" replaces analysis and leaders become "brokers." Although the model describes a large share of reality in any plural society, it also risks becoming, in effect, a learned apology for a prodigiously wasteful system of government incapable of disciplining its own claims on the society's resources, or of leading the public to rational choices in the country's long-range interest. A view of politics that proscribes the very concept of national interest and reduces statesmanship to barter is not well-suited to guide a political system through any but the most benign periods of opulence and security. The reform of American institutions might well begin, therefore, with the rejuvenation of American political and economic theory.

History over the past thirty years has been remarkably indulgent to the United States. Even the turbulence of the seventies was accompanied by remarkable prosperity. Until now, the American public has not been hurt enough by inflation or stagflation to embrace remedies that seemed worse than the disease. Whether history will continue to be so obliging seems improbable.

The consequences of adversity may not be all bad. That drift to inflation that characterized the past two decades reflects a prosperity so prolonged that even economists seem to have forgotten about scarcity—the fundamental fact that lies at the root of their discipline and of the social order itself. With bipolar parity and the rise of other powers in the world, as well as the end of cheap energy and painless inflation at home, history is finally presenting America with its bill. Paying up will doubtless require getting rid of some comfortable illusions and self-indulgences. The new era will be less carefree than the old. It may, however, be more worthy of self-respect. A harsher world may cure the sickness afflicting America's political elites since the collapse of Kennedy's dreams. Pressed by a more imperious necessity, Americans may hope to find the ideas and leadership to build a new consensus, one based on a more profound and balanced notion of welfare at home, as well as a more realistic and measured view of power abroad.

Acknowledgments
Tables
Selected Bibliography
Notes
Index

Acknowledgments

A book that covers so many theoretical and historical questions requires a great deal of help tracking down and interpreting sources. It also benefits greatly from the criticism and insights of others who have analyzed and participated in the events described. I have been well served on both counts. The Lehrman Institute kindly provided, once more, a series of meetings to discuss draft chapters as they emerged. A wide range of scholars, businessmen, and public officials took part. As is usual in that lively establishment, the participants were generous both with specific information and with broader insights. In particular, I wish to acknowledge the kind interest and encouragement of my colleagues at the institute, Nicholas Rizopoulos and Lewis Lehrman.

Another important source of criticism and insight has come from my colleagues and students here at the Johns Hopkins School of Advanced International Studies. In particular, the European Area Research Seminar has patiently endured several drafts and many revisions.

From among my students, several research assistants have given indispensable help. For major contributions at early stages, I should particularly like to thank John Harper, Paul Higdon, and Orme Wilson III. I must also mention Proctor Reid, who shepherded the text and notes through the final drafts, and Thomas

Row, who prepared the index. Among the many others, over several years, are Jonathan Aldrich, Jordan Barab, David Haettenschwiller, Leonard Nihan, William Nylen, Spyros Papas, David Rowe, and Gordon Vieth. Without their interest and friendship, I should certainly never have finished. Thanks, too, are owed to Winifred Williams, who patiently and accurately typed the many drafts.

Tables

1. US economic growth, inflation, and unemployment rates, 1960–1980

Year	GNP (1972 dollars; % change from prior year)	CPI	Unemployment (% of total civilian work force)
1960	2.2	1.6	5.5
1961	2.6	1.0	6.7
1962	5.8	1.1	5.5
1963	4.0	1.2	5.7
1964	5.3	1.3	5.2
1965	6.0	1.7	4.5
1966	6.0	2.9	3.8
1967	2.7	2.9	3.8
1968	4.6	4.2	3.6
1969	2.8	5.4	3.5
1970	− .2	5.9	4.9
1971	3.4	4.3	5.9
1972	5.7	3.3	5.6
1973	5.8	6.2	4.9
1974	− .6	11.0	5.6
1975	− 1.1	9.1	8.5
1976	5.4	5.8	7.7
1977	5.5	6.5	7.0
1978	4.8	7.7	6.0
1979	3.2	11.3	5.8
1980	− .2	12.6	7.1

Source: *ERP 1981*, pp. 233, 267, 293.

2. Federal budget outlays and balances in constant (1972) dollars, 1960–1980

	Outlays (billion dollars)					
Year	Total	National defense	Total nondefense[a]	Payments for individuals[b]	Net interest[c]	Aid to state and local gov.
1960	150.6	73.8	76.8	33.1	16.3	11.4
1965	173.0	69.3	103.7	42.5	16.7	15.7
1970	220.6	90.3	130.3	68.8	15.0	27.0
1971	222.9	81.2	141.7	81.5	15.2	29.5
1972	232.0	76.6	155.5	90.8	15.5	34.4
1973	233.3	70.0	163.3	98.1	15.4	39.6
1974	232.0	67.9	164.0	103.7	14.3	37.8
1975	253.6	67.2	186.4	119.5	14.6	39.1
1976	266.6	65.6	201.0	131.0	16.4	43.1
1976[f]	66.8	15.9	50.9	32.3	4.1	11.2
1977	272.2	66.5	205.7	132.7	17.4	45.9
1978	282.0	66.6	215.4	133.1	17.8	48.5
1979	280.0	69.3	210.7	132.8	17.0	47.2
1980 est.	286.3	70.7	215.6	138.6	16.3	45.8

a. Includes other items, not shown separately.
b. Includes small grants-in-aid to state and local governments.
c. Total interest less interest received by trust funds.
d. GNP as of fiscal year.

2. continued

		% of total outlays				
National defense	Total nondefense[a]	Payments for individuals[b]	Net interest[c]	Aid to state and local gov.	% of GNP[d]	Budget surplus or deficit[e]
49.0	51.0	22.0	10.8	7.6	18.5	.3
40.1	60.0	25.6	9.7	9.1	18.0	– 1.6
40.9	59.1	31.2	6.8	12.2	20.5	– 2.8
36.4	63.6	36.6	6.8	13.2	20.7	–23.0
33.0	67.0	39.1	6.7	14.8	20.9	–23.4
30.0	70.0	42.0	6.6	17.0	20.0	–14.8
29.3	70.7	44.7	6.2	16.3	19.8	– 4.7
26.5	73.5	47.1	5.8	15.4	22.4	–45.1
24.6	75.4	49.1	6.2	16.2	22.6	–66.4
23.8	76.2	48.4	6.1	16.8	—	–13.0
24.4	75.6	48.8	6.4	16.9	21.8	–45.0
23.6	76.4	47.2	6.3	17.2	21.9	–48.8
24.8	75.3	47.4	6.1	16.8	21.3	–27.7
24.7	75.3	48.4	5.7	16.0	22.4	–39.8

e. Billions of current dollars.
f. Transition quarter, July-September.
Source: US Department of Commerce, *Statistical Abstract of the United States* (1980), pp. 258–259.

3. Growth rates in real GNP, 1960–1980 (% change)

Country[a]	1960–73 annual average	1974	1975	1976	1977	1978	1979	1980[b]
United States	4.2	– .6	–1.1	5.4	5.5	4.8	3.2	– .2
Canada	5.4	3.6	1.2	5.5	2.2	3.4	2.8	– .5
Japan	10.5	– .6	1.5	6.5	5.4	6.0	5.9	5.0
France	5.7	3.2	.2	5.2	2.8	3.6	3.3	1.8
West Germany	4.8	.4	–1.8	5.3	2.6	3.5	4.5	1.8
Italy	5.2	4.1	–3.6	5.9	1.9	2.6	5.0	3.8
United Kingdom	3.2	–1.2	– .8	4.2	1.0	3.6	1.5	–2.3

a. For Italy, the United Kingdom, France, and the developing countries, data relate to real gross domestic product.
b. Preliminary estimates.
Source: *ERP 1981*, p. 353.

4. GNP per capita, 1960–1979

Country	GNP per capita (US dollars)[a]				Real GNP growth per capita (%)		
	1960 (GDP)	1970 (GDP)	1975	1979	1960–68 (GDP)	1968–73	1974–79
Canada	2,196	3,676	6,935	9,257	3.5	4.0	2.0
France	1,336	2,901	6,386	10,656	4.4	5.2	2.4
West Germany	1,300	3,034	6,842	12,387	3.4	4.2	3.0
Italy	701	1,727	3,074	5,604	4.3	3.6	1.5
Japan	463	1,911	4,425	8,891	–	8.4	4.0
United Kingdom	1,357	2,128	4,089	7,054	2.3	2.5	1.6
United States	2,817	4,734	7,099	10,739	3.7	2.6	2.4

a. Based on current prices and exchange rates.
Source: US Department of Commerce, *Statistical Abstract of the United States* (1971) p. 806; (1972) p. 813; (1974) p. 824; (1976) p. 877; (1980) p. 910.

5. Consumer prices, major industrial countries, 1964–1980 (1967 = 100)

Year	United States	Japan	France	West Germany	Italy	United Kingdom
1964	92.9	85.0	92.5	92.0	90.1	89.6
1965	94.5	91.5	94.8	95.0	94.2	93.9
1966	97.2	96.2	97.4	98.4	96.4	97.6
1967	100.0	100.0	100.0	100.0	100.0	100.0
1968	104.2	105.3	104.5	101.6	101.4	104.8
1969	109.8	110.8	111.3	103.5	104.1	110.3
1970	116.3	119.3	117.1	107.1	109.2	117.4
1971	121.3	126.8	123.5	112.7	114.4	128.5
1972	125.3	133.0	131.1	119.0	121.0	137.7
1973	133.1	148.5	140.7	127.2	134.0	150.2
1974	147.7	183.0	160.0	136.1	159.7	174.3
1975	161.2	204.5	178.9	144.2	186.8	216.5
1976	170.5	223.7	196.1	150.4	218.1	252.4
1977	181.5	243.0	214.5	155.9	255.2	292.4
1978	195.4	252.3	233.9	160.2	286.2	316.6
1979	217.4	261.3	259.1	166.8	328.5	359.0
1980	246.8	282.2	294.2	175.9	398.1	423.6

Source: *ERP 1981*, p. 355; US Department of Commerce, *International Economic Indicators*, June 1981, p. 43.

**6. Growth in money supply of major industrial countries, 1964–1980 (%
change over corresponding period of prior year)**

Year	United States	Japan	France	West Germany	Italy	United Kingdom
1964	3.7	38.2	10.3	8.6	8.3	5.4
1965	4.1	16.9	9.0	9.5	13.4	3.1
1966	4.6	16.9	8.9	4.4	14.5	3.1
1967	4.2	13.4	6.3	3.3	13.6	3.9
1968	7.5	14.6	5.5	7.9	13.4	4.5
1969	5.2	18.4	6.2	10.0	14.9	– .5
1970	3.6	18.3	1.6	6.4	21.8	7.1
1971	6.7	25.2	13.8	12.4	22.8	13.3
1972	7.3	22.1	13.1	13.7	18.0	16.8
1973	6.8	26.1	9.9	5.3	21.1	10.0
1974	4.4	13.2	12.6	5.9	16.6	3.5
1975	4.5	10.3	9.9	14.1	8.3	15.1
1976	5.1	14.2	14.9	10.2	20.5	14.6
1977	7.2	7.0	7.4	8.2	19.8	13.5
1978	7.3	10.8	11.3	13.5	23.8	20.3
1979	5.7	9.9	12.3	7.2	23.9	12.2
1980	6.7	.8	8.0	2.4	15.8	4.5

Source: IMF, *International Financial Statistics Yearbook* (1980), pp. 54–55.

7. **Exchange rates of major advanced industrial countries, 1950–1979 (currency unit per US dollar, end of year)**

Currency	1950	1960	1970	1971	1973	1975	1977	1979
British pound sterling[a]	2.800	2.804	2.394	2.553	2.323	2.024	1.906	2.224
French franc	3.499	4.903	5.520	5.224	4.708	4.486	4.705	4.020
German mark	4.200	4.171	3.648	3.268	2.703	2.622	2.105	1.7315
Italian lira	624.8	620.6	623.0	594.0	607.9	683.6	871.6	804.0
Canadian dollar	1.060	.996	1.011	1.002	1.000	1.016	1.094	1.168
Japanese yen	361.1	358.3	357.7	314.8	280.0	305.2	240.0	239.7
Swiss franc	4.289	4.305	4.316	3.915	3.244	2.620	2.000	1.580
US dollar[b]	1.000	1.000	1.000	1.086	1.206	1.171	1.215	1.317

a. US dollars per pound.
b. US dollar/SDR rate.
Source: IMF, *International Financial Statistics Yearbook* (1980).

8. US reserves and the world capital market, 1964–1979 (billions of dollars)

Year	Net size of Eurodollar market (est.)	US reserves	US basic balance
1964	9.0	16.67	– .100
1965	11.5	15.45	–1.817
1966	14.5	14.88	–1.474
1967	17.5	14.83	–3.303
1968	25.0	15.71	–1.297
1969	44.0	16.96	–3.943
1970	57.0	14.48	–3.989
1971	71.0	12.16	–10.478
1972	91.0	13.15	–11.580
1973	132.0	14.38	.97
1974	177.0	16.06	–5.586
1975	205.0	15.88	–1.239
1976	247.0	18.32	–10.693
1977	300.0	19.39	–27.612
1978	377.0	19.58	–26.079
1979	475.0	20.20 (Nov.)	–18.967

Source: Bank of International Settlements, *Annual Reports,* nos. 39, 40, 43, 47; *ERP 1973*, p. 299; *ERP 1976*, pp. 275, 278; *ERP 1980*, p. 324; IMF, *Balance of Payments Yearbook,* vol. 23 (1966–1970), p. 9; vol. 28 (1970–1976), p. 633; vol. 31 (1980), p. 605.

9. Money market and eurodollar rates (% per annum)

Country	1965	1966	1967	1968	1969	1970	1971	1972	1973	1974	1975	1976	1977	1978	1979
United States	4.07	5.12	4.22	5.67	8.21	7.18	4.66	4.43	8.73	10.50	5.82	5.05	5.54	7.93	11.20
Canada	3.99	4.99	4.64	6.27	7.19	5.99	3.56	3.56	5.47	7.83	7.40	8.87	7.33	8.67	11.68
Japan	6.97	5.84	6.39	7.88	7.70	8.29	6.42	4.72	7.16	12.54	10.67	6.98	5.68	4.36	5.86
France	4.21	4.78	4.80	6.15	8.96	8.68	5.84	4.95	8.91	12.91	7.92	8.56	9.07	7.98	9.04
West Germany	4.07	5.34	3.35	2.58	4.81	8.65	6.06	4.30	10.19	8.87	4.41	3.89	4.14	3.36	5.87
Italy	–	–	–	–	5.00	7.38	5.76	5.18	6.93	14.57	10.64	15.68	14.03	11.49	11.86
United Kingdom	5.91	6.10	5.82	7.09	7.64	7.01	5.57	5.54	9.34	11.37	10.18	11.12	7.68	8.51	12.98
Eurodollar London	4.81	6.12	5.46	6.36	9.76	8.52	6.58	5.46	9.24	11.01	6.99	5.58	6.00	8.73	11.96

Central Government Bond Yields
(average yields to maturity in % per annum)

Country	1965	1966	1967	1968	1969	1970	1971	1972	1973	1974	1975	1976	1977	1978	1979
United States	4.27	4.77	5.01	5.46	6.33	6.86	6.12	6.01	7.12	8.06	8.19	7.87	7.67	8.49	9.33
Canada	5.21	5.69	5.94	6.75	7.58	7.91	6.95	7.23	7.56	8.90	9.04	9.18	8.70	9.30	10.26
Japan	–	6.86	6.91	7.03	7.09	7.19	7.28	6.70	7.26	9.26	9.20	8.72	7.33	6.09	7.69
France	5.27	5.40	5.66	5.86	7.64	8.06	7.74	7.35	8.25	10.49	9.49	9.16	9.61	8.96	9.48
West Germany	7.10	8.10	7.00	6.50	6.80	8.30	8.00	7.90	9.30	10.40	8.50	7.80	6.20	5.80	7.40
Italy	6.94	6.54	6.61	6.70	6.85	9.01	8.34	7.47	7.42	9.87	11.54	13.08	14.62	13.70	14.05
Switzerland	3.95	4.16	4.61	4.37	4.90	5.82	5.27	4.97	5.60	7.15	6.44	4.99	4.05	3.33	3.45
United Kingdom	6.56	6.94	6.80	7.55	9.04	9.22	8.90	8.91	10.72	14.77	14.39	14.33	12.73	12.47	12.99

Source: IMF, *International Financial Statistics Yearbook* (1980), p. 52.

10. Productivity, 1960–1979 (output per hour; 1967 = 100)

Year	United States	Canada	Japan	United Kingdom	France	West Germany	Italy
1960	78.8	75.5	52.6	76.8	68.7	66.4	65.1
1961	80.7	79.6	59.3	77.4	71.9	70.0	67.4
1962	84.5	83.9	61.9	79.3	75.2	74.4	74.1
1963	90.4	87.1	67.1	83.6	79.7	78.4	76.5
1964	95.2	90.9	75.9	89.7	83.7	84.5	81.5
1965	98.2	94.4	79.1	92.4	88.5	90.4	91.6
1966	99.7	97.2	87.1	95.7	94.7	94.0	96.0
1967	100.0	100.0	100.0	100.0	100.0	100.0	100.0
1968	103.6	107.3	112.6	107.1	111.4	107.6	108.4
1969	104.9	113.3	130.0	108.4	115.4	113.8	112.2
1970	104.5	115.2	146.5	109.1	121.2	116.6	117.8
1971	110.3	122.9	151.7	114.3	127.5	122.5	123.5
1972	116.0	127.4	163.9	121.2	135.9	130.3	132.9
1973	119.4	132.2	184.3	128.1	142.2	138.6	147.8
1974	114.7	132.3	187.5	127.9	146.1	145.6	155.6
1975	118.8	133.7	202.9	125.7	151.9	151.6	152.9
1976	124.0	140.2	221.9	129.6	164.3	161.3	166.0
1977	127.7	147.3	241.5	129.1	171.7	170.2	167.8
1978	128.2	151.9	258.0	130.7	180.2	176.3	173.0
1979	129.4	153.7	279.0	132.9	188.7	185.5	189.1

Source: International Economic Report of the President, 1977, p. 144; US Department of Commerce, International Economic Indicators, March 1981, p. 64.

11. Unit labor cost in manufacturing, 1960–1980 (US dollar basis, 1967 = 100)

Year	United States	Canada	Japan	United Kingdom	France	West Germany	Italy
1960	97.8	106.3	82.5	85.7	81.7	78.1	76.5
1961	98.3	99.1	84.8	91.4	85.9	85.9	78.3
1962	97.9	91.8	92.8	94.1	90.5	91.7	83.4
1963	94.5	90.7	95.6	93.1	94.3	93.3	96.1
1964	93.8	90.2	94.8	92.8	96.6	93.6	101.0
1965	92.7	91.3	102.5	98.7	98.3	95.7	97.1
1966	95.5	95.7	102.4	103.1	97.6	100.2	95.1
1967	100.0	100.0	100.0	100.0	100.0	100.0	100.0
1968	103.3	100.1	103.8	87.4	101.1	98.3	99.0
1969	108.6	101.9	107.2	93.0	98.8	103.1	104.3
1970	116.5	111.5	113.3	106.0	98.9	124.6	119.2
1971	117.8	115.6	130.7	117.8	105.5	141.8	135.6
1972	118.4	122.1	160.2	127.9	120.8	162.5	151.9
1973	124.5	126.7	194.1	134.9	148.1	207.3	171.3
1974	142.4	144.5	234.6	153.7	162.0	237.6	183.1
1975	146.5	165.6	249.2	196.9	204.6	266.4	245.1
1976	151.6	186.2	244.5	181.8	194.1	262.2	212.5
1977	160.3	185.5	274.1	196.2	205.5	295.8	234.9
1978	172.0	180.3	350.5	246.2	241.5	358.3	271.7
1979	186.7	190.6	329.1	313.1	278.0	396.8	307.8
1980	207.4	–	–	–	–	–	–

Source: *International Economic Report of the President, 1976*, pp. 143–144; US Department of Commerce, *International Economic Indicators*, June 1981, p. 64.

12. Hourly compensation, major industrial countries, 1960–1979 (1967 = 100)[a]

Year	United States	Canada	Japan	France	West Germany	Italy	United Kingdom
1960	78.0	80.3	43.3	56.0	51.8	46.8	65.9
1961	80.2	78.9	50.3	61.7	60.5	51.8	70.8
1962	83.3	77.0	57.5	67.9	68.8	61.1	74.6
1963	85.8	79.0	64.1	75.0	73.6	72.3	77.9
1964	89.3	82.0	72.0	80.7	79.5	80.4	83.2
1965	91.1	86.2	81.1	86.9	85.7	86.0	91.2
1966	95.2	93.0	89.2	92.5	94.3	89.8	98.7
1967	100.0	100.0	100.0	100.0	100.0	100.0	100.0
1968	107.1	107.4	116.9	112.6	105.9	106.8	93.3
1969	114.2	115.5	139.3	111.6	117.3	121.1	101.7
1970	122.3	128.2	165.9	117.2	145.9	145.0	115.3
1971	129.9	142.6	197.4	131.3	173.1	169.7	134.3
1972	136.6	156.6	261.2	159.9	210.8	206.0	154.4
1973	146.5	170.5	359.9	208.5	288.3	261.7	167.8
1974	161.7	200.6	439.5	231.3	340.9	291.6	197.8
1975	181.1	221.4	505.5	310.7	404.0	374.7	247.5
1976	196.1	261.0	542.6	319.0	422.9	352.7	235.6
1977	212.7	273.2	661.8	353.0	503.6	394.3	253.3
1978	229.9	273.8	904.2	435.2	631.6	469.9	321.8
1979	250.8	292.9	918.2	524.5	736.0	582.0	416.2

a. Hourly compensation in manufacturing, US dollar basis. Data relate to all employed persons (wage and salary earners and self-employed) in the United States and Canada, and to all employees (wage and salary earners) in the other countries. For France and United Kingdom, compensation is adjusted to include changes in employment taxes that are not compensation to employees but are labor costs to employers.

Data for United States have not been revised to incorporate benchmark revisions in national income and product accounts.

Source: ERP 1981, p. 355.

13. Civilian employment, 1960–1979 (adjusted to US concepts, 1965 = 100)

Country	1960	1965	1970	1975	1980
France	96.3	100	104.3	106.4	114.9
West Germany	97.7	100	99.2	94.2	95.4
Italy	105.0	100	98.1	99.5	103.3
Japan	93.8	100	108.5	111.5	110.2
United Kingdom	95.5	100	97.8	98.2	97.1
United States	92.5	100	110.6	119.3	136.8

Source: Computations based on data supplied by US Bureau of Labor Statistics preliminary figures, September 1981, for forthcoming *Handbook of Labor Statistics, 1981* (Washington D.C.: GPO).

14. Export unit values, 1965–1979 (1975 = 100)

Country	1965	1966	1967	1968	1969	1970	1971	1972	1973	1974	1975	1976	1977	1978	1979
United States	49	50	51	52	54	57	59	60	70	89	100	104	108	115	131
Canada	47	49	50	51	52	56	58	61	69	94	100	106	104	106	124
Japan	49	49	51	51	53	55	58	65	79	100	100	99	109	134	141
France	46	48	47	47	48	49	52	58	72	84	100	98	105	120	139
West Germany	40	41	40	40	41	48	52	58	73	88	100	102	112	129	145
Italy	48	47	47	47	49	51	54	60	70	89	100	94	107	119	143
United Kingdom	51	53	53	50	51	55	59	65	71	86	100	97	112	135	165

Source: IMF, *International Financial Statistics Yearbook* (1980), p. 71.

15. World trade balance, 1965–1980 (billions of US dollars)

Country	1965	1970	1975	1977	1978	1979	1980[a]
United States	4.3	.8	4.2	–36.3	–39.4	–37.1	–34.3
Canada	–.2	2.5	–2.1	1.3	1.9	1.4	2.9
Japan	.3	.4	–2.1	9.7	18.4	–7.5	–12.1
France	–.2	–1.0	–.8	–5.5	–2.4	–6.3	–18.6
West Germany	.3	4.3	15.2	16.6	20.7	12.2	3.5
Italy	–.2	–1.8	–3.6	–2.8	–.4	–5.7	–18.4
United Kingdom	–2.3	–2.4	–9.6	–6.3	–6.9	–11.9	–3.2

a. Preliminary estimates.
Source: *ERP 1981*, p. 351.

16. Relative Price of Oil, 1950–1980 (% changes from prior period)

Year	US consumer price index	Price of oil per barrel[a]	Dollar depreciation SDR	DM
1950	—	—	—	—
1960	23.0	–12.3	—	– 0.7
1970	31.0	–15.4	—	–12.5
1971	4.3	21.2	–0.4	–10.4
1972	3.5	15.2	–7.7	– 1.8
1973	6.2	42.1	–8.9	–15.6
1974	11.0	261.5	–0.9	–10.9
1975	9.1	9.8	–0.9	8.9
1976	5.8	7.4	5.2	– 9.9
1977	6.5	7.7	–1.1	–10.9
1978	7.7	2.4	–6.7	–13.2
1979	11.3	33.6	–3.1	– 5.3
1980	12.5	65.4	–0.9	10.9
				(November)

a. Saudi Arabian Light Crude (34 – 34.9°) in 1975 dollars.
Source: *ERP 1981*, p. 289; IMF, *International Financial Statistics,* November 1960, pp. 130–131; September 1977, pp. 148–149; January 1981, pp. 10, 52, 133–134.

17. Total commercial energy consumption per capita, 1950–1974 (kilograms of coal equivalent)

Year	World	United States	United Kingdom	France	West Germany
1950	1,004	7,316	4,358	1,912	2,490
1960	1,423	8,172	4,861	2,474	3,695
1970	1,908	11,020	5,336	3,956	5,419
1974	2,059	11,485	5,464	4,342	5,698

Source: UN Department of Economic and Social Affairs, "World Energy Supplies, 1950–1974," Statistical Papers (New York, 1976), pp. 3, 42–43, 97–98.

18. Retail prices (including taxes) of gasoline (standard grade) and heating oil, 1963–1973 (US cents per gallon)[a]

Country		1963	1965	1970	1972	1973
United Kingdom:	gasoline	—	—	62	62	72
	heating oil	18	18	16	21	23
United States:	gasoline	30	31	35	35	39
	heating oil	16	16	19	20	23
West Germany:	gasoline	54	54	57	69	87
	heating oil	12	10	12	13	26
France:	gasoline	75	72	72	83	95
	heating oil	14	13	15	20	24

a. Qualities and specifications of heating oil differ among countries. The Italian quality in particular is lower than that of other countries.

Source: "The Oil Crisis in Perspective," Daedalus (Fall 1975), p. 287.

Selected Bibliography

A COMPLETE BIBLIOGRAPHY on American policy and its effects from 1960 to 1980 would be a major work in itself. Listed here are some general secondary sources particularly useful in shaping my own general analysis. More specific studies are mentioned in the notes. I have also made extensive use of the annual *Economic Report of the President* (*ERP*), not only for its statistical sources but also for its analysis of economic issues and government policies.

Barraclough, Geoffrey. "The Struggle for the Third World," *New York Review of Books,* Nov. 9, 1978, pp. 47–58.

Cagan, Philip. *Recent Monetary Policy and Inflation in the Sixties.* Washington, D.C.: American Enterprise Institute, 1972.

Calleo, David P. *The Atlantic Fantasy.* Baltimore: Johns Hopkins University Press,1970.

_____. "Inflation and American Power," *Foreign Affairs* 59 (Spring 1981): 781–812.

_____, ed. *Money and the Coming World Order.* Lehrman Institute Book. New York: New York University Press, 1976.

_____, and Benjamin Rowland. *America and the World Political Economy.* Bloomington: Indiana University Press, 1973.

Chace, James. *Solvency: The Price of Survival.* New York: Random House, 1981.

Cleveland, Harold van B. "How the Dollar Standard Died," *Foreign Policy* 5 (Winter 1971–72): 41–51.

_____. "Reflections on International Monetary Order," *Columbia Journal of Transnational Law,* Nov. 3, 1972, pp. 403–419.

_____, and W. H. Brittain. *The Great Inflation: A Monetarist View.* Washington, D.C.: National Planning Association, 1976.

Coffey, Kenneth. *The Strategic Implications of the All-Volunteer Force.* Chapel Hill: University of North Carolina Press, 1979.

Cohen, Stephen D. *International Monetary Reform, 1964–1969: The Political Dimension.* New York: Praeger, 1970.

Corden, William M. *Inflation Exchange Rates and the World Economy.* Chicago: University of Chicago Press, 1977.

Crozier, Michel, ed. *The Crisis of Democracy: Report on the Governability of Democracies to the Trilateral Commission.* New York: New York University Press, 1975.

De Carmoy, Guy. *The Foreign Policies of France, 1944–1968.* Chicago: University of Chicago Press, 1970.

Dunn, Robert N., Jr. "Exchange Rates, Payments Adjustment, and OPEC: Why Oil Deficits Persist," *Princeton Essays in International Finance,* no. 137, December 1979.

Eckstein, Otto. *The Great Recession.* Amsterdam: North Holland, 1978.

Fabra, Paul. *Mutations dans la structure financière après Bretton Woods.* Madrid: Instituto de Cooperacion, and Amsterdam: Fondation Européene de la Culture, 1980.

Fallows, James. *National Defense.* New York: Random House, 1981.

Friedman, Milton. *Dollars and Deficits: Living with America's Economic Problems.* New Jersey: Prentice-Hall, 1968.

_____. "The Role of Monetary Policy," *The American Economic Review,* no. 1 (1968): 1–17.

Galbraith, John Kenneth. *The New Industrial State.* Boston: Houghton Mifflin, 1967.

_____. "The Conservative Onslaught," *New York Review of Books,* Jan. 22, 1981, pp. 30–36.

Gardner, Richard N. *Sterling Dollar Diplomacy in Current Perspective.* New York: Columbia University Press, 1980.

Goodwin, Cranfurd D., ed. *Energy Policy in Perspective: Today's Problems, Yesterday's Solutions.* Washington, D.C.: The Brookings Institution, 1981.

Haberler, Gottfried, and Thomas E. Willett. *A Strategy for U.S. Balance of Payments Policies.* Washington, D.C.: American Enterprise Institute, 1971.

Harris, Seymour E. *Economics of Kennedy Years.* New York: Harper and Row, 1964.

Harriss, C. Lowell, ed. *Inflation: Long-Term Problems.* Proceedings of the Academy of Political Science, vol. 31, no. 4. New York: The Academy of Political Science, cosponsored by The Lehrman Institute, 1975.

Hayek, F. A. von. *Full Employment at Any Price?* Occasional Papers no. 45. London: Institute of Economic Affairs, 1975.

Heilbroner, Robert L. *An Inquiry into the Human Prospect.* New York: Norton, 1974.

Hicks, Sir John. *The Crisis in Keynesian Economics.* Oxford: Basil Blackwell, 1974.

Ingelhart, Ronald. "The Silent Revolution in Europe: Intergenerational Change in Post-Industrial Societies," *American Political Science Review* 65, no. 4 (December 1971): 991–1017.

Johnson, Harry G. "The Case for Flexible Exchange Rates," *Federal Reserve Bank of St. Louis, 1969 Report,* June 1969.

_____. *Inflation and the Monetarist Controversy.* Amsterdam-London: North Holland, 1972.

_____. "The Monetary Approach to Balance of Payments Theory," *Intermountain Economic Review* 3, no. 2 (March 1972). 1–13.

Kaufman, Henry. "America's Economic and Financial Dilemma," *Bond Market Research,* Salomon Brothers, February 1980.

_____. "The Disregard for Capital," *Bond Market Research,* Salomon Brothers, May 1980.

Kindleberger, C. P. "Money Illusion and Foreign Exchange." In *Leading Issues in International Policy,* ed. F. Bergsten and W. Tyler. Lexington, Mass.: Lexington Press, 1973.

_____. *The World in Depression, 1929–1939.* Los Angeles: University of California Press, 1973.

Kondratieff, M. D. "The Long Waves in Economic Life," *The Review of Economic Statistics* 17, no. 6 (November 1935): 105–115.

Krause, Laurence B. "A Passive Balance of Payments Strategy," *Brookings Papers on Economic Activity,* no. 3 (1970): 339–360.

Lawrence, Robert E. "An Analysis of the 1977 US Trade Deficit," *Brookings Papers on Economic Activity,* no. 1 (1978): 159–189.

_____. "Toward a Better Understanding of Trade Balance Trends — The Cost-Price Puzzle," *Brookings Papers on Economic Activity,* no. 1 (1979):191–210.

Lehrman, Lewis E. "Monetary Policy, the Federal Reserve System and Gold," Morgan Stanley *Investment Research Memorandum,* Jan. 25, 1980.

MacKintosh, Malcolm. "The Impact of the Middle East Crisis on Super-Power Relations," *Adelphi Papers,* no. 114 (Spring 1975): 1–19.

McCracken, Paul, ed. *Towards Full Employment and Price Stability.* Paris: OECD, 1977.

Meier, Gerald M. *Problems of a World Monetary Order.* London: Oxford University Press, 1974.

Moynihan, Daniel P. *The Politics of a Guaranteed Income.* New York: Random House, 1973.

Mundell, Robert A., and Jacques J. Polak, eds. *The New International Monetary System.* New York: Columbia University Press, 1977.

Okun, Arthur. *The Political Economy of Prosperity.* Washington, D.C.: The Brookings Institution, 1970.

Perry, George. "Changing Labor Markets and Inflation," *Brookings Papers on Economic Activity,* no. 3 (1970): 411–448.

Peterson, Peter G. *The United States in the Changing World Economy,* vols. 1–2. Washington, D.C.: GPO, 1971.

Phillips, A. W. "Employment, Inflation and Growth," *Economica,* n.s. 29 (February 1962): 1–16.

Preeg, Ernest H. *Traders and Diplomats.* Washington, D.C.: The Brookings Institution, 1970.

Riedel, James. "The Symptoms of Declining US International Competitiveness: Causes and Consequences," *The International Economy: US Role in a World Market, Special Study on Economic Change,* vol. 9. Washington, D.C.: GPO, Dec. 17, 1980, pp. 230–250.

Rolfe, Sidney E., and James Burtle. *The Great Wheel: The World Monetary System: A Reinterpretation.* New York: Quadrangle New York Times Book, 1973.

Roosa, Robert V. "Reforming the International Monetary System," *Foreign Affairs* 42 (October 1963): 107–123.

_____. *The Dollar and World Liquidity.* New York: Random House, 1967.

Rostow, Walt W. *The World Economy: History and Prospect.* Austin: University of Texas Press, 1978.

Rothschild, Emma. "Regan and the Real America," *New York Review of Books,* Feb. 5, 1981, pp. 12–18.

Rowland, Benjamin M., "Economic Policy and Development: The Case of Latin America." In *Retreat from Empire? The First Nixon Administration,* ed. Robert Osgood. Baltimore: Johns Hopkins University Press, 1973.

_____, ed. *Balance of Power or Hegemony: The Interwar Monetary System.* Lehrman Institute Book, New York: New York University Press, 1976.

Rueff, Jacques. *Les Doctrines monétaires a léprèuve des faits.* Paris: Alcan, 1932. Trans. in Rueff. *The Age of Inflation.* Chicago: Regnery, 1964.

_____. *The Balance of Payments.* New York: Macmillan, 1967.

_____. *The Monetary Sin of the West.* New York: Macmillan, 1972.

Rustow, Dankwart A. "US-Saudi Relations and the Oil Crisis in the 1980's," *Foreign Affairs* 55 (April 1977): 494–516.

Schmitt, Hans O. "Mercantilism: A Modern Argument," *The Manchester School* 47, no. 2 (June 1979): 93–111.

Schultz, George B., and Kenneth W. Dam. *Economic Policy Beyond the Headlines.* New York: Norton, 1977.

Schultze, Charles, ed. *Setting National Priorities: The 1971 Budget.* Washington, D.C.: The Brookings Institution, 1971.

Schumpeter, Joseph A. *Business Cycles: A Theoretical, Historical and Statistical Analysis of the Capitalist Process,* vols. 1–2. New York and London: McGraw-Hill, 1939.

Skidelsky, Robert J. A. *Politicians and the Slump: The Labour Government of 1921–1931.* London: Macmillan, 1967.

Solomon, Robert. *The International Monetary System, 1945–1976: An Insider's View.* New York: Harper and Row, 1977.

Sorenson, Theodore C. *Kennedy.* New York: Bantam Books, 1966.

Stein, Herbert. *The Fiscal Revolution in America.* Chicago: University of Chicago Press, 1969.

Stobaugh, Robert, and Daniel Yergin, eds. *Energy Future: Report of the Energy Project at the Harvard Business School.* New York: Random House, 1979.

Strange, Susan. "International Monetary Relations." In *International Economic Relations of the Western World, 1959–1971,* ed. Andrew Shonfield. London: Oxford University Press, 1976.

Thurow, Lester C. "Undamming the American Economy," *New York Times Magazine,* May 10, 1981, pp. 38–60.

_____. "How to Wreck the Economy," *New York Review of Books,* May 14, 1981, pp. 3–8.

Tobin, James. *The New Economics One Decade Older.* Princeton: Princeton University Press, 1979.

Triffin, Robert. *Gold and the Dollar Crisis.* New Haven: Yale University Press, 1960.

_____. *The World Money Maze.* New Haven: Yale University Press, 1966.

Tsoukalis, Loukas. *The Politics and Economics of European Monetary Integration.* London: Allen and Unwin, 1977.

Ture, Norman B. " 'Supply-Side' Analysis and Public Policy," paper presented to the Economic Policy Round Table of The Lehrman Institute, New York, Nov. 12, 1980.

Tucker, Robert W. *The Inequality of Nations.* New York: Basic Books, 1977.

Tufte, Edward. *Political Control of the Economy.* Princeton: Princeton University Press, 1978.

Volcker, Paul. "Statements to Congress on October 17, 1979," *Federal Reserve Bulletin* 65 (November 1979): 888–889.

Whitman, Marina von N. "Global Monetarism and the Monetary Approach to the Balance of Payments," *Brookings Papers on Economic Activity,* no. 3 (1975): 491–555.

Williamson, John. *The Failure of World Monetary Reform, 1971–1974.* New York: New York University Press, 1974.

Yeager, Leland B. *International Monetary Relations: Theory, History and Policy.* New York: Harper and Row, 1976.

Notes

1. Kennedy's Grand Design

1. For Eisenhower's economic policies, see Herbert Stein, *The Fiscal Revolution in America* (Chicago: University of Chicago Press, 1969), chs. 11-13. For his foreign policy, see Michael A. Guhin, *John Foster Dulles: A Statesman and His Times* (New York: Columbia University Press, 1972). For new material on his Administration, see Robert H. Ferrell, *The Eisenhower Diaries* (New York: Norton, 1981). For recent Eisenhower studies, see Stephen E. Ambrose, "The Ike Age," *The New Republic,* May 9, 1981, pp. 26-34; Ronald Steel, "Two Cheers for Ike," *New York Review of Books,* Sept. 24, 1981, pp. 54-57.

2. See W. W. Rostow, *The Stages of Economic Growth: A Non-Communist Manifesto* (Cambridge: Cambridge University Press, 1960). For foreign aid policy, see Robert A. Packenham, *Liberal America and the Third World: Political Development Ideas in Foreign Aid and Social Science* (Princeton: Princeton University Press, 1973).

3. For the Administration's views on the relationships of growth, productivity, investment, and trade, see *ERP 1962* (esp. pp. 108-143), *1963,* and *1964* (Washington, D.C.: GPO). See also Seymour E. Harris, *Economics of the Kennedy Years* (New York: Harper and Row, 1964).

4. The 1950s opened with a boom stimulated by defense spending in the Korean War. A mild recession from mid-1953 to the end of 1954 was followed by a boom until mid-1957. A subsequent recession ended in early 1958. A slight expansion followed until May 1960, succeeded by a slight contraction until February 1961. Through these various mild cycles, the Eisenhower Administration ran large economic countercyclical deficits but feared more active stimulus, from either government projects or tax cuts. Eisenhower saw the climate as basically in-

flationary. He thus rejected the tax cut pressed by Nixon and Burns in 1958. Stein, *Fiscal Revolution.*

5. Other measures, like The Trade Expansion Act of 1962, sought to encourage domestic investing for export rather than foreign investment. *ERP 1963,* pp. 135–144.

6. "More than anyone else, the highly articulate and intelligent Heller won the President over to modern views of economics. He accomplished this despite many obstacles, especially since the President in 1960 had not been convinced of the usefulness of budgetary deficits." Harris, *Kennedy Years,* p. 23. Kennedy made far more use of economists than his predecessor, and these sought not merely to advise but to initiate policy: "They were assiduous in mobilizing support for their views, inside and outside the government, in order to increase the likelihood that the President's decision would be their decision." Stein, *Fiscal Revolution,* pp. 379–381. See also James Tobin, *The New Economics One Decade Older* (Princeton: Princeton University Press, 1979), esp. pp. 1–39; Theodore C. Sorenson, *Kennedy* (New York: Bantam Books, 1966), pp. 447–449.

7. To apply the concept practically required some working definition of full employment. The Kennedy Administration set a figure of 4% unemployed, raised by the end of the decade to 4.6%. In the 1970s the figure rose still further, which underscored the elusive nature of the concept itself. For the evolution of the concept from its appearance in the New Deal to the sixties, see Stein, *Fiscal Revolution.*

8. *ERP 1963,* pp. IX–XXV. Unemployment remained high in 1962 and 1963, when the tax cut began to be considered seriously. *ERP 1965,* pp. 62–66.

9. *ERP 1981,* p. 235.

10. Kennedy also ran deficits in 1961, 1962, and 1963, but these were presumably justified by more conventional countercyclical practice. *ERP 1981,* p. 316.

11. See Tables 5, 10, 11, 12.

12. The Trade Expansion Act of 1962 authorized the President: to reduce up to 50% tariffs on goods from any country; to reduce to zero duties on products where the United States and EEC together account for 80% or more of the free world exports and on agricultural goods where the President determines such restrictions will help maintain or expand US exports; to reduce by more than 50% duties on tropical, agricultural, and forest commodities if not produced significantly in the United States as long as the EEC did the same; and to eliminate *ad valorem* duties of 5% or less. *ERP 1963,* pp. 135–136. Other provisions established adjustment assistance to distressed industries and tests and arrangements for escape clauses. For the Kennedy Round and its implications, see Ernest H. Preeg, *Traders and Diplomats* (Washington, D.C.: The Brookings Institution, 1970); John W. Evans, *The Kennedy Round in American Trade Policy: The Twilight of GATT?* (Cambridge: Harvard University Press, 1971).

13. Except for aircraft and margarine, the Trade Expansion Act's 80% provision (see note 12) was inoperative without British exports being added to the US-EEC export total. Preeg, *Traders and Diplomats.* For Britain's application and de Gaulle's 1963 veto, see Miriam Camps, *Britain and the European Commu-*

nity (Princeton: Princeton University Press, 1964); David P. Calleo, *Britain's Future* (New York: Horizon Press, 1968).

14. See e.g. Lloyd C. Gardner, *Economic Aspects of New Deal Democracy* (Boston: Beacon Press, 1971), pp. 1–46; Herbert Feis, *1933: Characters in Crisis* (Boston: Little, Brown, 1966), pp. 108–115.

15. Both domestic expansion and liberal internationalism were traditional goals with powerful constituencies. Kennedy was not unaware of the difficulties in this traditional Democratic combination: "The president stressed increased investment, rising productivity, continuing cost and price stability and also faster growth," while at the same time hoping for "some inflation abroad." Harris, *Economics of the Kennedy Years,* p. 151.

16. The basic difference between the EEC and the US was in the area of agriculture. American wheat and other agricultural products, if sold freely, would drastically undercut European prices and wipe out the more marginal European producers. Food and Agricultural Organization of the United Nations, *Production Yearbook 1968,* XXII, 532, 534–536.

17. For the importance the French attached to agriculture, see Guy de Carmoy, *The Foreign Policies of France, 1944–1968* (Chicago: University of Chicago Press, 1970), pp. 416–429. See also Edward L. Morse, *Foreign Policy and Interdependence in Gaullist France* (Princeton: Princeton University Press, 1973), pp. 77–83. For political problems affecting the Kennedy Round, see Evans, *Kennedy Round,* pp. 265–279.

18. For the views of Keynes and White and the final arrangements at Bretton Woods, see Gerald M. Meier, *Problems of a World Monetary Order* (London: Oxford University Press, 1974), pp. 18–48. See also Richard N. Gardner, *Sterling Dollar Diplomacy in Current Perspective* (New York: Columbia University Press, 1980), pp. 71–100.

19. For the US loan to Britain, see Gardner, *Sterling Dollar Diplomacy,* pp. 189–347.

20. For the European Payments Union, see Robert Triffin, *The Future of the European Payments System,* Wiksell Lecture Series (Stockholm: The Wiksell Lecture Society, 1958); Leland B. Yeager, *International Monetary Relations: Theory, History and Policy* (New York: Harper and Row, 1976), pp. 407–430.

21. For balance-of-payments figures, see *ERP 1965,* pp. 282–283. For 1960 crisis in the London Gold Market, see Susan Strange, "International Monetary Relations," in *International Economic Relations of the Western World, 1959–1971,* vol. II, ed. Andrew Shonfield (London: Oxford University Press, 1976), pp. 65–89.

22. For the gold-exchange standard, see Yeager, *International Monetary Relations;* Meier, *Problems of a World Monetary Order.*

23. For the Gold Pool, see *1964 Annual Report of the Directors of the IMF,* pp. 131–132; Robert Solomon, *The International Monetary System, 1945–1976: An Insider's View* (New York: Harper and Row, 1977), pp. 114–127.

24. See Table 8.

25. For the official view, see *ERP 1962,* pp. 144–166. See also Tobin, *New Economics,* pp. 27–34; Harris, *Kennedy Years,* pp. 147–175.

26. See Strange, "International Monetary Relations," pp. 66–68, 80–86, 270–275.

27. See Jim F. Heath, *John F. Kennedy and the Business Community* (Chicago: University of Chicago Press, 1969), p. 41; "Speech to the National Association of Manufacturers," Dec. 6, 1961, *Public Papers of the Presidents of the United States, John F. Kennedy (1961)*, pp. 778–779.

28. Though the Administration made no efforts to curb short-term capital outflows directly, it began in 1961 to manipulate the interest-rate structure. Short-term rates were to be raised to discourage capital outflows, while long-term rates were to be kept easy to promote domestic investment in business and housing. The policy was dubbed "Operation Twist." To invert the yield curve (raise short-term rates relative to long-term rates), the Federal Reserve and the Treasury adopted rather abnormal behavior. The Treasury had to sell a greater number of short-term Treasury bills than Treasury bonds in order to drive up the short-term rates, which contradicted the Treasury's normal efforts to lengthen the maturity of the national debt. The Fed, on the contrary, had to give up its practice of conducting open-market operations strictly on a "bills only" or a short-term basis so that it could buy up Treasury bonds and maintain easy credit in the long-term markets. As the CEA wrote in 1964: "Actions were taken to raise short-term interest rates and to maintain them at levels that would reduce outflows of funds to money markets abroad. Within the limits established by this policy, the Federal Reserve provided money and bank credit to support the expansion and generally avoid placing upward pressure on long-term rates." *ERP 1964,* p. 47. Other policies also exerted upward pressure on short-term rates while holding down long-term rates. Changes in Regulation Q in January 1962, July 1963, and November 1964 allowed banks to offer higher rates on deposits in time and savings accounts, and thereby brought funds into commercial banks. These additional funds were to be available for mortgages and state and local government bonds, thus pressuring long-term rates downward. In addition, the Fed raised the discount rate from 3% to 3.5% in July 1963 and from 3.5% to 4% in November 1964, largely to push up short-term rates and to help the US balance of payments. Finally, beginning in 1961, the Treasury engaged, for the first time since the mid-1930s, in foreign exchange operations in cooperation with foreign central banks. This meant transactions in both spot and forward markets designed to increase the cost to speculators and traders of exchange risk cover on sales of dollars, thereby reducing the incentive to sell dollars and buy foreign currencies. *ERP 1962,* p. 164.

29. The Interest Equalization Tax (IET) was essentially an excise tax on purchases in the United States of new or outstanding foreign stocks and bonds. Kennedy proposed it on July 18, 1963, as a temporary measure to discourage the rapidly rising outflows of long-term capital from American purchases of foreign securities (from $523 million in 1961 to a seasonally adjusted $1.9 billion in the first half of 1963). Borrowing costs were effectively raised for foreigners in the American capital market. Investment yields to American investors in foreign securities were reduced by about 1%. Portfolio investment abroad by Americans was thus to be discouraged without directly affecting domestic long-term interest

rates. The IET was thus consistent with "Operation Twist" which aimed at keeping long-term interest rates high enough to discourage outflows of short-term capital. The tax was passed in August 1964 and made retroactive to July 1963 to prevent any mass rush to invest in foreign securites before the tax became law. *ERP 1964,* pp. 125–130; *ERP 1965,* pp. 76–77. Securities of underdeveloped nations as well as of Japan and Canada were generally exempt. In 1965, the IET was extended to apply, on a voluntary basis, to most long-term lending (one year or more) by banks and other financial corporations, such as insurance companies. While effective in closing off New York as a capital market accessible to foreigners, the IET helped the offshore dollar markets. *ERP 1964,* p. 125; *ERP 1965,* pp. 76–77; *ERP 1966,* pp. 165–167; Sidney E. Rolfe and James Burtle, *The Great Wheel: The World Monetary System* (New York: Quadrangle, 1973), pp. 85–86, 95, 152–153.

30. The overall results of policies such as the IET and Operation Twist were mixed during the years 1961–1964. US private long-term capital flowed out of the country at an increasing net rate — from $2.6 billion in 1961 to $2.9 billion in 1962, $3.7 billion in 1963, and $4.4 billion in 1964. The Johnson Administration imposed voluntary capital controls in 1965 and made them mandatory in 1968. Short-term outflows were held to $.5 billion and $.8 billion in 1962 and 1963 respectively, down from an outflow of $1.6 billion in 1961, but in 1964 short-term outflows jumped to $2.1 billion. Errors and omissions remained above $1 billion in 1961, 1963, and 1964, indicating further hot money flows. *ERP 1966,* pp. 164–166.

31. The Eurodollar Market is a system by which dollar accounts, building up in European banks, are reloaned abroad without being converted into some currency other than dollars. Most of these loans are short-term. Considerable technical controversy exists over the actual size of the Eurodollar Market and its relation to US balance-of-payments deficits. Throughout the sixties and seventies, the Eurodollar Market was unregulated by reserve requirements. Hence, the usual process of pyramiding credit was controlled only by bankers' notions of what constituted prudent reserves and margins. Though the initial credit base presumably consisted of dollar outflows from the United States, the unregulated system permitted rapid expansion of credit beyond those outflows. Money "leaked out" of the system only when it was actually spent in the United States or converted into a foreign currency. The scale of "creation" and "leakage" are both disputed among experts. In due course, the Eurodollar Market has become more and more integrated with the US banking system. Initially in the early 1960s, American bankers were leery of the unregulated banking systems in London, Luxembourg, the Cayman Islands, and elsewhere that allowed banks to set their own reserve requirements and spreads and hence intensify competition. The 1929 crash in the United States had left a legacy of both strict federal legislation limiting banking competition and fear among bankers themselves of overextension and risk of failure. As the Eurodollar Market grew to such huge proportions, however, American bankers lost their inhibitions. This evolution was hastened by the progress of domestic inflation which made US banking regulations increasingly onerous. Reg-

ulation Q, for example, imposed a ceiling upon the interest offered on savings deposits and prohibited interest upon checking accounts. In 1966 and 1969, when interest rates climbed on Treasury bills and commercial paper, banks were prevented from paying competitive short-term interest rates. The consequent reduction in deposits forced American commercial banks to Eurodollar borrowing to keep up their reserves. In the 1969 credit crunch, for example, US banks' holdings of Eurodollars increased from virtually nothing to $15 billion, and because of the pressure, Eurodollar interest rates climbed from 6.25% in September 1968 to 11.31% in September 1969. The change in the 1970s from fixed to floating exchange rates boosted the Eurodollar market tremendously as bank participation in hedging practices through the forward exchange markets became active speculation in exchange rate fluctuations. The Eurodollar Market received a further giant boost by the "recycling" of oil profits to debtor countries after 1973. For a span of views from the vast literature, see Milton Friedman, "The Eurodollar Market: Some First Principles," *Morgan Guarantee Survey,* October 1969; Fritz Machlup, "Eurodollar Creation: A Mystery Story," *Banca Nationale del Lavoro, Quarterly Review,* September 1970, pp. 219-260; Helmut Mayer, "Multiplier Effects and Credit Creation in the Eurodollar Market," *Banca Nationale del Lavoro, Quarterly Review,* September 1971, pp. 233-262; Carl H. Stem, John H. Makin, and Dennis E. Logue, eds., *Eurocurrencies and the International Monetary System* (Washington, D.C.: American Enterprise Institute, 1976); Strange, "International Monetary Relations," ch. 6; Gunter Duffy and Ian H. Giddy, *The International Money Market* (Englewood Cliffs, N.J.: Prentice-Hall, 1978).

2. From Boom to Stagflation

1. For growth and employment statistics, see *ERP 1964,* p. 234; *ERP 1965,* pp. 189, 192. For new plant and equipment expenditures, see US Department of Commerce, *Survey of Current Business,* December 1975, statistical supplement, p. 2.

2. In 1964, M1 grew 4%, the largest annual growth rate since 1951, and bank credit grew 8%. International factors, however, caused considerable fluctuation in the Federal Reserve's policy throughout 1964. "Bank Credit and Monetary Development in 1964," *Federal Reserve Bulletin,* February 1965, pp. 213-225.

3. "Federal Fiscal Policy in the 1960's," *Federal Reserve Bulletin,* September 1968, pp. 701-718.

4. *ERP 1980,* p. 263; *ERP 1966,* p. 235; *ERP 1967,* p. 263.

5. See Table 2; Charles Schultze, ed., *Setting National Priorities: The 1971 Budget* (Washington, D.C.: The Brookings Institution, 1971), pp. 11-12. For defense spending and its relations to GNP, see Charles McLure, Jr., in Philip Cagan, ed., *Economic Policy and Inflation in the Sixties* (Washington, D.C.: American Enterprise Institute, 1972), pp. 40-45.

6. Johnson did propose and Congress did pass the inadequate Tax Adjustment Act of 1966. In addition, in November 1966, the investment tax credit was

temporarily suspended. *ERP 1966,* p. 11; *Federal Reserve Bulletin,* September 1968, pp. 705–706. For 1966–1968 monetary and fiscal policies and the politics behind them, see Arthur Okun, *The Political Economy of Prosperity* (Washington, D.C.: The Brookings Institution, 1970) pp. 69–99.

7. For the Fed's actions and consequent credit crunch in 1966, see Okun, *Political Economy,* pp. 69–70, 79–82; Robert A. Gordon, *Economic Instability and Growth: The American Record* (New York: Harper and Row, 1974), pp. 150–159; "Recent Bank Credit and Monetary Developments," *Federal Reserve Bulletin,* February 1967, pp. 187–200. The *Federal Reserve Bulletin* for any month in 1967 has complete statistics on interest rates and credit availability during 1966. See also the *Annual Report of the Board of Governors of the Federal Reserve System, 1966.*

8. Okun, *Political Economy,* pp. 84–86; *ERP 1968,* p. 268; International Institute for Strategic Studies, *The Military Balance, 1970–71,* p. 110; *ERP 1973,* p. 268.

9. Okun, *Political Economy,* pp. 86–89; Strange, "International Monetary Relations," pp. 264–265.

10. For wage and inflation rates, see *ERP 1980,* pp. 244, 263. For Kennedy "guideposts," see Gordon, *Economic Instability and Growth,* pp. 143–146; Arthur Burns and Paul Samuelson, *Full-Employment, Guideposts and Economic Stability* (Washington, D.C.: American Enterprise Institute, 1967).

11. For an insider's view, see Okun, *Political Economy,* pp. 62–99. See also Tobin, *New Economics,* pp. 34–35. For the concomitant effects of monetary policy, see Philip Cagan, *Recent Monetary Policy and the Inflation* (Washington, D.C.: American Enterprise Institute, 1971), pp. 101–103.

12. See Table 6; remarks by William McC. Martin in the Joint Economic Committee of Congress, *Hearings on the 1968 Economic Report of the President,* pt. I, pp. 177–178; *Annual Report of the Board of Governors of the Federal Reserve, 1969,* p. 6. For interest rate and money supply figures, see statistical appendices to the *Federal Reserve Bulletin.* For effects of the 1968 tax increase and the influence of monetary policy, see Okun, *Political Economy,* pp. 91–96; Gordon, *Economic Instability and Growth,* pp. 166–170. See also P. Cagan, "Monetary Policy," in *Economic Policy and Inflation in the Sixties,* ed. Cagan, pp. 98–103.

13. Charles E. McClure, Jr., "Gradualism and the New Economic Policy," in P. Cagan, ed., *A New Look at Inflation* (Washington, D.C.: American Enterprise Institute, 1973), pp. 46–47. See also *ERP 1970,* pp. 25–27.

14. See Table 1. For unemployment in December 1970, see *ERP 1971,* p. 225. For the Penn-Central bankruptcy, see *New York Times,* June 23, 1970, pp. 1, 42.

15. On Sept. 14, 1970, nearly 400,000 GM workers walked off the job, with no settlement until January 1971. Costs were staggering. In the third and fourth quarters of 1970, GM posted losses of $77 million and $135 million, the largest in its history. Costs to the national economy were estimated at $160 million per day in wages, car sales, tax revenue, and suppliers' sales. Strikes in 1970 lost 62 million man-days—the highest level in 10 years, one quarter of which was attributable to the GM strike. *New York Times,* Oct. 19, 1970, p. 65; Jan. 12, 1971, p. 28.

16. See Table 1. For classic studies of modern corporations and the unresponsive nature of prices in manufacturing, see Adolph A. Berle, Jr., and Gardiner C. Means, *The Modern Corporation and Private Property* (New York: Macmillan, 1948); J. Kenneth Galbraith, *The New Industrial State* (Boston: Houghton Mifflin, 1978).

17. See Tables 6 and 9. For detailed interest rate and money-supply figures, see *ERP 1973*, pp. 47–51, 261. For controversial analyses of the Fed's policies during 1972, see Sanford Rose, "The Agony of the Federal Reserve," *Fortune*, July 1974, pp. 90–93; Paul Lewis, "Challenging the Olympian Fed," *New York Times*, Aug. 18, 1974, sec. III, pp. 1, 5. For a rebuttal by Milton Friedman, Alan Greenspan, George Schultz et al, see "Controversy over Burns and Fed's Role," *New York Times*, Sept. 1, 1974, sec. III, p. 10.

18. For the dollar's position from 1968 to August 1971, see Strange, "International Monetary Relations," pp. 321–353.

19. Real GNP declined 2.2% in 1970 and rose only 3.4% in 1971. See Table 1. For 1971, the Administration wanted a business recovery but without more inflation. The CEA set an unusually ambitious target of 9.1% GNP growth and suggested a 7–8% growth in money supply. Arthur Burns claimed the Fed would continue the more moderate monetary growth of about 6% pursued throughout 1970. From February to July, however, as the Fed tried to resist a cyclical rise in interest rates that threatened recovery, the money supply spurted at a 10.8% rate. Speculative dollar outflows were enormous as foreign exchange markets began anticipating a devaluation. Upturn nevertheless started very slowly in the first half of 1971. Midyear saw little progress in reducing unemployment. Commentators began to talk about controls. Growth in dollar GNP was to be induced by more expansive monetary and fiscal policy; controls were to stop price inflation and thus make the growth real. P. Cagan, "Controls and Monetary Policy, 1969–1973," in *A New Look at Inflation*, ed. Cagan, pp. 8–13.

20. See Table 1.

21. See Table 1. For military expenditures and inflation in 1965, see *ERP 1967*, pp. 45–47.

22. A "simulation" of what economic performance would have been, with taxes adjusted to maintain full-employment balance from 1966 to 1968, projects rather meager results. Otto Eckstein, *The Great Recession* (Amsterdam: North Holland, 1978), ch. 3, pp. 23–38.

23. For the Phillips Curve, see A.W. Phillips, "Employment, Inflation and Growth," *Economica*, n.s. 29 (February 1962); 1–16.

24. By 1973, four major changes in the work force had occurred: male participation went up from 42.7 million in 1947 to 53.3 million in 1972, an increase of about 25%, whereas female participation nearly doubled, rising from 16.7 million to 33.3 million; the 16–17 and 18–19 male groups increased from 2.5 million in 1947 to 4.5 million in 1972, nearly doubling, whereas the number of prime age workers, 20–64 years old, only increased from 38.2 million to 46.8 million, or 22.5% over the same period; nonwhite male participation rates went up from 4.2 million in 1954 to 5.3 million in 1972, an increase of 26%, whereas white male

participation went up around 20% from 39.8 million to 47.9 million over the same period; and nonwhite females increased from 2.6 million in 1954 to 4.2 million in 1972, about 75%, whereas white females increased from 17.0 million to 29.0 million, about 70% over the same period. US Bureau of Labor Statistics, *Handbook of Labor Statistics 1973*, pp. 33–36. For the "shift to the left" and its inflationary consequences, see George Perry, "Changing Labor Markets and Inflation," *Brookings Papers on Economic Activity*, no. 3, 1970, pp. 411–448; Charles Schultze, "Has the Phillips Curve Shifted? Some Additional Evidence," *Brookings Papers on Economic Activity*, no. 2, 1971, pp. 452–467.

25. *ERP 1971*, pp. 77–78.

26. Nixon introduced his new welfare proposal in a televised speech in August 1969. The current Aid to Families with Dependent Children (AFDC) was said to be defective for its geographic inequality of aid distributed, insufficient work incentive, and destabilizing effects of increased benefits for fatherless families. Nixon's remedy, the new Family Assistance Plan (FAP), incorporated a negative income tax that guaranteed income at a $1600 level for a family of four on welfare with no outside income. Outside earnings would be encouraged by allowing the new worker to keep the first $60 a month of outside earnings without a reduction in benefits; beyond that, benefits would be reduced by only fifty cents of each dollar earned. The FAP, somewhat amended in the Ways and Means Committee, passed the House in April 1970 by an almost 2 to 1 vote but failed to emerge from the Senate Finance Committee. Senate attacks came from both liberal Democrats who found its benefits insufficient and conservative Republicans who found its work incentives too weak. Its reintroduction in 1971 faced increasing opposition in Congress and diminishing commitment from the Administration. "Transcript of Nixon's Address to Nation Outlining Proposals for Welfare Reform," *New York Times*, Aug. 9, 1969, p. 10; *ERP 1970*, p. 64. For the FAP and its reception in Congress, see Daniel P. Moynihan, *The Politics of a Guaranteed Income* (New York: Random House, 1973).

27. The Natural Rate of Unemployment is explained thus: "At any moment of time, there is some level of unemployment which has the property that it is consistent with equilibrium in the structure of *real* wage rates. At that level of unemployment, real wage rates are tending on the average to rise at a 'normal' secular rate, i.e., at a rate that can be indefinitely maintained so long as capital formation, technological improvements, etc., remain on their long-run trends. A lower level of unemployment is an indication that there is an excess demand for labor that will produce upward pressure on real wage rates. A higher level of unemployment is an indication that there is an excess supply of labor that will produce downward pressure on real wage rates." Milton Friedman, "The Role of Monetary Policy," *The American Economic Review*, no. 1 (1968): 8. Money illusion is defined as a mistaken view that, as prices are changing, behavior "should be guided by money quantities, such as money income or money wealth, rather than real variables." C.P. Kindleberger, "Money Illusion and Foreign Exchange," in *Leading Issues in International Economic Policy*, ed. F. Bergsten and W. Tyler (Lexington, Mass.: Lexington Press, 1973), p. 51.

28. Ronald Inglehart, "The Silent Revolution in Europe: Intergenerational Change in Post-Industrial Societies," *American Political Science Review*, no. 65, December 1971. See also Michel Crozier, ed., *The Crisis of Democracy, Report on the Governability of Democracies to the Trilateral Commission* (New York: New York University Press, 1975). For the relationship between welfare spending, social change, and inflation, see Morris Janowitz, *Social Control of the Welfare State* (Chicago: The University of Chicago Press, 1976).

29. See Table 4.

30. See Tables 10, 13.

31. The shift in the labor force of the major OECD countries is illustrated by the following percentage changes:

Country	Civilian labor force in agriculture		Women in civilian labor force	
	(1958)	(1969)	(1958)	(1969)
Belgium	8.7	5.2	30.7	32.6
Canada	14.3	8.2	25.3	32.2
France	23.7	15.1	—	—
West Germany	15.7	9.6	37.5	36.3
Italy	32.7	20.3	31.2	27.2
Japan	32.8	18.8	41.1	39.4
United Kingdom	4.5	2.9	33.8	36.7
United States	8.9	4.6	32.7	37.3

The figures for Belgium are from 1960 and 1969. The figures for Italy are from 1959 and 1969. OECD, *Labour Force Statistics: 1958-1969* (Paris, 1971), pp. 19, 29, 40, 48, 65, 91, 97, 127, 194.

For the migration of blacks and its impact on employment, see Vivian W. Henderson, "Regions, Race, and Jobs," in *Employment, Race, and Poverty*, ed. A.M. Ross and Herbert Hill (New York: Harcourt, Brace and World, 1967), pp. 90–97.

32. For how inflation stunts growth, see C. Lowell Harriss, "Causes and Effects of Inflation," and G.L. Bach, "The Economic Effects of Inflation," in *Inflation: Long-term Problems*, ed. C.L. Harriss, Proceedings of The Academy of Political Science, vol. 31, no. 4 (New York: The Academy of Political Science in conjunction with the Lehrman Institute, 1975), pp. 3–33.

33. Paul McCracken, ed., *Towards Full Employment and Price Stability* (Paris: OECD, 1977), p. 147.

34. According to Hicks, inflation causes social disruption by overturning customary income differentials. The last twenty years have seen two stages of inflation: demand-pull and cost-push. The first resulted from Keynesian demand management that raised the general level of economic activity at both ends of the business cycle and hence produced not only less unemployment during recessions but more inflation during booms. The second, cost-push stage came from wage increases. Social pressure for rising wages has been such that various occupations

have been able to indulge in competitive "leap-frogging," and labor scarcity is no longer needed for inflationary wage increases. In prolonged inflation, the need for continual upward adjustment of income calls into question customary income differentials and results in increasing social and economic discord. Sir John Hicks, *The Crisis in Keynesian Economics* (Oxford: Basil Blackwell, 1974), pp. 59–85.

35. See e.g. Joseph Spengler, *Population Change, Modernization, and Welfare* (Englewood Cliffs, N.J.: Prentice Hall, 1974); Robert Heilbroner, *An Inquiry into the Human Prospect* (New York: Norton, 1974); Anne and Paul Ehrlich, *The End of Affluence* (New York: Ballantine Books, 1974); Dennis Meadows et al, *The Limits to Growth* (New York: Universe Books, 1972).

3. The Decline and Fall of the Dollar

1. *ERP 1965*, pp. 75–77; *ERP 1980*, p. 317.

2. *ERP 1965*, p. 75.

3. See Table 9.

4. *ERP 1966*, pp. 165–168.

5. The dollar came under severe pressure during the first two months of 1965. The reasons included the deteriorating situation in Vietnam, rumors that the United States would remove the gold reserve requirement against deposits with the Federal Reserve and Fed notes, and French attacks on the dollar's reserve role in the international monetary system. Pressure peaked on March 5 when gold reached $35.17 per ounce. Johnson lifted the gold cover on Fed deposits, which freed some $5 billion in gold for possible use. IMF, *Annual Report, 1965*, pp. 100–101. See also Strange, "International Monetary Relations," pp. 281–299.

6. For de Gaulle's policies, see David P. Calleo, *The Atlantic Fantasy* (Baltimore: Johns Hopkins University Press, 1970).

7. General Charles de Gaulle, *Major Addresses, Statements and Press Conferences* (New York: French Embassy and Information Division, 1967) II, 179–181.

8. For Rueff's views in the context of the political and economic events of the interwar period, see Judith L. Kooker, "French Financial Diplomacy: The Interwar Years," in *Balance of Power or Hegemony: The Interwar Monetary System*, ed. Benjamin M. Rowland, The Lehrman Institute (New York: New York, University Press, 1976). Rueff's initial critique of the gold-exchange standard was linked to Anglo-French political and financial rivalry in Eastern Europe during the twenties: "The application of the gold-exchange standard had the considerable advantage for Britain of masking its real position for many years. During the entire postwar period, Britain was able to loan to Central European countries funds that kept flowing back to Britain, since the moment they had entered the economy of the borrowing countries, they were deposited again in London. Thus, like soldiers marching across the stage in a musical comedy, they could reemerge indefinitely and enable their owners to continue making loans abroad, while, in fact, the inflow of foreign exchange, which in the past had made such loans possi-

ble, had dried up." Jacques Rueff, *Les doctrines monétaires à l'épreuve des faits* (Paris: Alcan, 1932); trans. in Jacques Rueff, *The Age of Inflation* (Chicago: Regnery, 1964), p. 30. See also the edition of his writings, ed. E.M. Claassen and Georges Lane (Paris: Librairie Plon): *De l'aube au crépuscule* (1977); *Théorie monétaire* (1979); *Politique économique* (1980); *L'ordre sociale* (forthcoming). For an English version, see *The Collected Works of Jacques Rueff*, ed. W.H. Bruce Brittain and E.M. Claassen (The Lehrman Institute, forthcoming). For weaknesses of the gold-exchange standard and link to unsound domestic practices, see Rueff, *Balance of Payments*, trans. J. Clement (New York: Macmillan, 1967); Rueff, *Monetary Sin of the West* (New York: Macmillan, 1972).

9. Rueff's proposals for a return to the gold standard involved doubling the official price of gold, with the windfall permitting the United States to pay its external debt and the Europeans to fund the sterling balances. Rueff, *Monetary Sin of the West*, pp. 283–287. Throughout 1963–1965, Rueff's proposals competed with another French proposal, closely associated with then Minister of Economics, Valéry Giscard d'Estaing, for a multilateral Composite Reserve Unit (CRU) to substitute for the reserve currency roles of sterling and the dollar. Under this proposal, CRU would be created and allocated by the Group of Ten in strict proportion to each country's existing gold reserves (one CRU for every nine units of gold). International payment accounts would then be settled in gold and CRU's in fixed proportion. Hence, the United States would suffer an immediate gold loss unless it corrected its deficit. In February 1965, de Gaulle proclaimed the need for a return to the gold standard, and the CRU plan was abandoned. Strange, "International Monetary Relations," pp. 205–207, 218–220; Loukas Tsoukalis, *The Politics and Economics of European Monetary Integration* (London: Allen and Unwin, 1977), pp. 64–66.

10. "Now that most countries have abandoned the gold standard, the supply of the metal would, if the chief user of it restricted its holdings to its real needs, prove largely redundant. The United States has not been able to let gold fall to its 'natural' value, because it could not face the resulting depreciation of its standard. It has been driven, therefore, to the costly policy of burying in the vaults of Washington what the miners of the land have laboriously brought to the surface. Consequently, gold now stands at an 'artificial' value, the future course of which almost entirely depends on the Federal Reserve Board of the United States." J.M. Keynes, *A Tract on Monetary Reform* (London: Macmillan, 1924), p. 167. See also Robert Triffin, *Europe and the Money Muddle* (New Haven: Yale University Press, 1957), p. 299.

11. For an American exposition of this view, see C.P. Kindleberger, *The World in Depression, 1929–1939* (Los Angeles: University of California Press, 1973), pp. 28, 291–308.

12. For the "Triffin Paradox," see Robert Triffin, *Gold and the Dollar Crisis* (New Haven: Yale University Press, 1960). See also Triffin, *The World Money Maze* (New Haven: Yale University Press, 1966).

13. For an early version, see Robert V. Roosa, "Reforming the International Monetary System," *Foreign Affairs* 42 (October 1963): 107–123. For further de-

velopment, see Robert V. Roosa, *The Dollar and World Liquidity* (New York: Random House, 1967), pp. 109–126. See also Strange, "International Monetary Relations," p. 214.

14. Under the arrangements finally agreed upon at the IMF conference at Rio de Janeiro in 1967, the United States was to receive about $250 million out of each $1 billion of SDR's created. Common Market countries taken as a group were to receive about $180 million; the United Kingdom $116 million; Canada and Japan, about $35 million each; other developed countries, $280 million; and the less-developed countries $280 million. Final approval required an 85% majority of the voting power of the participating countries. This gave veto power not only to the United States but also to the Common Market countries as a group. *ERP 1968*, pp. 185–186. See also IMF, *Summary Proceedings, Annual Meeting 1967*, pp. 271–279; Stephen D. Cohen, *International Monetary Reform, 1964–1969: The Political Dimension* (New York: Praeger, 1970), pp. 50–69; Solomon, *The International Monetary System*, pp. 128–150; Strange, "International Monetary Relations," pp. 225–254; John Williamson, *The Failure of World Monetary Reform, 1971–1974* (New York: New York University Press, 1974).

15. SDR creation bore the following relation to world liquidity in millions of SDR's:

Total reserves	1970	1971	1972	1973
All countries	93,247	123,235	146,519	152,240
Industrial countries	65,806	88,793	97,461	95,750
SDR's	2,423	4,586	6,575	6,601

IMF, *International Financial Statistics,* December 1976, pp. 18, 20.

16. For liberal defenses of "benign neglect," see Gottfried Haberler and Thomas E. Willet, *A Strategy for US Balance of Payments Policies* (Washington, D.C.: American Enterprise Institute, 1971); Lawrence B. Krause, "A Passive Balance of Payments Strategy," *Brookings Papers on Economic Activity*, no. 3, 1970.

17. Strange, "International Monetary Relations," pp. 266–269. See also Charles A. Barrett, *Canada's International Trade: Trends and Prospects* (Ottawa: The Conference Board of Canada, 1976), esp. ch. 4.

18. The Kiesinger Great Coalition, which came to power in December 1966, was supposed to reduce defense spending and eliminate offset payments for American forces. On May 2, 1967, it signed a conciliatory tripartite agreement with the United States and United Kingdom which included a written assurance by Karl Blessing, the President of the *Bundesbank*, not to convert Germany's dollar holdings into gold; and to convert $500 million of the *Bundesbank's* dollar holdings into medium-term US government securities. Substantial arms purchases were to continue to cover US military expenditures in Germany. Despite continual pressure for D-mark revaluation, the Christian Democrats refused to adjust the

exchange rate. It was not until the Social Democrats won the Sept. 29, 1969, elections that the German government announced a revaluation of 9.29%. Strange, "International Monetary Relations," pp. 270–275, 323–332; Solomon, *The International Monetary System*, p. 111.

19. For the "black hole" metaphor, see Strange, "International Monetary Relations," pp. 275–278. For Japanese tactics and American relations, see Warren S. Hunsberger, *Japan and the United States in World Trade* (New York: Harper and Row, 1964) pp. 88–101. See also Calleo and Rowland, *America and the World Political Economy*, ch. 8.

20. In January 1967, British Chancellor of the Exchequer James Callaghan earnestly requested a reduction of interest rates in the United States, France, West Germany, and Italy. The US Treasury bill rate dropped to 3½% in mid-1967, from a September 1966 high of 5½%. Strange, "International Monetary Relations," p. 205.

21. Johnson's Jan. 1, 1968, State of the Economy address announced a seven-point policy to reduce the balance-of-payments deficit. The most important temporary measure was a mandatory program, effective immediately, to restrain direct foreign investment. This was expected to reduce the deficit by $1 billion. It included annual limits on the amount of new capital transfers, repatriation at least once per year of a specific share of income from foreign assets, and reduction of the net position on short-term assets to the average level of 1965–1966. Other temporary measures included reduction of overseas lending from US financial institutions (an expected $500 million reduction in the deficit), voluntary reduction of nonessential travel by US citizens, and reduction of US government expenditures abroad by increases in "offset" payments and investment in long-term US securities by foreign governments. The request for removing the gold cover came in Johnson's Jan. 17, 1968 State of the Union message. Removal was meant to emphasize the commitment to maintain the price of gold at $35 per ounce. *New York Times*, Jan. 2, 1968, p. 16; Strange, "International Monetary Relations," p. 269.

22. For the last quarter of 1967, balance on a liquidity basis was negative by $1,850 million, on official reserve transactions basis by $1,200 million; total 1967 deficit was $3,575 million (liquidity basis), or $3,400 million (reserve transactions basis). Moreover, the fourth quarter's decline in gold reserves was the largest in ten years. US Department of Commerce, *Survey of Current Business*, March 1968, pp. 15–16. As speculation reached its climax, from Mar. 10–14, private gold purchases totaled $850 million. On Mar. 12, the United States released $450 million in gold from Fort Knox to support the Gold Pool. On the same day the US Senate agreed to abolish the statutory gold backing for Federal Reserve notes. With private demand running at $200 million on Mar. 14, rumors began to circulate that France might opt out of the Gold Pool. Johnson was finally forced to appeal to Harold Wilson to close the London Gold Market. The central bank governors of Germany, Britain, Italy, the Netherlands, Belgium, and Switzerland were summoned to a weekend meeting in Washington. Strange, "International Monetary Relations," pp. 289–290.

23. Strange, "International Monetary Relations," p. 245.

24. See Strange, "International Monetary Relations," pp. 270–275, 323–332.

25. The "two-tier" gold market separated the official fixed dollar price for gold from the fluctuations of the private market. Central banks agreed not to buy or sell on the private gold market and thus could only convert their dollars through the US government, hence increasing ability to exert pressure. The dollar became effectively inconvertible for any country under US military protection. Rueff, *Monetary Sin of the West*, pp. 184–189. See also Strange, "International Monetary Relations," pp. 292–295.

26. For the French devaluation and the German revaluation, see Strange, "International Monetary Relations," pp. 323–332; Solomon, *The International Monetary System*, pp. 151–165.

27. See Strange, "International Monetary Relations," pp. 320–322. See also Tsoukalis, *The Politics and Economics of European Monetary Integration*.

28. *ERP 1973*, p. 294. By early 1971, drastic improvement in the American balance-of-payments deficits seemed improbable. An election-year decline in American interest rates and massive increase in the money supply accelerated the outflow of short-term capital. Harold van B. Cleveland, "How the Dollar Standard Died," *Foreign Policy* 5 (1971–72): 45. Early reports made a US trade deficit, the first since 1893, seem inevitable. In May, the dollar crisis began anew. On May 3 and 4, the *Bundesbank* was forced to buy $2 billion in dollars to defend the parity of the mark, and an additional $1 billion during the first 40 minutes of trading on May 5, after which the mark was allowed to float upward. Switzerland, Austria, the Netherlands, and Belgium followed. But the rush to sell dollars continued. European and other central banks began to demand that the United States settle its debts. Despite swaps and other measures, the United States paid out $3.1 billion to foreign official dollar holders in the first eight months of 1971 (mostly during July–August), including $864 million in gold, $394 million in foreign currencies, $480 million in SDR's, and $362 million against US reserves in the IMF. In addition, $600 million of US securities denominated in foreign currency were issued, bringing the total of such instruments to $2.1 billion. Charles A. Coombes, "Treasury and Federal Reserve Foreign Exchange Operations," *Federal Reserve Bulletin*, October 1971, pp. 783–814.

29. *ERP 1973*, p. 294.

30. US exports increased from $25,501 million in 1964 to $43,319 million in 1971. US imports rose from $18,700 million in 1964 to $45,579 million in 1971. *ERP 1980*, p. 316.

31. *ERP 1980*, p. 316. Deteriorating trade balances for 1965 and 1966 came essentially from an accelerating rise in imports, encouraged by the expanding economy. Imports of capital goods in 1966, for example, jumped 50%, a natural development with the US economy at full capacity. After the pause in 1966, the trade balance might have been expected to improve in 1967. The concurrent European recession, however, limited Europe's demand for imports. As the Johnson boom resumed in later 1967, 1968 saw the US trade surplus nearly eliminated. Domestic prices shot up in tandem with imports. US exports also rose, although

not nearly as much. *ERP 1967*, pp. 179–182; *ERP 1968*, pp. 167–170; *ERP 1970*, pp. 124–125.

32. The average Kennedy Round tariff reduction by all major industrial countries was 36–39% on a wide range of individual products. About two-thirds of the tariff cuts were 50% or more. The agricultural negotiations, however, achieved mixed results. Negotiations in special groups, such as grains, meats, and dairy products in particular, were generally unsuccessful. In addition, initial reductions in nontariff barriers were made with the establishment of an international anti-dumping code. See Preeg, *Traders and Diplomats*; Evans, *Kennedy Round*.

33. Evans, *Kennedy Round*, pp. 265–279; "Pressure Mounting for Import Quota Legislation," *Congressional Quarterly Weekly Report*, Feb. 2, 1968, pp. 155–160.

34. In its 1972 Report, the Council of Economic Advisers attributed the deterioration of the US trade balance to "the relatively poor price-cost performance of the US economy associated with the inflationary developments after 1965." *ERP 1972*, p. 151. See Tables 11 and 14. During the first half of the 1960s, US price stability made American goods more competitive in world markets. Through 1964, unit labor costs in manufacturing fell, while those in other countries remained unchanged. The unit value of US manufactured exports remained on par with competitors' export prices, developments which contributed to rising US trade surpluses through 1964. During the latter part of the 1960s, however, domestic price inflation eroded American price and cost competitiveness. From 1964 to 1969, unit labor costs in manufacturing rose 2.5% per annum in the United States, twice as fast as the 1.2% among competitors. Unit values of US manufactured exports also increased twice as fast as among competitors. In 1970, the anti-inflationary policies of the Nixon Administration brought some recovery to the US price and cost position. By 1971, the fall of the dollar against foreign currencies and the wage-price restraints of Aug. 15 kept unit labor cost rises in the United States substantially lower than in foreign countries, resulting in an overall improved American position. *ERP 1972*, pp. 151–152. For the view that income elasticity of foreign demand for US exports was abnormally low, and that the US trade balance would therefore worsen over time, see Hendrick S. Houthakker and Stephen P. Magee, "Income and Price Elasticities in World Trade," *Review of Economics and Statistics*, May 1969, pp. 111–125. See Table 11.

4. Nixon's Revolution

1. For Nixon's view, see Strange, "International Monetary Relations," pp. 336–337; Meier, *Problems of a World Monetary Order*, pp. 164–167.

2. The six measures announced were: a 90-day freeze on rents, wages, and prices (but not dividends) with a Cost of Living Council for enforcement; tax cuts of $6.2 billion; government spending cuts of $4.7 billion to bring a 5% cut in federal employment and a 10% cut in foreign aid; 10% job-development tax credits for buying American-produced capital goods, to be reduced to 5% in one year; a 10% import surcharge on 50% of total US imports, exempting only those subject

to nil duty or under mandatory quotas, which added about $2 billion to the cost of American imports (the surcharge, Nixon said, was a temporary measure to compensate American exports for "unfair exchange rates . . . when the unfair treatment is ended, the import tax will end as well"); and the gold convertibility of the dollar was suspended at the Treasury, the Federal Reserve suspended the swap network through which other central banks could change dollars for other currencies, and even the exchange of American-held SDR's for other assets was strictly limited. "Transcript of President's Address on Moves to Deal with Economic Problems," *New York Times*, Aug. 16, 1971, p. 14.

3. For Connally's personality and performance, see Solomon, *The International Monetary System*, pp. 190–191. For his link of overseas military spending to US payments deficits, see "Remarks of the Honorable John B. Connally, Secretary of the Treasury, at the International Banking Conference of the American Bankers Association, Munich, Germany," *Department of the Treasury News*, May 28, 1971. This link was plausible, as the comparison of US basic balance and net military transactions figures from 1960–1970, in millions of dollars, suggests:

Year	US basic balance	US net military transactions
1960	−1,155	−2,752
1961	20	−2,596
1962	−979	−2,449
1963	−1,262	−2,304
1964	28	−2,133
1965	−1,814	−2,122
1966	−1,614	−2,935
1967	−3,196	−3,138
1968	−1,349	−3,140
1969	−2,879	−3,341
1970	−3,038	−3,371

US Department of Commerce, *Survey of Current Business*, June 1971, table 1.

4. Pompidou and Nixon met on Dec. 13 and 14, 1971, and agreed that the dollar would be devalued by raising the price of gold from $35 to $38 per ounce. Discussions were to follow to realign exchange rates and establish wider margins. Without admitting it officially, Pompidou also agreed not to press for an early return to dollar convertibility, the American precondition for officially raising the gold price. Also unmentioned was US agreement to drop the import surcharge following general currency realignment. On Dec. 17, the ministers and governors of the Group of Ten convened in Washington at the Smithsonian Institution. New temporary margins of 2.25% above and below were agreed upon. Countries changing their parities in terms of gold might adopt "central rates" instead of parities. The former implied less fixity than the old "par value." Solomon, *The International Monetary System*, pp. 207–208. Changes in central rates for national currencies in terms of the dollar were agreed upon: Belgium +11.57, France +8.57, Italy +7.48, Germany +13.58, Japan +16.88, Netherlands +11.57,

Sweden +7.49, and Britain +8.57. Strange, "International Monetary Relations," p. 343.

5. *ERP 1974*, p. 279; *ERP 1981*, pp. 235, 293.

6. The US balance of payments in millions of dollars during 1970–1972 was:

Year	Long-term capital flows, net US gov.	Private	Nonliquid short-term private capital flow, net	Liquid private capital flows, net	Official reserve transactions balance
1970	−2,018	−1,429	−482	−5,988	−9,839
1971	−2,359	−4,401	−2,347	−7,788	−29,753
1972	−1,339	−152	−1,637	3,542	10,340

ERP, 1974, p. 351.

7. Connally's resignation was announced abruptly on May 16, 1972. He was replaced by George Schultz, the first professional economist to occupy the post of Secretary of the Treasury. Schultz was a specialist in labor problems and a monetarist partial to the "free market" in general and to floating exchange rates in particular. He won the President's confidence and the leadership of economic policymaking. Solomon, *The International Monetary System*, p. 220. For Schultz's view of this period, see George B. Schultz and Kenneth W. Dam, *Economic Policy Beyond the Headlines*, (New York: W. W. Norton, 1977).

8. A hint of coming changes in the US position appeared in a speech by Arthur Burns, then Chairman of the Federal Reserve, at the American Bankers Association's Annual International Monetary Conference in May 1972, just before Connally's resignation. Schultz's proposals at the opening session of the Sept. 25, 1972, IMF meeting called for wider bands of permissible fluctuation, stressed the importance of the SDR, underscored the asymmetry of the existing system, and proposed that a "surfeit of reserves" should also induce pressures for adjustment. Solomon, *The International Monetary System*, pp. 220, 226–227.

9. Peter G. Peterson, *The United States in the Changing World Economy*, vol. I (Washington, D.C.: GPO, 1971). For US share of total world exports and of world exports of manufactures, see US Department of Commerce, *International Economic Indicators*, March 1977, pp. 56–57.

10. See Tables 10–12.

11. See chapter 2, nn. 24, 31; Tables 10, 13; *ERP 1965*, pp. 121–131. For a later analysis of the changing work force and its consequences for productivity, see Emma Rothschild, "Reagan and the Real America," *New York Review of Books*, Feb. 5, 1981, pp. 12–18.

12. See chapter 3, nn. 17, 19.

13. Peterson, *Changing World Economy*, II, 47.

14. Peterson, *Changing World Economy*, I, 1–5.

15. For the theory of "free riders," see Kindleberger, *World in Depression*, pp. 301–308; Kindleberger, "Systems of International Economic Organization," in *Money and the Coming World Order*, ed. David P. Calleo, Lehrman Institute Book (New York: New York University Press, 1976).

16. Peterson, *Changing World Economy*, I, 12.

17. See Table 7.

18. For a mercantilist position, see Hans O. Schmitt, "Mercantilism: A Modern Argument," *The Manchester School* 47, no. 2 (June 1979): 93–111. For continuity between "benign neglect" of the late sixties and Nixon's devaluation, see H. Houthakker, *The Wall Street Journal*, Mar. 16, 1973.

19. See Table 7.

20. For a model to explain the behavior of surplus and deficit-prone countries under fixed and flexible exchange rates, see William M. Corden, *Inflation, Exchange Rates and the World Economy* (Chicago: University of Chicago Press, 1977).

21. For Keynes's early views on full employment and fixed exchange rates, see Robert J.A. Skidelsky, *Politicians and the Slump: The Labour Government of 1921–1931* (London: Macmillan, 1967), pp. 23–26. For the politics of monetary stabilization after World War I, see Charles S. Maier, *Recasting Bourgeois Europe: Stabilization in France and Italy after World War I* (Princeton: Princeton University Press, 1975).

22. Milton Friedman, Statement before Joint Economic Committee, US 88th Congress, 1st session, The US Balance of Payments, p. 3, Nov. 14, pp. 452–459, cited in Meier, *Problems of a World Monetary Order*, pp. 236–242. See also Harry G. Johnson, "The Case for Flexible Exchange Rates," *Federal Reserve Bank of St. Louis, 1969 Report*, June 1969. For monetarist dissenters from the enthusiasm for floating rates, aside from Rueff, see F.A. von Hayek, *Full Employment at Any Price?* Occasional Papers no. 45 (London: Institute of Economic Affairs, 1975); Robert A. Mundell, "Concluding Remarks," in *The New International Monetary System*, ed. Robert A. Mundell and Jacques J. Polak (New York: Columbia University Press, 1977), pp. 237–244. See also *Oxford Economic Papers* 28 (March 1976): 1–24.

23. See Strange, "International Monetary Relations," pp. 4–7.

24. See Table 8.

25. For a case study of Belgium, see "Politique de change — choix et implications," *Bulletin de la Banque Nationale de Belgique* I, no. 4 (April 1978): 1–67. See also *Oxford Economic Papers* 28 (March 1976): 1–24.

26. Edward Tufte, *Political Control of the Economy* (Princeton: Princeton University Press, 1978). Big mistakes in economic policy, Tufte notes, may be traced to covert aims and concealed priorities, such as the Vietnam financing in 1965-1967 and Nixon's all-out electoral stimulation. See also M. Kalecki, "Political Aspects of Full Employment," *Political Quarterly* 14 (October-December 1943): 322–331; William E. Nordhaus, "The Political Business Cycle," *Review of Economic Studies* 42 (April 1975): 169–190; Assar Lindbeck, "Stabilization Policy in Open Economies with Endogenous Politicians," *American Economic Review* 66 (May 1976): 1–19. Otto Eckstein, *The Great Recession*, ch. 4, notes the singularity of Nixon's success in manipulating the economy for the election, a success that apparently eluded the incumbent party in 1960 and 1968 (not to mention 1976 and 1980).

27. For impact of the 1971 dollar devaluation on US competitiveness, see James Riedel, "The Symptoms of Declining US International Competitiveness: Causes and Consequences," in the Joint Economic Committee of the Congress of the United States, *The International Economy: US Role in a World Market, Special Study on Economic Change* (Washington, D.C.: GPO, 1980), IX, 230–250. See also Robert E. Lawrence, "Toward a Better Understanding of Trade Balance Trends: The Cost Price Puzzle," *Brookings Papers on Economic Activity*, no. 1 (1979): 199–210.

28. US Senate Committee on Foreign Relations, Subcommittee on International Economic Policy, *International Debt, the Banks, and US Foreign Policy* (Washington, D.C.: GPO, 1977), pp. 9–12.

29. The United States is said to have enjoyed "seignorage" gains from issuing a reserve currency and hence to have had an extra incentive to inflate. Critical to this argument is the belief that interest rates do not adequately compensate foreign holders of dollars for American inflation and, in a floating-rate system, for currency depreciation. This may be seen as the consequence of structural factors that sustain demand for dollars, such as the absence of other vehicle currencies, political pressures, and "dirty floating" to prevent trade damage. Robert Mundell has argued that seignorage gains continue under floating rates as an "inflation tax"; that is, the rate of dollar inflation is inadequately compensated by interest and forward rates. Corden, *Inflation, Exchange Rates and the World Economy*, p. 91; Robert A. Mundell, "The Optimum Balance of Payments Deficit," in *Stabilization Policies in Interdependent Economies*, ed. E. Claassen and P. Salin (Amsterdam: North Holland, 1972).

30. The international investment position of the United States at the end of selected years from 1970 to 1979, in billions of dollars, was:

Assets	1970	1972	1974	1976	1977	1978	1979
US private abroad	118.8	149.7	201.5	282.4	314.1	378.0	435.8
Nonofficial foreign	80.7	98.7	117.1	159.1	168.7	200.7	257.9

ERP 1981, p. 349.

31. See chapter 2, n. 18; chapter 3, n. 27.

32. See e.g. the editorial "Monetary Responsibility," *New York Times*, July 21, 1972, p. 30.

5. The Revolution in Retrospect

1. Hans O. Schmitt, "Mercantilism: A Modern Argument." For a critical response, see David Vines, "Competitiveness, Technical Progress, and Balance of Trade Surpluses," and Schmitt's reply, "Rejoinder on Mercantilism," *Manchester School* 48, no. 4 (December 1980): 378–395.

2. London was the principal center of the international system before 1914, but after World War I was increasingly rivaled and constrained by New York.

American loans were, for example, the principal source of international liquidity for Germany. The United States had a large proportion of the world's gold (44% in 1923), and the British reserve position (9% in 1923) was precarious in view of the country's economic weakness after the war. The pound's collapse in 1931 brought down the system. The United States ended dollar convertibility into gold in 1933. American stabilization in 1934, with the dollar devalued to 59% of its former parity, and the tripartite agreement of the United States, Britain, and France in 1936 restored a semblance of the gold-exchange standard but within the general protectionist climate of the time. W. Arthur Lewis, *Economic Survey, 1919–1939* (London: G. Allen and Unwin, 1970); W. Adams Brown, Jr., *The International Gold Standard Reinterpreted, 1914–1934* (New York: National Bureau of Economic Research, 1940); Rueff, *The Monetary Sin of the West*, pp. 48–49; *Balance of Power or Hegemony*, ed. Rowland.

3. For a classification of political-monetary relationships, see Susan Strange, *Sterling and British Policy* (London: Oxford University Press, 1971), esp. ch. 1. See also Calleo and Rowland, *America and the World Political Economy*, ch. 5, 10; Calleo, "The Historiography of the Interwar Period: Reconsiderations," *Balance of Power or Hegemony*, ed. Rowland.

4. For domestic politics of monetary stabilization after World War I, see Maier, *Recasting Bourgeois Europe*. For US involvement in Italian stabilization, see Gian Giacomo Migone, *Gli Stati Uniti e il fascismo* (Milan: Feltrinelli, 1980).

5. A natural-law view prevails throughout the writing of Jacques Rueff. For his perspectives on scientific method, see e.g. Rueff, *The Gods and the Kings: A Glance at Creative Power* (New York: Macmillan, 1973).

6. Meier, *Problems of a World Monetary Order*, pp. 104–107.

7. Economists have three broad analytical approaches to explain the balance of payments: the relative prices, absorption, and monetary approaches. The first approach focuses on relative prices and ignores the influence of important macro variables such as income flows and stocks of assets. For an imbalance, relative price adjustment is recommended through exchange rate changes or demand-management policies. The absorption approach sees payments balances characterized, if not caused, by differences, *ex ante*, between an economy's aggregate income and its aggregate domestic spending (absorption). In effect, this approach extends to an open economy the Keynesian model for a closed economy. Income and expenditure flows are emphasized, and monetary variables and relative prices are ignored. Though the model's explanatory power is weak, linking the balance of payments to domestic income and expenditure is at least suggestive to policymakers. The third, monetary approach, is described in the text. D. G. Pierce and D. M. Shaw, *Monetary Economic Theories, Evidence and Policy* (London: Butterworth, 1976), pp. 337–355. See also chapter 6, n. 14; Corden, *Inflation, Exchange Rates, and the World Economy*.

8. See Kevin Allen and Andrew Stevenson, *An Introduction to the Italian Economy* (London: Barnes and Noble, 1974), pp. 151–171; Yoshio Suzuki, *Money and Banking in Contemporary Japan* (New Haven: Yale University Press, 1980), esp. pp. 203–216.

9. See chapter 4, n. 3.

10. See Table 8. For US liquidity and basic balances, see *ERP 1973*, p. 294. For net capital flows, see *ERP 1981*, p. 345.

11. For economic impact of the Vietnam War, see Eckstein, *The Great Recession*, pp. 23–28. For defense expenditures, see chapter 5. The increments in US direct investment abroad compare to increments in foreign direct investment in the United States, in millions of US dollars during 1961–1972, as follows:

Year	US direct investment abroad	Foreign direct investment in US
1961	2,852	482
1962	2,559	220
1963	3,460	332
1964	3,744	419
1965	4,994	434
1966	5,325	257
1967	4,692	869
1968	5,492	892
1969	6,050	1,003
1970	7,145	1,452
1971	8,020	385
1972	7,833	708

IERP 1974, p. 103.

12. American officials spoke confidently of restoring America's international payments to balance. In July 1965, for example, Secretary of the Treasury Henry Fowler predicted, "The deficit will be reduced by half by the end of 1965 and fully eliminated by the end of 1966." That accomplished, it would be essential to begin "the deliberate creation of a new reserve instrument (the special drawing right) to replace the additional liquidity arising out of the US balance-of-payments deficit, which is not expected to continue." Quoted in Rueff, *Monetary Sin of the West*, p. 200.

13. Paul McCracken et al., *Towards Full Employment and Price Stability* (Paris: OECD, 1977); *ERP 1977*, pp. 118–119.

14. For the argument that a balance-of-payments deficit is "exported inflation," see Rueff, *Balance of Payments*; Rueff, *Monetary Sin of the West*, pp. 159–167. Rueff defines inflation as excessive monetary growth, with rising domestic prices an epiphenomenon. Such a definition made irrelevant the frequent American rejoinder to Rueff in the 1960s that the United States could not be exporting inflation since its rate of domestic price increases was lower than in most countries in Europe, France included. But Rueff's definition also makes inflation difficult to measure. It is difficult enough to measure in a single country, as the controversy over measurements of the US money supply makes clear. And insofar as inflation is exported through the balance of payments, it presumably does not show up in domestic price increases or even in measurements of the money

supply. Complications in measuring growth in the national money supply are compounded in comparing rates among countries, each with its distinct banking structure, statistical system, and rate of real GNP growth. For all these reasons, comparing traditional national computations of rates of price inflation or monetary growth is highly misleading. See Tables 5–6.

15. Sir John Hicks, *The Crisis in Keynesian Economics*, pp. 59–85.

16. Lewis Lehrman, "International Monetary Order," in *Money and the Coming World Order*, ed. D. P. Calleo, pp. 71–120. Whether the external monetary system acts to check a particular country's inflation depends essentially on the systemic norm. Even countries with strong domestic coalitions averse to inflation, like Germany or Switzerland, have had great difficulty in arresting their inflation at a level much below the systemic norm, despite willingness in recent years to appreciate their currencies.

17. Milton Friedman, *Dollars & Deficits: Living with America's Economic Problems* (New Jersey: Prentice-Hall, 1968).

18. International Institute for Strategic Studies, *The Military Balance, 1963–64*, p. 32; *1968–69*, pp. 55–56; *1971–72* pp. 60–61.

19. For inflationary consequences of increasing military expenditures, see Emma Rothschild, "Reagan and the Real America," *New York Review of Books*, Feb. 5, 1981, p. 15. Rothschild points out with respect to the Reagan "remilitarization" program that the normally inflationary effects of military spending are even further exacerbated by the high-technology, big "systems" concentration (e.g. the MX system, nuclear submarines). Fewer, more specialized jobs and greater expenditures are the inflationary result.

20. David P. Calleo, "Inflation and American Power," *Foreign Affairs* 59, no. 4 (Spring 1981): 781–812.

21. Comparative Studies Staff, Office of International Policy, Social Security Administration. Country data are generously provided by the International Social Security Association and include old age, survivors' and invalidity, public health insurance, workmen's compensation, unemployment insurance, family allowances, public employee programs, and public assistance. The figures for Canada, Japan, the United Kingdom, and United States are adjusted to the fiscal year.

22. W. E. Kuhn, "Guest Workers as an Automatic Stabilizer of Cyclical Unemployment in Switzerland and Germany," *International Migration Review* 12 (Summer 1978): 210–224.

23. See chapter 2, n. 24, 28, 31; chapter 4, n. 11.

24. IMF, *International Financial Statistics*, December 1968, pp. 134, 136, 182, 320, 326; December 1974, pp. 142, 146, 204, 370, 374.

25. For the *Bundesbank's* legal structure and its relations with the federal government, see Bank for International Settlements, *Eight European Central Banks* (London: Praeger, 1963), pp. 54–96. For the constitutional barrier to central budget deficits, see *The Basic Law of the Federal Republic of Germany*, Articles 110–115.

26. See e.g. Strange, *Sterling and British Policy*; Kindelberger, *The World in Depression*.

6. Shocks at Home and Abroad

1. In 1971, unemployment averaged 5.9%, the consumer price index 4.3%, and real GNP growth 3.4%. *ERP 1981*, pp. 235, 271, 294. Eckstein, *The Great Recession*, pp. 40–75.

2. *ERP 1974*, p. 351.

3. *ERP 1974*, p. 304; *ERP 1980*, p. 284. See also Eckstein, *The Great Recession*, pp. 40–43.

4. *ERP 1974*, pp. 254, 261, 263. See also Eckstein, *The Great Recession*, pp. 72–73.

5. IMF, *International Financial Statistics*, December 1974, p. 34.

6. Eckstein, *The Great Recession*, p. 73.

7. *ERP 1974*, pp. 251, 318; *ERP 1980*, p. 263. See also Eckstein, *The Great Recession*, p. 73.

8. Eckstein, *The Great Recession*, pp. 49–54.

9. *ERP 1976*, p. 191; Eckstein, *The Great Recession*, p. 68, fig. 6.3.

10. By the time the OPEC embargo was lifted in March 1974, the acquisition cost of imported crude oil had risen from three to twelve dollars per barrel. Eckstein, *The Great Recession*, pp. 112–113.

11. *ERP 1975*, pp. 143–144, 251, 277, 304.

12. Cited in Harold van B. Cleveland and W. H. Bruce Brittain, *The Great Inflation: A Monetarist View* (Washington, D.C.: National Planning Association, 1976), p. 26.

13. French policy was rather special. The franc devalued 10.9% against the dollar and 17.8% against the revalued DM, thus helping to reduce the international consequences of the sharp wage increases. At the same time, the government reduced its own deficits while still increasing expenditures, and the money supply was kept very tight. For French inflation and money supply figures, see IMF, *International Statistical Yearbook*, 1979, p. 55. For wage increases, see Table 12. For government expenditures and financing figures, see IMF, *International Financial Statistics*, 1968–1974.

14. See e.g. Cleveland and Brittain, *The Great Inflation,* from which a good part of the chapter's analysis is derived. For internationalist-monetarist approach, see Marina von N. Whitman, "Global Monetarism and the Monetary Approach to the Balance of Payments," *Brookings Papers on Economic Activity*, no. 3 (1975): 491–555. See also Robert A. Mundell, *Monetary Theory: Inflation, Interest, and Growth in the World Economy* (Santa Monica, Cal.: Goodyear Publishing, 1971); Harry Johnson, "The Monetary Approach to Balance to Payments Theory," *Journal of Financial and Quantitative Analysis*, March 1972; Johnson, *Inflation and the Monetarist Controversy* (Amsterdam-London: North Holland, 1972).

15. For the observation that the duplicating mechanisms of the gold-exchange standard, as described by Rueff, had come to characterize big private American banks as well, see Paul Fabra, *Mutations dans la structure financière après*

Bretton Woods, (Instituto de Cooperacion Intercontinental: Madrid and, in French, Fondation Européene da la Culture: Amsterdam, 1980). See also Fabra's regular articles in *Le Monde*. Fabra is skeptical that the extraordinary expansion of the Eurodollar market can be explained primarily by a higher ratio of deposits to credits. The monetary base for the Eurodollar market, he argues, is in the form of deposits in domestic US banks. Because the deposits are maintained in a domestic US bank at the same time as dollar credits based on those deposits are issued by a Eurodollar bank, the duplicating mechanism of the gold-exchange standard is extended to the private sphere. No reduction takes place in the deposit base of the US bank, while an increase occurs in the deposit base of the Eurodollar bank. Inflation becomes inevitable, particularly in a period where the dislocation of oil price increases creates a desperate demand for liquidity to finance debts.

16. Cleveland and Brittain, *The Great Inflation*, pp. 14–15. See also Harold van B. Cleveland, "Reflections on International Monetary Order," *Columbia Journal of Transnational Law*, Nov. 3, 1972, pp. 403–419.

17. See Tables 5, 7.

18. For the inflation-devaluation spiral, see chapter 4, n. 26.

19. *ERP 1980*, p. 263. See also Eckstein, *The Great Recession*, p. 52; "Commodities: Something Has to Give," *Fortune*, April 1974, p. l2; "Trend of American Business," *US News and World Report*, May 27, 1974, p. 70.

20. Whereas the period from the Korean War to Vietnam was essentially free of exogenous shocks and consequently a time of stable economic growth, "since 1965, the shocks have come thick and fast, and have been the decisive movers of the economy." Eckstein, *The Great Recession*, p. 146.

21. Walt W. Rostow gives an exhaustive and fascinating analysis of the Kondratieff Cycle's implications for the world economy. The 1973–1977 price rise is seen as the upswing of the fifth Krondratieff cycle. Previous cycles peaked in the 1790s, 1860s, 1910s, and late 1940s as Malthusian shortages and anxieties effected a shift in terms of trade against manufactured goods, a shift that elicited new investment in producing or substituting for raw products and, generally in a couple of decades, a reversal. Rostow, *The World Economy: History and Prospect* (Austin: University of Texas Press, 1978), pp. 578, 626–643. See also N. D. Kondratieff, "The Long Waves in Economic Life," *The Review of Economic Statistics*, 17, no. 6 (November 1935): 105–115.

22. Walter Heller, "Taxes and Capital Shortfall," *Wall Street Journal*, Aug. 19, 1975; Rostow, *The World Economy*, pp. 635–643.

23. For prices, see Rostow, *The World Economy*, pp. 248–249.

24. Eckstein, *The Great Recession*, pp. 61–65.

25. The influence of the Texas Railroad Commission waned as domestic demand for petroleum began to outstrip supply and as the major oil companies expanded into other less well-controlled states. Texas, however, still produced 35% of the country's output into the mid-1960s. John M. Blair, *The Control of Oil* (New York: Pantheon Books, 1976), pp. 159–186.

26. Blair, *The Control of Oil*, pp. 169–204. For international comparison of

retail oil prices and of taxes as a percentage of the total price of oil, see *The Economist*, Mar. 1, 1980, p. 73. See also Table 18.

27. See Table 17.

28. From 1947 to 1965, US energy consumption grew at 2.8% annually; from 1965 to 1973, at 4.2% per year. With domestic production almost at peak capacity in 1972, the mandatory oil import quotas were removed. By 1973, the United States received one-third of its oil imports from the Arab nations. Eckstein, *The Great Recession*, pp. 114–115; Blair, *The Control of Oil*, pp. 159–188.

29. Eckstein, *The Great Recession*, pp. 1–4. For monthly figures, see *ERP 1974*, pp. 304, 318.

30. *ERP 1978*, p. 381. See also Table 7.

31. For changes in the US trade balance, investment income, and oil imports, see *ERP 1980*, pp. 316, 319, 320. For US manufactures balance, see US Department of Commerce, *International Economic Indicators*, March 1977, p. 51. See also Eckstein, *The Great Recession*, pp. 107–110. For US oil company profits, see US Department of Commerce, *Survey of Current Business*, Sept. 1974, pp. 14–17; Jan. 1975, pp. 13–14.

32. For increasing role of US banks in petrodollar recycling in the years immediately after 1974, see Paul A. Volcker, "The Recycling Problem Revisited," *Challenge*, July/August 1980, pp. 3–14. See also Fabra, *Mutations dans la structure financière*.

33. For the American attempt to use the oil crisis to reinforce its Western hegemony, see David P. Calleo, "The European Coalition in a Fragmenting World," *Foreign Affairs* 54 (October 1975): 103–112. For US proposals on the safety net, see Thomas O. Enders, "The Role of Financial Mechanisms in the Overall Oil Strategy," *Department of State Bulletin*, Mar. 10, 1975, pp. 312–317. The net was to have consisted of a $25 billion Solidarity Fund, of which the United States was to put up a 25% or 30% share. This share reflected voting power as well as lending obligations and borrowing rights. Borrowing was to be conditional on pursuit of "responsible" policies. For the French stance at the Washington Conference and Kissinger's response, see "Text of Communique to Washington Energy Conference and Summary Statement," and "Secretary Kissinger's News Conference of February 13," *Department of State Bulletin*, Mar. 4, 1974, pp. 220–230.

7. The Nixon-Kissinger World System

1. David P. Calleo, "The Political Economy of Allied Relations: The Limits of Interdependence," *Retreat from Empire? The First Nixon Administration*, ed. Robert E. Osgood (Baltimore: The Johns Hopkins University Press, 1973), pp. 207–239. See also articles in the same volume by Herbert S. Dinerstein, George Liska, Robert E. Osgood, and Robert W. Tucker. For the Nixon Administration's official attempts to define and explain its policies, see *United States Foreign Policy for the 1970's: A New Strategy for Peace* (Washington, D.C.: GPO, 1970); *United States Foreign Policy for the 1970's: The Emerging Structure of Peace* (Washington, D.C.: GPO, 1972).

2. Henry Kissinger, "Industrial Democracies and the Future," speech on Nov. 11, 1975, in *Department of State Bulletin*, Dec. 1, 1975, pp. 757–769; Kissinger, interview with Barbara Walters, May 5–8, 1975, *Department of State Bulletin*, May 26, 1975, pp. 665–675.

3. For American policy in the Third World, see Benjamin M. Rowland, "Economic Policy and Development: The Case of Latin America," *Retreat from Empire?* ed. Osgood, pp. 241–277.

4. For an early analysis of the liberal dilemma, see Robert W. Tucker, *The Inequality of Nations* (New York: Basic Books, 1977).

5. In 1979, roughly one-quarter of US exports went to non-OPEC developing countries, a share close to that taken by Western Europe. The dependence of Japan and the EEC on trade with the Third World is substantially greater. Geoffrey Barraclough, "The Struggle for the Third World," *New York Review of Books*, Nov. 9, 1978, pp. 47–58. See also *ERP 1981*, p. 347.

6. For Kissinger's views, see his speech "Energy, Raw Materials and Development: The Search for Common Ground," *Department of State Bulletin*, Jan. 12, 1976, pp. 37–48.

7. Solomon, *International Monetary System*, pp. 309–319. See also "The Spirit of Rambouillet," *The Economist*, Nov. 22, 1975, pp. 77–78; "Jawing in Jamaica," *The Economist*, January 1976, p. 81.

8. "How the Snake Lost Its Charm," *The Economist*, Mar. 20, 1976, pp. 69–70.

9. *ERP 1981*, pp. 343, 344.

10. See McCracken et al., *Towards Full Employment and Price Stability*.

11. For an American critique of the "locomotive" theory, see Geoffrey E. Wood and Nancy Ammon Jianakoplos, "Coordinated International Expansion: Are Convoys or Locomotives the Answer?" *Federal Reserve Bank of St. Louis*, 60, no. 7 (July 1978). See also *Annual Report of the Deutsche Bundesbank, 1976*, p. 48.

12. *New York Times*, Nov. 1, 1979, p. D1. Comparing the annual percentage increases of US and West German GNP growth, interest, and inflation rates shows the changes in German policy and situation:

| | West German % change from prior year | | | US % change from prior year | | |
Year	GNP growth	CPI	Discount rate	GNP growth	CPI	Discount rate
1976	5.4	4.3	3.5	5.9	5.8	5.25
1977	2.8	3.7	3.0	5.3	6.5	6.00
1978	3.6	2.8	3.0	4.4	4.7	9.50
1979	4.5	4.1	6.0	2.3	11.3	12.00

German GNP growth is in 1972 prices; US GNP growth is in 1967 prices. IMF, *International Financial Statistics*, Dec., 1980, pp. 160, 405; US Department of Commerce, *International Economic Indicators* (Washington, D.C.: GPO, 1980), pp. 7, 43.

13. "The Raging Fight over Burke-Hartke," *Business Week*, Feb. 12, 1972, p. 14.

14. The bill restored presidential power to make limited tariff reductions and eliminated the American Selling Price as a basis for setting import duties. It also proposed "new authority to act against countries that employ export subsidies in competition with the US exports in third markets" and liberalized adjustment assistance "to workers and businesses adversely affected by imports." *ERP 1971*, pp. 154–158; *ERP 1969*, pp. 4–126.

15. Calleo and Rowland, *America and the World Political Economy*, ch. 8, esp. pp. 210, 216.

16. Riedel, "Symptoms of Declining US International Competitiveness"; US Department of Commerce, *International Economic Indicators* (Washington, D.C.; GPO, March 1981), p. 36.

17. Robert E. Lawrence, "An Analysis of the 1977 US Trade Deficit," *Brookings Papers on Economic Activity*, no. 1 (1978): 182; "Toward a Better Understanding of Trade Balance Trends—The Cost-Price Puzzle," *Brookings Papers on Economic Activity*, no. 1 (1979): 191–210. See also Riedel, "The Symptoms of Declining US International Competitiveness."

18. See Table 15.

19. US Department of Commerce, *International Economic Indicators*, March 1981, pp. 12, 15.

20. The Nixon Administration's initial "Project Independence" stressed reducing dependency on foreign oil. Research and development was to increase domestic energy production, and decontrol of oil prices was to control consumption, with a windfall profits tax to rectify inequities. Watergate paralyzed the President, and Congress provided no alternative overall program. *ERP 1974*, pp. 122–125. For Ford's program, see *ERP 1975*, pp. 20–24. The program was finally passed in a much diluted form as the "Energy Policy and Conservation Act" in 1975. *ERP 1976*, pp. 23–24; *The New York Times*, Dec. 23, 1975, p. 1. See also Cranfurd D. Goodwin, ed., *Energy Policy in Perspective: Today's Problems, Yesterday's Solutions* (Washington, D.C.: The Brookings Institution, 1981).

21. US Department of Commerce, *Survey of Current Business*, September 1974, pp. 14–17; January 1975, pp. 13–14.

22. US Department of Commerce, *International Economic Indicators*, March 1981, pp. 20, 38, 40.

23. For comparative US energy situation, see International Energy Agency, *Energy Policies and Programmes of IEA Countries*, (Paris: OECD Annual Publication): Robert Stobaugh and Daniel Yergin, eds., *Energy Future, Report of the Energy Project at the Harvard Business School* (New York: Random House, 1979); Hans H. Landsberg, et al., *Energy: The Next Twenty Years*, report sponsored by Ford Foundation (Cambridge: Ballinger, 1979).

24. See Table 17.

25. See Table 18.

26. See Table 16.

27. Loring Allen, *OPEC Oil* (Cambridge: Oelgeschlager, Gunn and Hain, 1979), pp. 93–101.

28. Malcolm MacKintosh, "The Impact of the Middle East Crisis on Super-

Power Relations," *Adelphi Papers* (London: International Institute for Strategic Studies, Spring 1975), no. 114, pp. 1–19.

29. Leslie M. Pryor, "Arms and the Shah," *Foreign Policy* 31 (Summer 1978): 56–71; Geoffrey Kemp, "The Military Build-up: Arms Control or Arms Trade?" *Adelphi Papers* (London: The International Institute for Strategic Studies, Spring 1975), no. 114, pp. 31–37.

30. By 1976, the Saudis' production averaged 8.2mb/d, while their installed capacity was estimated at 11.8mb/d. Their excess capacity, more than two-thirds of Iran's production and more than the total production of any of OPEC's other eleven members, guaranteed them the role of OPEC's regulator. In a price war among the cartel members, the Saudis could increase production until the price dropped as much as 44% and still make a profit, while other OPEC members with smaller excess capacity (Iran 18%, Algeria 16%, Indonesia 14%) would begin losing money if the price dropped more than 14–18%. Conversely, the Saudis could prevent price increases by threatening to increase production. Dankwart A. Rustow, "US-Saudi Relations and the Oil Crisis in the 1980's," *Foreign Affairs* 55 (April 1977): 503–505.

31. US Senate Committee on Foreign Relations, Subcommittee on International Economic Policy, *International Debt, the Banks and US Foreign Policy* (Washington, D.C.: GPO, 1977), pp. 9–12, 43; Volcker, "The Recycling Problem Revisited."

32. Rueff, *Mutations dans la structure financière après Bretton Woods.*

33. Robert N. Dunn, Jr., "Exchange Rates, Payments Adjustment, and OPEC: Why Oil Deficits Persist," *Princeton Essays in International Finance*, no. 137, December 1979.

34. For mercantilist strategy, see Schmitt, "Mercantilism: A Modern Argument." See also Dunn, "Exchange Rates."

35. "EMS Brief," *The Economist*, Mar. 17, 1979, pp. 74–75. For different countries' views and possible implications for US-European relations, see W. Kohl, G. Basevi, S. Papas, and J. McDonald, eds., *The Political Economy of the EMS*, Occasional Paper no. 3 (Bologna: Bologna Center Research Institute, Johns Hopkins University, 1980).

36. Throughout the 1970s several countries exhibited the phenomenon of current account and basic deficits accompanied by increasing national reserves which were financed through short-term capital flows. See e.g. external accounts of Belgium, Sweden, Italy, Brazil, Israel, and Peru in IMF, *Balance of Payments Yearbook, 1980*, vol. 31.

37. US Senate Committee on Foreign Relations, Subcommittee on International Economic Policy, *International Debt, the Banks and US Foreign Policy*, pp. 59–68.

8. The Carter Cycle

1. See Table 3.

2. *ERP 1975*, p. 279; *ERP 1977*, pp. 203, 221, 236. For Ford period, see Eck-

stein, *The Great Recession*, much of which is reflected in the text.

3. *ERP 1976*, pp. 50–58.

4. *ERP 1976*, p. 239.

5. *ERP 1976*, p. 173. For rise in the Dow Jones Average, see "Market Is Climbing at a Record Pace," *New York Times*, June 6, 1975, pp. 41, 46.

6. Growth presumably slowed as soon as depleted inventories adjusted. The growth rate for 1976's last three quarters fell to 3.75%. Though business investment was high in many industries, the Ford Motor strike discouraged spending in the huge automobile sector. Fiscal policy remained stimulating, with a federal deficit of $58.3 billion. Monetary conditions were relatively moderate. M1 grew by 5%, and with demand limited and inflationary expectations sharply diminished, interest rates were low. Inflation fell to 5%. Real personal income grew 4.1% for the year with wages up 2%. *ERP 1977*, pp. 58–99.

7. *OECD Economic Outlook*, December 1976, p. 77.

8. "The Final Stretch—and Both Men Are Behind," *The Economist*, Oct. 30, 1976, pp. 45–46.

9. *ERP 1977*, pp. 31–32, 268–269.

10. *ERP 1978*, pp. 13, 16–20, 46, 82.

11. *ERP 1978*, pp. 54, 86–87.

12. For Carter's original energy proposals, see *OECD Economic Survey: United States*, July 1978, pp. 53–54. To contrast them with the final product, see "Seven Years after the Embargo, U.S. Has an Energy Policy," *Congressional Quarterly Weekly Report*, Oct. 25, 1980, pp. 3207–3212.

13. "Administration Sees 1980 Budget Surplus with Inflation, Unemployment Rates at 5%," *New York Times*, July 2, 1977, pp. 1, 27; "Lance on US Economy: Pleased, But Not Satisfied," *New York Times*, July 8, 1977, p. D5; "Carter Begins Talks on Tightening Budget for 1979," *New York Times*, June 25, 1977, p. 7.

14. *ERP 1978*, p. 35.

15. *ERP 1978*, pp. 73–75, 340.

16. *ERP 1979*, pp. 46–47, 77–85; *New York Times Supplement*, New York Times News Service, Oct. 25, 1978, pp. 25–27.

17. *ERP 1979*, pp. 25–27; *ERP 1980*, pp. 207, 263.

18. *ERP 1981*, pp. 343–345. See also Table 3.

19. *ERP 1979*, pp. 153–156.

20. The Council of Economic Advisers predicted that the budget would "move significantly toward restraint in the next fiscal year." *ERP 1980*, p. 68. Their record for prediction was erratic, as shown by their projected and the actual balances of federal receipts and outlays in millions of dollars in the period:

Fiscal Year	Projected	Actual
1978	−61,847	−48,807
1979	−37,379	−27,694
1980	−29,013	−59,563

ERP 1978, p. 340; *ERP 1979*, p. 263; *ERP 1981*, p. 316.

21. "Nation Faces Mild Recession, Administration, CBO Agree; Caution Urged on Stimulus," *Congressional Quarterly Weekly Report*, July 14, 1979, pp. 1381-1382.

22. For quarterly shifts in exchange rates, see *ERP 1980*, p. 315. For monthly rises in interest rates, see *ERP 1980*, p. 279. For official explanation, see *ERP 1980*, pp. 174-179.

23. US interest rates and money stock during 1976-1980 were:

Year	Prime rate charged by banks	Growth of money supply (M1) % change from prior year	
		Target	Actual
1976	6.84	4.5 - 7.5	5.8
1977	6.83	4.5 - 6.5	7.9
1978	9.06	4 - 6.5	7.2
1979	12.67	3 - 6	5.5
1980	15.27	4 - 6.5 (M-1B)	7.1

ERP 1981, pp. 53, 308. For the Fed's policies, see *ERP 1977,* pp. 33-35; *ERP 1978,* pp. 56-60.

24. By 1974, for example, the growing use of Electronic Funds Transfer (the use of computers to transmit debt and credit) began to make it easy to circumvent such 1930s banking legislation as the ban on interest for demand deposits, limits on interest rates for time deposits, and limits on access or competition within the banking system. Similarly, the Negotiable Order of Withdrawal (NOW account – an interest-bearing checking account or a savings account with check-cashing privileges), begun in 1972 in Massachusetts, drew money out of checking accounts into interest-paying but equally flexible instruments. The first effect was that the money supply became much more difficult to define, since the money usually counted in M1 as demand deposits shifted to other instruments. The second effect was an increase in the velocity of money. Thus, a $1 increase in M1 led to a $5.11 in GNP in early 1975, and a $5.60 increase in May 1977. Increased velocity and decreased ability to gauge monetary aggregates made the Fed's control of the money supply tenuous. "More Bang for the Buck," *Fortune*, May 1977, pp. 202-228; *Fortune*, Apr. 24, 1978, p. 82; *ERP 1979*, pp. 47-53; *ERP 1980*, pp. 51-58. For a radical critique of the Fed's pretension to control the money supply, see Lewis E. Lehrman, *Monetary Policy, the Federal Reserve System, and Gold*, Morgan Stanley, Investment Research Memorandum, Jan. 25, 1980.

25. *ERP 1980*, pp. 51-58, 263, 271, 315.

26. For Volcker, see *New York Times Magazine*, Dec. 2, 1979, pp. 58, 62. For chronology of the cabinet shuffle, see "Letters of Resignation and Acceptance," *The New York Times*, July 20, 1979, p. 10; "Carter Replaces Bell, Blumenthal, Califano; Miller Goes to Treasury," *New York Times*, July 20, 1979, pp. 1, 8.

27. *ERP 1980*, pp. 54-55; Paul Volcker, "Statements to Congress on October

17, 1979," *Federal Reserve Bulletin* 65, (November 1979): 888–889.

28. The figures show the simultaneous rise of interest rates and the dollar:

Date	Prime rate charged by banks	US dollar multilateral trade-weighted average (March 1973 = 100)
March 1979	11 3/4 - 11 3/4	88.4
June 1979	11 3/4 - 11 1/2	89.6
December 1979	15 1/2 - 15 1/4	86.3
March 1980	16 3/4 - 19 1/2	90.3

ERP 1981, pp. 309, 343.

29. Edward Meadows, "Volcker Takes on the Money Serpent," *Fortune*, Nov. 19, 1979, pp. 46–50; "Why Wall Street Looks Oversold," *The Economist*, Oct. 20, 1979, pp. 111–112.

30. See e.g. "Manic Gold Trading Poses a Global Threat," *Business Week*, Oct. 1, 1979, p. 56; "More Shocks for the Monetary System," *Business Week*, Jan. 21, 1980, pp. 86–89.

31. World petroleum prices in US dollars per barrel of Saudi Arabian light crude during 1977–1980 were:

Date	Price
December 1977	$12.40
December 1978	12.70
December 1979	24.00
April 1980	28.00
December 1980	32.00
April 1980	32.00

IMF, *International Financial Statistics,* March 1980, p. 52; June 1981, p. 52.

32. *ERP 1980*, pp. 54–55; Volcker, *Federal Reserve Bulletin* 65 (November 1979): 888–889.

33. Thanks to inflation and the consequent "fiscal drag," revenues would increase sharply. If expenditures could be held and a deep recession avoided, the budget would naturally move close to balance. With Congress passing a windfall tax on oil company profits from deregulation, a major boost to federal revenue could be expected as early as fiscal 1982. Furthermore, US gasoline excise taxes were still by far the lowest in the industrial world. A fifty cent tax on gasoline was all that was needed, budget planners argued, to balance the 1981 budget. In short, an Administration seriously determined to bring inflation under control might well have hoped to achieve a balanced budget in fiscal 1981. Steven Rattner, "50¢ Tax on Gasoline Urged; Stricter Utility-Fuel Plan Due," *New York Times*, Dec. 7, 1979, p. D4.

34. The rise in oil prices "has at least set back the timetable for visible and sustained relief from inflation a quarter or two." Paul Volcker, speech on Jan. 2, 1980, *New York Times*, Jan. 3, 1980, pp. D1, D3. See also *ERP 1981*, p. 134.

35. Hendrick Smith and Edward Cowan, "Carter Increases Arms Funds and Foresees Mild Recession in $616 Billion Budget for '81," *New York Times*, Jan. 29, 1980, pp. 1, 11–12. The relative significance of US defense expenditures in relation to overall budget deficits, 1975–1981, in millions of US dollars, was:

Year	Defense expenditures	Budget deficits
1975	85,552	–45,154
1976	89,430	–66,413
Transition quarter	22,307	–12,956
1977	97,501	–44,948
1978	105,186	–48,807
1979	117,681	–27,694
1980	135,856	–59,563
1981	161,088	–55,215

ERP 1981, pp. 314–315.

36. For the Administration's view of events and the confusing problems posed for its policies, see *ERP 1981*, esp. pp. 132–138, 146–152, 173–174.

37. "Carter Seeks 'Prudent' 1981 Spending Plan," *Congressional Quarterly Weekly Review*, Feb. 2, 1980, pp. 235–245; "Carter and Congress Weigh New Steps to Fight Inflation," *Congressional Quarterly Weekly Review*, Mar. 1, 1980, pp. 587–589.

38. US Congressional Budget Office, "Entering the 1980's: Fiscal Policy Choices," January 1980, p. 44, table 18.

39. *ERP 1981*, pp. 158–162, 293, 309; *Federal Reserve Bulletin*, June 1980, p. A26.

40. *ERP 1981*, p. 169.

41. Robert M. Bleiberg, "Independent Fed: Credit Restraint Yields to Election-Year Pump-Priming," *Barron's*, Sept. 29, 1980, p. 7; "Is the Fed Fueling the Carter Campaign?" *Business Week*, Oct. 6, 1980, pp. 20–22.

42. "US Finds the Economy in 3rd Quarter," *New York Times*, Sept. 20, 1980, pp. 1, 35.

43. For Carter's revitalization plan, see *Business Week*, Sept. 8, 1980, pp. 34–35; *ERP 1981*, pp. 165–167.

44. For Reagan's "supply-side" economics, see Norman B. Ture, " 'Supply-side' Analysis and Public Policy," paper presented to Economic Policy Round Table, The Lehrman Institute, November 1980. For a critique, see Robert L. Heilbroner, "The Demand for the Supply-Side," *New York Review of Books*, June 11, 1981, pp. 37–41. See also Leonard Silk, "The Republican Policy on Gold," *New York Times*, Aug. 1, 1980, p. D2; interview with Arthur Laffer, "Reagan's Economic Guru," *Euromoney*, August 1980, pp. 31–34.

45. Kenneth H. Bacon, "Better Economic News Helps Smother Flames of Fed-Carter Dispute," *Wall Street Journal*, Oct. 6, 1980, pp. 1, 32.

46. Though in certain circumstances rapid growth may take place along with inflation, in advanced societies the resistance to mounting inflation ultimately tends to generate restraining policies that make long-term investment increasingly unattractive. For harmful effects of inflation on growth, see chapter 3, n. 32, 34; Morris Janowitz, *Social Control of the Welfare State*, pp. 10–16.

47. Henry Kaufman, "The Disregard for Capital," *Bond Market Research*, Salomon Brothers, May 1980; Kaufman, "America's Economic and Financial Dilemma," *Bond Market Research*, February 1980.

9. Reagan's Temptation

1. For a critique of Thatcher's economic policy, see *The Cambridge Economic Policy Review* 7, no. 1 (April 1981).

2. Kissinger's interview "Kissinger Critique II," *The Economist*, Feb. 10, 1979, pp. 31–35.

3. For SALT I negotiations, see Raymond L. Garthoff, "SALT I: An Evaluation," *World Politics*, 31 (October 1978): 1–25; "Negotiating with the Russians: Some Lessons from SALT," *International Security* 1 (Spring 1977): 3–24.

4. "Kissinger Warns Soviets and Cuba on Aid to Angola," *New York Times*, Nov. 25, 1975, pp. 1, 5. For Kissinger's policy toward Angola, see Gerald Bender, "Angola, the Cubans and American Anxieties," *Foreign Policy* 31 (Summer, 1978): 3–30.

5. For Carter's early disarmament proposal, see John F. Lehman, "Reflections on the Quarter: SALT after Moscow," *Orbis*, 21 (Summer 1977): 187–190. For Carter's human rights initiatives, see "Letter to a Dissident," *The Economist*, Feb. 26, 1977, p. 41.

6. For chronology of US-European frictions in the wake of the Soviet invasion of Afghanistan, see *The Economist*: "How to Be a Good Ally Without Putting Oneself Out," Apr. 19, 1980, pp. 47–48; "The Wandering President Returns to Raised Eyebrows," May 24, 1980, pp. 59–60; "Fourteen Anxious Faces Watch as Schmidt Enters the Bear's Den," June 28, 1980, pp. 41–42.

7. For de Gaulle's 1958 proposals for a three-power directorate and US response, see David Schoenbrun, "De Gaulle and the Anglo-Saxons," *Le Figaro*, July 9–17, 1964. For a suggestion that the idea be revived, see my colleague, Michael Harrison, "Reagan's World," *Foreign Policy*, 43 (Summer 1981): 3–16.

8. For the significance of the volunteer army, see Kenneth Coffey, *The Strategic Implications of the All-Volunteer Force* (Chapel Hill: University of North Carolina Press, 1979), pp. 51–99. For figures on real US defense spending, see International Institute of Strategic Studies, *The Military Balance, 1978–79*, p. 87; *1980–81*, p. 94.

9. Defense spending increases were especially heavy in fiscal years 1979 ($12.5 billion), 1980 ($18.2 billion), and 1981 ($25.2 billion). In the same years, overall fiscal deficits were $27.7 billion, $59.6 billion, and $55.2 billion respectively.

(Figures for both 1980 and 1981 are estimates.) In a downswing, of course, deficits are greatly swollen by antirecession stabilizers as well as a relative decline in revenue. *ERP 1981*, pp. 314–315.

10. Karl Kaiser, "The Great Nuclear Debate: German-American Disagreements," *Foreign Policy* 30 (Spring 1980): 83–110. See also David P. Calleo, "Faulting Nuclear Diplomacy," *New York Times*, June 7, 1978, p. E23; Calleo, "Of Atoms and Allies," *New York Times*, June 18, 1978, p. E19. For a defense of the American position, see Joseph Nye, "Nonproliferation: A Long-Term Strategy," *Foreign Affairs* 56 (April 1978): 601–623.

11. In the initial Reagan proposals, a progressive series of "supply-side" tax cuts were to reach an annual sum of $100 billion by fiscal 1983. These were expected to restore prosperity and thus augment federal revenues and cut transfer payments. Widespread deregulation was to encourage long-range growth. To compensate for short-term losses of revenue, cuts of some $49.1 billion in civilian expenditures were proposed for fiscal 1982, with the total to rise to $79.9 billion in fiscal 1983. Large increases in military spending authorizations, however, were requested on March 4, but the impact on fiscal 1982 was estimated at only $4.8 billion. In general, tight monetary policy was counted upon to dampen any inflationary impulse from fiscal policy. The Fed would be helped, it was hoped, because the new Administration's manifest determination and competence would lower "inflationary expectations." The White House, Office of the Press Secretary, *America's New Beginning: A Program for Economic Recovery*, Feb. 18, 1981. For military requests, see *New York Times*, Mar. 5, 1981, p. A1.

12. See chapter 5.

13. International Institute for Strategic Studies, *The Military Balance 1981–1982*, pp. 112–113.

14. For the figures, see n. 11 above. For economic consequences, see Lester Thurow, "How to Wreck the Economy," *New York Review of Books*, May 14, 1981, pp. 3–8. For criticism of America's defense strategy and its budgets, see James Fallows, *National Defense* (New York: Random House, 1981). For American foreign policy and its economic costs, see James Chace, *Solvency: The Price of Survival* (New York: Random House, 1981).

15. Whereas from fiscal 1977 through fiscal 1980, expenditures for strategic forces increased from $9.4 billion to $10.8 billion, expenditures for General Purpose Forces jumped from $40.2 billion to $50 billion (current dollars). *Department of Defense Annual Reports, FY 1977*, p. A13; *FY 1980*, p. 320. Conventional forces are a much larger proportion of the defense budget than strategic forces. A precise breakdown between the two is complicated because major programs, such as Research and Development, Central Supply and Maintenance, Intelligence and Communication, or Administration and General Personnel Activities, encompass both. Nevertheless, Strategic Forces, in comparison with programs strictly defined as conventional (General Purpose Forces, Airlift and Sealift, Guard and Reserve Forces), represent at most 15% of the total. Calculation based on TOA figures, *Department of Defense Annual Report, FY 1980*, p. 321.

16. A precise cost for US-NATO forces cannot be provided since most force

elements have more than one purpose and, in any major confrontation with the Warsaw Pact, all US forces would be made available. Nevertheless, a recent US response to the NATO Defense Planning Questionnaire estimates the cost of forces formally committed to NATO at approximately $81.1 billion, or around 51% of the total defense budget for FY 1981. The "formal commitment" figure is derived by adding the total cost of $57 billion for "forces rapidly available to NATO" (General Purpose Forces forward deployed in Europe and US-based forces ready to deploy solely for the defense of Europe), and a sizable fraction of the total cost for "Multi-purpose forces," namely $24.1 billion out of $74.8 billion. (General Purpose Forces that would be used in a NATO conflict but made available for other conflicts: Strategic Reserves, Strategic Forces, Intelligence and Communication facilities). Included in these figures, in addition to the direct cost of the combat forces, is an allocated share of the cost of new equipment, a proportionate share of US-based training and logistics support, research, development, testing and evaluation, and Department of Defense administration. *Department of Defense Estimates, 1981.*

17. In spring 1981, Congressional analysts assumed an immediate annual saving of $2.28 billion for each NATO division disbanded, with double the annual savings possible from reductions in infrastructure and equipment costs within three years. The figure of $2.28 billion assumes a saving of $1.35 billion from the combat element (at full strength), $450 million from the sustaining increment (estimated at 75% of full strength), and $450 million from the tactical support increment (estimated at 60% of full strength). Such calculations are inevitably complex and approximate but give a rough idea of the magnitude of US-NATO costs. The figure of $30 billion presupposes cutting six divisions, but not US-NATO naval or tactical air forces. After the cuts, four divisions would remain for NATO purposes, presumably to cover one of the two sectors on the central front for which the United States was exercising direct responsibility. Basic data for the projections come from Office of the Comptroller of the Army, *The Armed Forces Planning Cost Handbook* (Washington, D.C.: GPO, 1979).

18. Comparisons of defense expenditures and military manpower in 1980 were:

Country	$ million (1980)	$ per head (1980)	% of GNP (1980)	Nos. in armed forces (thousands) (1980)
United States	142,700	644	5.5	2,050.0
United Kingdom	24,448	437	5.1	329.2
France	20,220	374	3.9	494.7
West Germany	25,120	410	3.2	495.0

West German expenditures exclude aid to West Berlin. International Institute for Strategic Studies, *The Military Balance, 1981–82*, pp. 112–113.

To say West Germany spends proportionately less of its GNP on defense is not to say it lacks impressive military forces. In addition to 495,000 men under arms,

West Germany has a well-trained reserve force of 750,000 men, which is capable of being mobilized within 36 hours. Its military force probably seems more formidable when seen from Moscow than from Washington. German military figures are courtesy of German Information Center, New York, 1981.

Conclusion. The American Disease and Its Cures

1. Edmund Burke, *The Works of Edmund Burke* (Boston: C. C. Little and J. Brown, 1839), III, 310, 312.

2. Lester C. Thurow, "Undamming the American Economy," *New York Times Magazine*, May 10, 1981, pp. 38–60; Thurow, *The Zero-Sum Society* (New York: Basic Books, 1980), ch. 4.

3. John A. Hobson, *Imperialism, a Study* (London: Allen Unwin, 1902). Hobson's theories about the evolution of capitalism in Britain are perhaps more elaborate than suggested in the text.

4. John Kenneth Galbraith, *The New Industrial State* (Boston: Houghton Mifflin, 1967). See also Galbraith's critique of contemporary libertarian enthusiasm for free markets: "The Conservative Onslaught," *New York Review of Books*, Jan. 22, 1981, pp. 30–36.

5. On what it would take to end the stagflation caused by such "imperfections," see Eckstein, *The Great Recession*, pp. 152–184.

6. See Joseph A. Schumpeter, *Business Cycles: A Theoretical, Historical and Statistical Analysis of the Capitalist Process*, 2 vols. (New York: McGraw Hill, 1939).

7. On a philosophical level, a revival of conservative idealism, with its respect for individual freedom, appreciation for the moral role of the state, and skeptical view of the state's capacity for direct action, would be salutary. See e.g. Bernard Bosanquet, *The Philosophical Theory of the State* (London: Macmillan, 1889).

Index